LANDSCAPE
AS SYMBOL
IN THE
POETRY
OF
T. S. ELIOT

LANDSCAPE AS SYMBOL IN THE POETRY OF T. S. ELIOT

Nancy Duvall Hargrove

UNIVERSITY PRESS
OF MISSISSIPPI
JACKSON
1978

THIS VOLUME IS AUTHORIZED
AND SPONSORED BY
MISSISSIPPI STATE UNIVERSITY

Copyright © 1978 by the
University Press of Mississippi
Manufactured in the United States of America
Designed by J. Barney McKee

The author wishes to thank the following for permission to use selections from copyrighted material:
Excerpts from the poetry and prose of T. S. Eliot are reprinted from his volumes *Collected Poems 1909–1962* and *Selected Essays* by permission of Harcourt Brace Jovanovich, Inc.; copyright, 1932, 1936, 1950, by Harcourt Brace Jovanovich, Inc.; copyright © 1943, 1960, 1963, 1964, by T. S. Eliot; copyright, 1971, by Esme Valerie Eliot.
Excerpts from *To Criticize the Critic* by T. S. Eliot, Copyright © 1965 by Valerie Eliot. Reprinted with the permission of Farrar, Straus and Giroux, Inc.
Excerpts from *On Poetry and Poets* by T. S. Eliot, Copyright © 1943, 1945, 1951, 1954, 1956, 1957 by T. S. Eliot. Reprinted with the permission of Farrar, Straus and Giroux, Inc.
An excerpt from "The Death of Saint Narcissus" from *Poems Written in Early Youth* by T. S. Eliot, Copyright © 1967 by Valerie Eliot. Reprinted with the permission of Farrar, Straus and Giroux, Inc.
Excerpts from *The Inferno* by Dante Alighieri, translated by John Ciardi. Copyright © 1954 by John Ciardi. Reprinted by arrangement with The New American Library, Inc., New York, N.Y.
An excerpt from "The Circus Animals' Desertion" from *Collected Poems* of William Butler Yeats. Copyright 1940 by Georgie Yeats, renewed 1968 by Bertha Georgie Yeats, Michael Butler Yeats and Anne Yeats. Reprinted with the permission of Macmillan Publishing Co., Inc.

Library of Congress Cataloging in Publication Data

Hargrove, Nancy Duvall.
    Landscape as symbol in the poetry of T. S. Eliot.

    Bibliography: p. 227
    Includes index.
    1. Eliot, Thomas Stearns, 1888—1965—Allegory and symbolism.   2. Eliot, Thomas Stearns, 1888–1965—Settings.   3. Landscape in literature.   4. Symbolism in literature.   I. Title.
PS3509.L43Z68159   821'.9'12   78-9270
ISBN 0-87805-077-9

For Guy,
Guy III,
and Meg,
and for Jane

Contents

List of Photographs

Acknowledgments

First of all I would like to thank Mrs. Valerie Eliot who has been both kind and generous in responding to my requests for advice, information, and permissions. The copyright in both published and unpublished material by T. S. Eliot belongs to Mrs. Eliot. I gratefully acknowledge her permission to use copyrighted material from the Eliot collections of King's College Library and Magdalene College Library, Cambridge University, and of the Houghton Library, Harvard University. Further, I am indebted to Mrs. Eliot and to the following for permission to quote from the poetry and prose of T. S. Eliot: Harcourt, Brace, Jovanovich, Inc. for excerpts from *Collected Poems: 1909–1962* and from *Selected Essays*; Farrar, Straus and Giroux, Inc. for excerpts from *On Poetry and Poets, Poems Written in Early Youth*, and *To Criticize the Critic*; Harvard University Press for excerpts from *The Use of Poetry and the Use of Criticism* (Copyright, 1933, By the President and Fellows of Harvard College); Faber and Faber, Ltd. for excerpts from Eliot's prefaces to Edgar A. Mowrer's *This American World*, to James B. Connolly's *Fishermen of the Banks*, and to Paul Valéry's *Le Serpent; Daedalus* for excerpts from "The Influence of Landscape upon the Poet," and the *St. Louis Post-Dispatch* for excerpts from the article "From a Distinguished Former St. Louisan." Mrs. Eliot has also granted me permission to quote excerpts from Eliot's "London Letter" in *The Dial*, from "The Three Provincialities" in *The Tyro*, from "The Significance of Charles Williams" in *The Listener*, from a letter to S. E. Morison in *The American Neptune*, and from an unpublished lecture on *Ulysses* (1933) quoted in Matthiessen's *The Achievement of T. S. Eliot*.

I wish to thank David Higham Associates Limited for permission to quote from Dorothy L. Sayers's translations of Dante's *Hell, Purgatory*, and *Paradise*, the New American Library, Inc. for permission to quote from John Ciardi's translation of Dante's *Inferno,* and the Macmillan Publishing Co., Inc. for permission to quote from W. B. Yeats's poem, "The Circus Animals' Desertion," from *Collected Poems.* Eudora Welty graciously consented to let me use a quotation from her essay, "Place in Fiction," originally published in the *South Atlantic Quarterly.* I am also grateful to Mrs. Diana Oakeley, the sister of John Hayward, who has granted me permission to quote from Mr. Hayward's letters to Frank Morley and from the drafts of his notes for the French translations of *The Waste Land* and *Four Quartets.* Both the letters and the notes are located in the Eliot collection of King's College Library, Cambridge University.

Portions of Chapters I, III, and IV were first published in somewhat different versions in the following journals, and I gratefully acknowledge the editors' permissions to include that material here. Parts of Chapter I appeared earlier as "Landscape as Symbol in Tennyson and Eliot," *Victorians Institute Journal,* 1 (July, 1974), 73–83 and as "T. S. Eliot: The Symbol in Theory and in Practice," *Illinois Quarterly,* 38 (Spring, 1976), 52–62. Much of the "Ash Wednesday" section of Chapter III was published as "Landscape as Symbol in T. S. Eliot's *Ash Wednesday,*" *Arizona Quarterly,* 30 (Spring, 1974), 53–62, and an early version of Chapter IV appeared as "Symbolism in T. S. Eliot's 'Landscapes,' " *Southern Humanities Review,* 6 (Summer, 1972), 273–83.

My husband and I took many of the photographs, but others were obtained from various sources. The photographs from the Henry Ware Eliot, Jr. collection of the Houghton Library are reprinted by permission of the Houghton Library, Harvard University. I would like to thank the Friends of Little Gidding and Tony Hodgson for permission to reproduce the photograph of the interior of the chapel at Little Gidding, John N. Cole for permission to use the photograph of the Virgin of Our Lady of Good Voyage Church in Gloucester, Massachusetts, and Mrs. Emily Morison Beck and *The American Neptune* for permission to reprint Samuel Eliot Morison's photograph of the Dry Salvages. The excellent work of the following photographers is greatly appreciated: Jerry Klinow of Gloucester, Massachusetts, Gitchell's Studio of Charlottesville, Virginia, W. H.

Rendell of Yeovil, England, and M. J. Hopkins of Chipping Campden, England. I wish to thank Lord Sandon, owner of Burnt Norton, for allowing Mr. Hopkins to photograph the house and grounds. The Scottish Tourist Board, the British Tourist Authority, the German Information Center, the St. Louis Regional Commerce and Growth Association, and Wide World Photos also supplied me with photographs.

I am also happy to acknowledge the following individuals and organizations who contributed to the book. When I was a student at Agnes Scott College, Jane Pepperdene first introduced me to Eliot's poetry and the debt I owe her is acknowledged in the dedication. I must also thank the great Eliot scholars whose works have been a constant source of inspiration: Helen Gardner, Elizabeth Drew, Cleanth Brooks, Grover Smith, and F. O. Matthiessen. I would like to express my gratitude to Mississippi State University for encouragement and financial assistance in the publication of this book, and to J. Chester McKee and the Office of Research at Mississippi State University for two grants which enabled me to complete my research in Great Britain and in New England. I am also indebted to the Missouri Historical Society; to the staffs of King's College Library and Magdalene College Library of Cambridge University, to W. H. Bond and Deborah Kelley of the Houghton Library of Harvard University, and to Martha Irby of the Mississippi State University Library; to Patti Abraham, Martha Chesser, and Sharon LaFleur, who typed portions of the manuscript; to Ashley Brown, E. O. Hawkins, Miriam Shillingsburg, and Peyton Williams, who gave me aid and advice at various stages of my work; to Warren French and Jac Tharpe, who read the manuscript and made valuable and perceptive suggestions; and to Barney McKee, the director of the University Press of Mississippi, who not only did the design for the book but always gave me encouragement and good advice.

Finally, I owe a special thanks to my husband, Guy, and to my children, Guy III and Meg, who have a very real share in this book; they cheerfully accompanied me to Eliot's settings, even the most remote and obscure, and my husband took many of the photographs.

Preface

Much has been written on both the content and the technique of T. S. Eliot's poetry. For some time now the thematic unity of Eliot's work has been acknowledged, and his remarks on Pascal serve as a significant comment on the meaning expressed in his poetry:

> He finds the world to be so and so; he finds its character inexplicable by any non-religious theory: among religions he finds Christianity, and Catholic Christianity, to account most satisfactorily for the world and especially for the moral world within; and thus, by what Newman calls "powerful and concurrent" reasons, he finds himself inexorably committed to the dogma of the Incarnation.
> . . . I know of no religious writer more pertinent to our time. . . . I can think of no Christian writer . . . more to be commended than Pascal to those who doubt, but who have the mind to conceive, and the sensibility to feel, the disorder, the futility, the meaninglessness, the mystery of life and suffering, and who can only find peace through a satisfaction of the whole being.[1]

Considerable critical effort has been spent on the technical aspects of Eliot's work and on his use of symbols in particular. However, as Father Genesius Jones points out, "the symbols have not been pinned down as the allusions have been. The provenance of certain symbols has been studied, but the main body of symbols remains unexplicated. . . ."[2] This observation holds especially true for landscape, one of Eliot's most complex and consistently used symbols. Despite the central role it plays throughout the poetry, landscape has not received the direct and sustained critical analysis that it deserves. Indeed, one of the foremost Eliot critics, Dame Helen Gardner, concludes an article on Eliot's landscapes by stating," if I were to rewrite my book on *The Art of T. S. Eliot* I should give much more space than I did to Eliot as a poet of places.''[3] It is my intent to provide in this book a close and thorough analysis of Eliot's use of landscape. Throughout the study I employ the term "landscape" in the broad sense of "setting," including interior as well as exterior and urban as well as rural scenes.

My own interest in this topic stems from a series of essays written a generation ago by Marshall McLuhan. In these essays, he not only indicates the importance of landscape technique in Eliot's work, but he also suggests that its roots are to be found in Tennyson and Baudelaire. With McLuhan's remarks as a starting point, I will discuss in the opening chapter Eliot's concept of the symbol in general, his use of landscape as symbol in particular, and his sources for this technique, Tennyson and Baudelaire. The following four chapters proceed through a chronological, poem-by-poem analysis with great emphasis on close reading. Chapter II concerns the urban landscapes of the early poems through *The Waste Land.* Chapter III focuses on the middle poems ("The Hollow Men," "Ash Wednesday," and the Ariel poems) and the shift to rural landscape. Chapter IV discusses the often overlooked but important series of poems entitled "Landscapes." The last chapter is devoted to the predominantly rural landscapes of the *Four Quartets.*

Throughout I have tried to analyze the lines as closely as possible. In my interpretations I rely on the context of the lines in the poem, on information about Eliot's life and time which seems significant, and particularly on the actual geographical locations which are the sources of the poetic landscapes. I have visited every major setting and many of the minor ones, including the remote Rannoch, by Glencoe in Scotland and Usk in Wales. It is my conviction that knowledge of these sites greatly increases the validity of interpretation.

The photographs of the settings are an integral part of the book, and indeed I feel that they are as important as the text. I have included photographs of all the major landscapes as well as many of the minor ones, and I hope they will be particularly helpful to those Eliot readers who have not been able to visit these locations.

LANDSCAPE
AS SYMBOL
IN THE
POETRY
OF
T. S. ELIOT

*From the dawn of man's imagination,
place has enshrined the spirit.*

EUDORA WELTY

*We shall not cease from exploration
And the end of all our exploring
Will be to arrive where we started
And know the place for the first time.*

T. S. ELIOT

1 · Landscape as Symbol in Eliot, Tennyson, and Baudelaire

By the mid-thirties T. S. Eliot's reputation as a modernist poet was well established, and his influence was felt by poets in places as widespread as India, Greece, and Brazil. For a generation he had been associated with the "men of 1914," James Joyce, Ezra Pound, and Wyndham Lewis, names which immediately evoke the great period of modernism in London from 1910–1920. The author of "Prufrock" and other startlingly new poems was regarded with both awe and admiration by poets, critics, and friends. Wyndham Lewis, for example, described his first meeting with Eliot in the following terms: "I looked up one day from a brooding interval, as I sat in the narrow triangle of Ezra's flat. And there, sitting down with a certain stealth, not above a couple of feet away from me, was the author of Prufrock—indeed, was Prufrock himself: but a Prufrock to whom the mermaids would decidedly have sung, one would have said, at the tops of their voices. . . ."[1] He was admired not only by his contemporaries but also by younger writers. The British poets of the 1920s and 1930s particularly emulated him. Stephen Spender speaks of "the aura Eliot's name . . . had for undergraduate poets. . . . Already, in 1928, T. S. Eliot was a legend to the young poets . . . [because] he wrote a new, a really new poetry. . . ."[2] W. H. Auden, too, experienced a "shock of recognition" upon discovering Eliot's poetry. Nevill Coghill relates an incident occurring in 1926 in which his student Auden confessed tearing up his poems because they were " 'no good. Based on Wordsworth.' " When pressed for further explanation, Auden replied, " 'You ought

3

to read Eliot. I've been reading Eliot. I now see the way I want to write.' "[3] Perhaps Wyndham Lewis and Hugh Ross Williamson best sum up the position of the poet. In his *Men Without Art* (1934), Lewis says, "There is no person today who has had more influence upon the art of literature in England and America than Mr. T. S. Eliot. . . . For ten years now countless young verse-makers both here and in America have modeled themselves upon *Ara Vos Prec, The Waste Land* or *Prufrock.*"[4] And Williamson in his *The Poetry of T. S. Eliot* (1932) makes an even more comprehensive statement when he asserts, "It is no exaggeration to say that there is no young poet at present writing who does not owe something to T. S. Eliot."[5]

The specific reason for this intense and far-reaching influence was the modernist element in Eliot's work. With "Prufrock" and the other early poems, Eliot introduced into poetry new techniques of expression as well as a new world view, a new attitude toward the human experience. Three aspects can be singled out as forming a major part of the poetic content. First, man in the twentieth century found himself in a new cultural situation. For the first time the whole of human history was available to all, particularly through the work of anthropologists such as Sir James Fraser who probed into the mythic consciousness of the past. Eliot himself has pointed out the importance of work such as Fraser's in giving modern man a nearly comprehensive view of himself,[6] and his poetry clearly reflects this attitude as he consistently uses mythic allusions to comment on modern experience. Second, psychological advances opened up fresh routes of exploration into the workings of man's mind and personality. Eliot incorporated these advances into his poetry, producing new realms of psychological realism in which his protagonists reveal their innermost souls. Finally, this modernist world view reflected the chaos and lack of direction in twentieth century life where the human being was lost amid the rush of metropolitan existence, the horror of world war, and the deterioration of established values. These three elements, then, composed the core of the modern sensibility presented in Eliot's poetry.

To convey this contemporary sensibility, the poet sought out new modes of expression, new poetic techniques; as F. O.

Matthiessen notes, Eliot felt that a new content necessitated a new form.[7] His many technical innovations are among his most outstanding contributions to literature. F. R. Leavis remarks on this accomplishment in his *New Bearings in English Poetry:* "To invent techniques that shall be adequate to the ways of feeling, or modes of experience, of adult, sensitive moderns is difficult in the extreme. Until it has been once done it is so difficult as to seem impossible. One success makes others more probable because less difficult. That is the peculiar importance of Mr. T. S. Eliot."[8]

Four techniques in particular have been singled out as specifically modernist. First, and perhaps most startling, is the new form composed of disjunctive sequences of images, events, and/or thoughts. Juxtaposition is used without connectives. This structural innovation is the essence of "Prufrock," "Gerontion," and especially *The Waste Land.*[9] Second, a remarkable fidelity to the materials shows that the artist does not attempt to elevate or glorify his subject matter. Thus, to quote a phrase from Yeats, "the foul rag-and-bone shop of the heart" is presented as it is; the poetry is filled with graphic realistic detail, which is carefully controlled by the form. Third, experimentation with the meaning and rhythm of language constitutes an important aspect of the poetry. Eliot combined a concern for finding the right word, "The common word exact without vulgarity,/The formal word precise but not pedantic,"[10] with a desire to "purify the dialect of the tribe." What Matthiessen calls an "intricately sensitive awareness of words" came from Eliot's belief that the artist must give "to the word a new life and to the language a new idiom."[11] In working with the rhythms of poetry, Eliot not only pointed out the need for new meters but also invented many himself. The irregularity of his verse reflects the essence of contemporary life, for there are, as Matthiessen points out, "connections between a poet's rhythm and what can loosely be called the rhythm of his age."[12] Furthermore, Eliot stressed the need for rhythms combining both regularity and irregularity because "this contrast between fixity and flux, this unperceived evasion of monotony, . . . is the very life of verse."[13] Fourth, a highly sophisticated technique of symbolizing emotional states, called the objective correlative, appears in the poetry. Concrete, sensory detail is used to communicate complex emotions objectively.

These vital modernist elements were certainly the most striking aspects of Eliot's poetry up to the mid-thirties. Indeed, his young poet-followers as well as his numerous critics were concerned exclusively with them. Edmund Wilson describes the way in which aspiring poets of the twenties and early thirties saturated themselves with both the milieu and the techniques of Eliot's modernist verse: "In London, as in New York, and in the universities both here and in England, [the young poets] for a time took to inhabiting exclusively barren beaches, cactus-grown deserts, and dusty attics overrun with rats—the only properties they allowed themselves to work with were a few fragments of old shattered glass or a sparse sprinkling of broken bones."[14] Critic after critic emphasized these new twentieth-century qualities, stressing the complete break between Eliot's poetry and that of the nineteenth century.

Leavis presents a typical viewpoint in his book published in 1932: "It is mainly due to [Eliot] that no serious poet or critic to-day can fail to realize that English poetry in the future must develop (if at all) along some other line than that running from the Romantics through Tennyson, Swinburne, *A Shropshire Lad*, and Rupert Brooke. He has made a new start, and established new bearings."[15] Eliot himself spoke of his "reaction against the poetry, in the English language, of the nineteenth and early twentieth centuries"[16] and complained that he could find no starting points in English poetry as a whole: "The kind of poetry that I needed, to teach me the use of my own voice, did not exist in English at all. . . ."[17]

If then Eliot totally rejected the techniques as well as the attitudes of Wordsworthian and Tennysonian poetry, where had he found his inspiration? The well known answer, given first by Eliot and then explored *ad infinitum* by the critics, was that to a great extent the French Symbolists had supplied the new direction. In his essay "American Literature and the American Language," Eliot recalls their influence on him: "In the first decade of the century the situation was unusual. I cannot think of a single living poet, in either England or America, then at the height of his powers, whose work was capable of pointing the way to a young poet conscious of the desire for a new idiom. . . . [But] there was something to be learned from the French poets of the Symbolist Movement. . . ."[18]

Specifically, it was Jules Laforgue who offered him the new voice, the new mode of expression which he had been unable to find in English poetry: Laforgue "was the first to teach me how to speak, to teach me the poetic possibilities of my own idiom of speech."[19] The discovery of Laforgue's form of expression gave Eliot a clue to the discovery of his own form. Eliot also found help in Mallarmé, Baudelaire, Corbière, and others. Thus it would *seem* that Eliot, the modernist poet, took his technique and tone from these French poets and found but little inspiration in the mainstream of the English tradition.[20]

However, a major aspect of Eliot's work, which has usually been overlooked in the welter of modernist poetic devices, descends directly from both English and French poetry of the nineteenth century. Landscape as symbol is a basic element in all of Eliot's poetry, and one that becomes more dominant as the poems pass out of the extremely modernist period. About the middle of the 1930s landscape comes to the forefront in "Ash Wednesday," in the Ariel poems, in the series of short poems entitled "Landscapes," and in *Four Quartets*. In addition, Eliot's essays on Tennyson, Baudelaire, and Dante indicate an interest in this device. Looking over his poetry as a whole, one realizes that use of a variety of landscapes serves symbolic ends: the elegance of upper class apartments, the squalor of backstreet slums, the filth of the commercial Thames are all parts of the urban landscape of the early poems. In the later poetry the landscape shifts to the countryside: the orchard of "New Hampshire," the temperate valley of "Journey of the Magi," the rose garden of "Burnt Norton," the sea coast of "Marina" and "The Dry Salvages." This pervasive use of landscape requires a reconsideration of Eliot's poetry and its sources. In a remarkable series of essays published in the 1950s, Marshall McLuhan sets forth the theory that Eliot's technique of using landscape as symbol descends directly from both French and English poetry of the nineteenth century and from Baudelaire and Tennyson in particular.[21] Baudelaire's general influence has been pointed out by Eliot himself and discussed by many critics, but the influence of his specific innovations in the use of symbolic landscape has not been greatly explored. On the other hand, the idea that Tennyson influenced Eliot at all has rarely been acknowledged. Yet, close investigation reveals that Tennyson's technique of using natural scenes as symbols appears in Eliot's poetry. A brief examination of Eliot's use of symbols in general and of landscape in particular, followed by an analysis of Tennyson's and Baudelaire's treatments of setting as symbol, will make clear the ways in which Eliot was able both to adopt and to adapt their highly developed techniques for his own poetry.

In *Romantic Image* Frank Kermode states, "The unique power of the poet, however one describes it, is to make images or symbols. . . ."[22] T. S. Eliot's ability to create symbols has long been recognized; being dissatisfied with the poetry of the past, poetry dominated by rumination, description, and decoration, he saw the symbol as a means of revitalizing verse, of recapturing concentration and true feeling, of evading what Arthur Symons calls " 'the old bondage of rhetoric . . . [and] exteriority.' "[23] Though the symbol is a major element in his work, Eliot never set forth a clearly defined theory of symbolism. However, scattered remarks in his essays do comprise a theory of sorts. And they help to explain his ideas about the creation, function, and general characteristics of the symbol.

Eliot's view of the function of the symbol is in part traditional: its purpose is to stand for something larger than itself, to be *"more in intention than [it is] in existence."*[24] Eliot remarks on this aspect in discussing Baudelaire: "It is not merely in the use of imagery of common life, not merely in the use of imagery of the sordid life of a great metropolis, but in the elevation of such imagery to the *first intensity*—presenting it as it is, and yet *making it represent something much more than itself*—that Baudelaire has created a mode of release and expression for other men." (The second group of italics is mine.)[25] It is in *what* the symbol represents that Eliot's "individual talent" manifests itself. For Eliot, the "something much more than itself" evoked by a clearly rendered symbol is a complex emotional/moral state or état d'âme. He felt that the intangible, almost inexpressible feelings and experiences of the human being (and of the modern human being in particular) could be communicated in poetry by means of the symbol. Eliot's own definition of this quality of the symbol is found in his famous passage on the objective correlative: "The only way of expressing emotion in the form of art is by finding an 'objective correlative'; in other words, a set of objects, a situation, a chain of events which shall be the formula of that *particular* emotion; such that when the external facts, which must terminate in sensory experience, are given, the emotion is immediately evoked."[26]

Where, however, does the poet find these concrete symbols with which to communicate inner experience? In an era with few meaningful traditional symbols, he is, for the most part, forced to find or make his own. (If he does employ a traditional symbol, he must recreate it and give it fresh life by using it in new ways and/or infusing it with new meanings.) In an unpublished lecture on *Ulysses* given in 1933, Eliot indicates that symbols (1) can be found in literary works and (2) can be created from one's personal experience: " 'In some minds certain memories, both from *reading* and *life,* become charged with emotional significance' " (italics mine).[27] Elaborating on the matter of reading, he says that a poet will "select and store up certain kinds of imagery from . . . books. And I should say that the mind of any poet would be magnetised in its own way, to select automatically, in his reading . . . the material—an image, a phrase, a word—which may be of use to him later."[28] Perhaps, however, the poet's own life with its myriad events provides the greater reservoir of symbols, as Eliot suggests in the final essay of *The Use of Poetry and the Use of Criticism:* "And of course only a part of an author's imagery comes from his reading. It comes from the whole of his sensitive life since early childhood. Why, for all of us, out of all that we have heard, seen, felt, in a lifetime, do certain images recur, charged with emotion, rather than others? The song of one bird, the leap of one fish, at a particular place and time, the scent of one flower, an old woman on a German mountain path, six ruffians seen through an open window playing cards at night at a small French railway junction where there was a water-mill: such memories may have symbolic value. . . ."[29]

Eliot restates this idea of the poet's creating symbols out of his own experience in an essay written seventeen years later: "From [Baudelaire], as from Laforgue, I learned that the sort of material that I had, the sort of experience that an adolescent had had, in an industrial city in America, could be the material for poetry; and that the source of new poetry might be found in what had been regarded hitherto as the impossible, the sterile, the intractably unpoetic."[30]

Beginning then with objects or experiences which are often personal, whether found in literature or in life, the poet subsequently transforms them into bearers of universal significance. In his introduction to Valéry's *Le Serpent*, Eliot defines this important step in the making of a symbol: ". . . personal emotion, personal experience, is extended and completed in something impersonal . . ." and ". . . not our feelings, but the pattern which we may make of our feelings, is the centre of value."[31] Thus, while Eliot's symbols begin in the particular, the concrete object or the private experience, they end in the universal, the unconsciously general, which belongs to humanity as a whole. He feels the poet "out of intense and personal experience, is able to express a general truth; retaining all the particularity of his experience, to make of it a general symbol."[32] That the symbols partake of both the concrete and the abstract, the tangible and the intangible, strengthens their power of communication. (They avoid the weakness of a system of symbolism which entirely excludes reality, as did, for example, some Georgian works, such as the poetry of Robert Graves and Robert Bridges and Yeats's *A Vision*.)

Finally, Eliot's symbols usually have a multiplicity of meanings in their original context, but they also gain in complexity as they appear again and again in the poetry. The modern symbol has multiple levels to begin with, as Robert Langbaum perceptively points out in *The Poetry of Experience:* "In the allegorical poetry of the Middle Ages and Renaissance, the symbol stands in a one-to-one relation for an external idea or system of ideas. But the modern symbol exists as an object for imaginative penetration. . . . Whereas Dante uses the three beasts, Beatrice, the purgatorial mount to point (even if obscurely) to definite ideas, Eliot, in *Ash Wednesday,* presents the three leopards, the Lady, the winding stair with a precision learned from

Dante, but lets their 'indefinite associations unfold variously in different readers' minds.' Eliot's symbols invite penetration as Dante's do not, because Eliot's symbols put forth an atmosphere of unlimited meaningfulness."[33] At its first appearance an Eliotean symbol cannot be pinned down to a single meaning; and its rich density is further increased in every subsequent poem in which it is used.

Thus, the characteristics of an Eliotean symbol may be summarized as follows: (1) it conveys a complex moral or emotional state, (2) it originates in the poet's personal experiences in literature and/or in life, (3) it is grounded in the real, the actual, but it expresses universal feelings, emotions, experiences, and (4) it has a multiplicity of meanings, both singly and as the sum of all its appearances. The symbol, then, in Eliot's hands is a powerful instrument capable of reflecting the complexity of modern human experience.

Landscape, or setting, is one of the most important of Eliot's basic recurring symbols, for it reflects with particular sensitivity both the outer and inner worlds; to quote Elizabeth Drew, "Although no poetry could be more concrete in detail, image and scenery, all are part of an inner world, a visionary and symbolic landscape."[34] An analysis of this major symbol will reveal each aspect of the theory at work.

Eliot uses landscape to represent much more than scenery or setting; it is a means of defining or suggesting emotional or moral states, a means of controlling and manipulating feeling. For example, in the opening two lines of "The Fire Sermon" in *The Waste Land,* the desolate riverside landscape of winter strikingly conveys an agonized state of emptiness and suicidal despair, with undertones of a human being in the last throes of drowning: 'The river's tent is broken: the last fingers of leaf/ Clutch and sink into the wet bank." On the other hand, the winter landscape of section one of "Little Gidding" communicates the elusive and complex state of spiritual ecstasy and union with the timeless:

> When the short day is brightest, with frost and fire,
> The brief sun flames the ice, on pond and ditches,
> In windless cold that is the heart's heat. . . .

In each case Eliot achieves a masterful suggestion of an inner état d'âme through the use of landscape.

The particular landscapes that Eliot chooses for symbols come, as he has noted, both from his voluminous reading in many literatures and from his experiences in life. Baudelaire and Tennyson were his foremost literary sources, providing him not only with landscape techniques but also with specific scenes. Baudelaire's teeming and decadent metropolitan settings appear often in Eliot's early poetry, while Tennyson's English countryside dominates the middle and later works. Indeed, Eliot's movement is consistently away from Baudelairean toward Tennysonian landscapes. In addition, the English writers Conan Doyle, Charles Dickens, and Lancelot Andrewes all furnished him with significant views of London. In French literature, he found particular inspiration in the Paris of Charles-Louis Philippe whose *Bubu de Montparnasse* conveyed myriad sense impressions of the Boulevard de Montparnasse. Classical works too suggested some landscapes which appear in Eliot's poetry, as in the following quotation from "Sweeney Erect":

> Paint me a cavernous waste shore
> Cast in the unstilled Cyclades,
> Paint me the bold anfractuous rocks
> Faced by the snarled and yelping seas.

Dante was also a major source of settings for the poet who had found so much else in him and had become perhaps his leading English advocate. Some of those "clear visual images" of Dante's which Eliot so admired as the means of realizing the inapprehensible found their way into his store of landscape symbols: the dark wood, the winding Mount of Purgatory, and aspects of the rose garden, to mention a few. Two less known sources of Eliot's settings were his readings in Sanskrit literature from which, as Howarth suggests, he probably took portions of the final section of *The Waste Land* "with its red glimpses of Indian landscape,"[35] and his acquaintance with certain Ferrarese artists. Of the latter, Georges Cattaui has noted that "[Eliot's] legendary Dantesque world, lit by a weird and spectral glow, evoke[s] the burnt, barbaric landscapes of the Ferrarese school of painters—the glassy deserts and rocky wildernesses of Cosimo

Tura, the petrified world of Francesco del Cossa, the spiky, metallic trees of Ercole de Roberti."[36]

While many of Eliot's landscapes came from his reading, an equal, if not greater, number came from the varied scenes of his own life. In an address to the American Academy of Arts and Sciences, Eliot said, "my personal landscape is a composite." He went on to describe the sources of his urban landscape as the St. Louis of his childhood and the Paris and London of his adult life: "[W]e lived on in a neighbourhood [in St. Louis] which had become shabby to a degree approaching slummi-ness. . . . So it was, that for nine months of the year my scenery was almost exclusively urban, and a good deal of it seedily, drably urban at that. My urban imagery was that of St. Louis, upon which that of Paris and London have been superimposed."[37] Although he neglected to mention it here, Boston is another important source of his urban landscape, particularly in the early poetry.

His rural landscape symbolism also had varied sources. One was the midwest area with "the long dark [Mississippi] river, the ailanthus trees, the flaming cardinal birds, the high lime-stone bluffs where we searched for fossil shell-fish. . . ."[38] Another, and more dominant, source was New England, as Eliot himself has noted: "My country landscape . . . is that of New England, of coastal New England, and New England from June to October."[39] Here the details of the scenery consist of "fir trees, the bay and goldenrod, the song-sparrows, the red granite and the blue sea of Massachusetts."[40] A third major source for his natural landscapes, especially in the later poems, was the countryside of England, as the garden of "Burnt Nor-ton," the village of "East Coker," and the country chapel of "Little Gidding" testify. Eliot's remarks on the importance of rural England are revealing: "I am not maintaining that early impressions are the only ones that count. Far from it: later impressions come to cover them, and to fuse, in some sort, with them. English landscape has come to be as significant for me, and as emotionally charged, as New England land-scape."[41] In addition to these three major sources are numer-ous minor ones such as areas in Wales, Scotland, and Virginia.

Thus the origins of Eliot's landscape symbols, both urban

and rural, are complex, rich, and varied. A "finished" symbol as found in the poetry can come from a single or multiple literary landscape, a single or multiple personal landscape, or from a fusion of the two.

Out of this complex of literary and personal landscapes, Eliot has forged powerful symbols both particular and universal, both concrete and abstract. They have a life, a reality, of their own, for they are real places with recognizable landmarks. In *The Waste Land*, for example, is a more or less literal geography of the City district of London. The City workers come up out of the tube station, climb a hill, go down King William Street, and pass St. Mary Woolnoth, all of which are real parts of London's City area. And in "Marina" is the actual shore of Maine in all its fragrant beauty of combined sea, granite islands, grey rocks, and towering pines, obscured somewhat by a light mist. Even the landscapes of nightmare or of "death's dream kingdom" are furnished with landmarks of real, perceived places, as for example in Section V of *The Waste Land* with its "hooded hordes swarming/Over endless plains, stumbling in cracked earth." While Eliot's landscapes are then actual places, they also stand for something more than themselves; they are symbolic of universal emotional or moral states. As Jay Martin notes, "It is the geography of the mind and imagination in which [Eliot] is really interested."[42] Thus *The Waste Land* setting of King William Street and St. Mary Woolnoth suggests the boredom, monotony, and emptiness in the lives of workers who daily trudge the same path. And the fragile loveliness of the coastal scene in "Marina" evokes first the sense of joy and ecstasy in Pericles's rediscovery of his daughter and on a deeper level indicates the rapture of rebirth of the spirit. Finally, the nightmarish plains of cracked, dried mud symbolize the horror of the complete loss of spirituality and the violence of total return to bestiality and barbarism. The landscape symbols are therefore both particular and general, a necessary characteristic, according to Eliot. In an essay on Mark Twain, he points out that a good literary work will combine a "strong local flavour" with "unconscious universality" and concludes by saying, "I doubt whether a poet or novelist can be universal without being local too."[43]

Finally, Eliot's landscape symbols possess many layers of meaning both in themselves and as they develop from poem to poem. One of the most outstanding examples of a symbol which of itself expresses many different concepts is the sea. Among its varied meanings in the poetry are eternity, destruction, creation, mystery ("The Dry Salvages," I), life ("The Dry Salvages," II), death (*The Waste Land*, IV), sterility (*The Waste Land*, I), and physical beauty ("Ash Wednesday," VI). On the other hand, the rose garden is a symbol which, while possessing some complexity of meaning on its own, gains in depth and significance at each successive appearance in the poems so that in "Little Gidding" it has come to be the symbol of the ultimate goal in Eliot's poetic search for the meaning behind human experience, the ecstasy and serenity of regained spiritual purity and fulfillment. Five major clusters of landscapes are found throughout Eliot's poetry from beginning to end; as such they have highly complex symbolic content and form the core of the landscape symbolism. These are the city (boredom, triviality, sterility), the country (release, fertility, rebirth), the desert (chaos, terror, emptiness), the garden (ecstasy, innocence, serenity), and the sea or river, with the associations detailed above.

Eliot's use of landscape is then a highly sophisticated technique, and, as pointed out in McLuhan's essays, he owes much to Tennyson and Baudelaire as sources of its development. The similar use of symbolic landscape by two poets as seemingly different as Tennyson and Baudelaire has been noted by W. H. Auden: " 'Both felt themselves to be exiles from a lost paradise, desert dwellers (the barren rocks and desolate fens of Tennyson correspond to the gas-lit Paris of Baudelaire); both shared the same nostalgia for the Happy Isles, *le vert paradis des amours enfantines,* to be reached only after long voyages over water. . . .' "[44] Yet before McLuhan no one had linked the names of Tennyson, Baudelaire, and Eliot as sharing the technique of landscape as symbol. However, a close look at this aspect of Tennyson's and Baudelaire's art reveals how perceptive McLuhan's suggestions are.

In many respects Tennyson is more modern than he seems

on the surface, and especially in his use of symbols. Eliot was clearly attracted to one particular feature of Tennyson's symbolism, his highly developed use of exterior landscape to evoke emotion. Eliot himself in his essay on *In Memoriam* indicates his awareness of this quality when he notes that "[Tennyson's] poems are always descriptive, and always picturesque. . . ." Being even more specific, he quotes the "Dark house" passage and then comments: "This is great poetry, economical of words, *a universal emotion related to a particular place* . . ." (italics mine).[45] Eliot, then, recognized Tennyson's ability to evoke feeling through significant setting.

Tennyson uses landscape, which for him means nature solely, in at least four different ways. On the most obvious level, he describes nature for itself, finding pleasure in precise and accurate delineation of details. Harold Nicolson, one of his early critics, notes that "his observation . . . smacks often of the microscope . . . [and] he place[s] accuracy of observation above the more imaginative qualities."[46] Being devoid of emotional content, these descriptions are pictorial and decorative. In "Ode to Memory," for example, is a detailed rendering of an English countryside:

> Come from the woods that belt the gray hillside,
> The seven elms, the poplars four
> That stand beside my father's door,
> And chiefly from the brook that loves
> To purl o'er matted cress and ribbed sand,
> Or dimple in the dark of rushy coves,
> Drawing into his narrow earthen urn,
>   In every elbow and turn,
> The filter'd tribute of the rough woodland. . . .[47]

The country landscape is beautifully drawn; yet its value lies solely in the accuracy of the description.

Second, Tennyson finds landscape to be a solace, a comfort, among the vicissitudes of life. He once confessed, "A known landskip is to me an old friend, that continually talks to me of my youth and half-forgotten things, and, indeed, does more for me than many an old friend that I know."[48] This use of natural settings is often sentimental:

> Sweet after showers, ambrosial air,
> That rollest from the gorgeous gloom
> Of evening over brake and bloom
> And meadow, slowly breathing bare
>
> The round of space, and rapt below
> Thro' all the dewy-tassell'd wood,
> And shadowing down the horned flood
> In ripples, fan my brows and blow
>
> The fever from my cheek. . . .

Third, he employs landscape for mood or atmosphere. In "Recollections of the Arabian Nights" the glittering landscape evokes an atmosphere of fantasy. Perhaps the best example, however, is found in "The Lotos-Eaters," where the scenery conveys the essence of languor and passivity:

> All round the coast the languid air did swoon,
> Breathing like one that hath a weary dream.
> Full-faced above the valley stood the moon;
> And, like a downward smoke, the slender stream
> Along the cliff to fall and pause and fall did seem.

Finally, as McLuhan suggests, the Victorian poet utilizes landscape as "a means of exploring and charting exactly discriminated mental states. . . ."[49] It is this aspect of Tennyson's landscape technique that seems to have directly influenced Eliot. Tennyson, like Eliot later, found himself in an era with few meaningful traditional symbols. Therefore, he had to create his own and use them repeatedly so that their meanings would become apparent to the reader. Landscape is one of the most powerful of these created symbols. His natural scenes, when used in this highly sophisticated mode, are, to quote McLuhan, "immediate impressionistic evocations of situations in which it is the state of mind of the protagonist that is central . . . [and thus] each brief vista is an objective correlative. . . ."[50] McLuhan's choice of Eliot's familiar terminology to describe Tennyson's technique is indeed valid and underlines this similarity between the two poets.

Further, Tennyson's symbolic landscapes are generally real places drawn from his personal experiences, a characteristic shared by Eliot's settings. Elizabeth Waterston notes that "the realities of [Tennyson's] own earliest memories, the realities most charged with emotional history for him [were] a narrow range of scenes which . . . recur throughout the poems with symbolic significance: high bushless fields, a sandy ridge, a cottage overlooking a marsh, a garden with dark alleys opening on plots of roses, lily, and lavender."[51] The Rectory garden at Somersby in particular provided him with the basic elements of many a symbolic setting, as did the New England coast, for example, in the case of Eliot. Thus the landscape symbols are based on reality and are described in graphic detail, but reach beyond themselves to express universal human experience.

Finally, as symbols, Tennyson's settings, like Eliot's later, are capable of numerous variations in meaning. Waterston says, "[H]is symbolism rarely has a one-to-one ratio, an equation value; the symbol creates emotion, but it may be used in different poems to create different emotions."[52] An outstanding example of this multiplicity of meaning is the ocean: its restlessness suggests the passion of human life, as in Part I, Section III of "*Maud*"; its vastness evokes thoughts of eternity, as in "Crossing the Bar"; and its mystery communicates the spirit of adventure, as in "Ulysses."

While a general review of Tennyson's landscape technique is helpful, brief analyses of several poems will suggest more concretely the similarities between the two poets. In "Mariana," *In Memoriam, Maud,* and *Idylls of the King,* poems which span Tennyson's career, symbolic setting is a highly effective element.

In "Mariana" Tennyson conveys the sense of isolation, loss, and decay basically through the description of landscape, reinforced by the refrain of Mariana's despairing moan. The landscape, consisting of the ruined farmhouse and the barren level waste which surrounds it, is a symbol for the quality of Mariana's existence. It skillfully catches up her emptiness and lone-liness.

As the poem develops, the setting gains its significance as symbol: "The symbol of the grange is not arbitrarily assigned to Mariana's state of mind; on the contrary the grange is a real house and its power to represent a mental state is built up within the poem itself by the same means as those used by Tennyson to evoke Mariana's state of mind. The impression of the house in decay is created for us so that we may enter into the mood of its inhabitant, and because of this the emotional and sensuous links between the house and Mariana's mood are so strong that, little by little, the house comes to stand for the mood. This use of evocative imagery for symbolic purposes is the foundation of Tennyson's distinctive poetic tech-nique. . . ."[53] Tennyson's method of making the landscape symbolic of Mariana's complex emotional state, so perceptively pointed out above by Valerie Pitt, begins with an objective exterior view of the house and its immediate grounds, as if described by an observer standing at the outer edge of the moat. The physical signs of decay are detailed:

> With blackest moss the flower-plots
> Were thickly crusted, one and all;
> The rusted nails fell from the knots
> That held the pear to the gable-wall.

So far only the rottenness of the place is conveyed, but in the next four lines the observer's description suggests a touch of sadness as well as a sense of isolation:

> The broken sheds look'd *sad* and strange:
> *Unlifted* was the clinking latch;
> Weeded and worn the ancient thatch
> Upon the *lonely* moated grange (italics mine).

The next two stanzas give details of information about Mariana, with the fourth stanza returning to landscape. There is, however, a subtle change. Whereas in the first stanza the setting is described as if from *outside* looking in, here it seems to be described from *inside* the house looking out at the stagnant moat waters and the surrounding sterile fields:

> About a stone-cast from the wall
>   A sluice with blacken'd waters slept,
> And o'er it many, round and small,
>   The cluster'd marish-mosses crept.
> Hard by a poplar shook alway,
>   All silver-green with gnarled bark:
> For leagues no other tree did mark
> The level waste, the rounding gray.

With extreme expertise Tennyson creates his symbols as the poem progresses, making stronger and stronger the link between landscape and emotion. The stagnant, dark waters, the flat, infertile lands *are* the blackness and emptiness of Mariana's life.

In the sixth stanza Tennyson focuses entirely on the interior of the house. He thus reveals not only the outer but also the inner decay, suggesting the mental as well as the physical ruin of Mariana. The only sounds actually in the house are those of creaking doors, buzzing flies, and shrieking mice:

> All day within the dreamy house,
>   The doors upon their hinges creak'd;
> The blue fly sung in the pane; the mouse
>   Behind the mouldering wainscot shriek'd. . . .

However, Mariana hears and sees the inhabitants of the past, "old faces," "old footsteps," "old voices." The setting thus symbolizes both Mariana's physical isolation and her complete emotional deterioration.

Landscape is also used symbolically in many sections of *In Memoriam*. Basil Willey notes that "exquisite landscapes . . . are here employed as vehicles or symbols of the poet's changing moods and share in his imaginative life; they never strike us, as often elsewhere, . . . as decoration, mechanically and coldly applied from without."[54] Symbolic forms are necessary to objectify the highly personal emotional changes which occur in this poem of a man's coming to terms with life, and Tennyson successfully employs setting as one means of controlling the feeling. This technique is illustrated particularly well in Section XI and its complementary Section XV. In Section XI the mood of calm or resigned despair is rendered through a morning autumn landscape seen from a Lincolnshire hilltop:

> Calm and still light on yon great plain
>   That sweeps with all its autumn bowers,
>   And crowding farms and lessening towers,
> To mingle with the bounding main;
>
> Calm and deep peace in this wide air,
>   These leaves that redden to the fall,
>   And in my heart, if calm at all,
> If any calm, a calm despair. . . .

Set over against this quiet, though troubled, mood is the feverish anguish and "wild unrest" of Section XV, symbolized by the same landscape seen at evening just before a storm:

> To-night the winds begin to rise
>   And roar from yonder dropping day;
>   The last red leaf is whirl'd away,
> The rooks are blown about the skies;
>
> The forest crack'd, the waters curl'd,
>   The cattle huddled on the lea;
>   And wildly dash'd on tower and tree
> The sunbeam strikes along the world. . . .

The section ends with an impassioned description of a thundercloud as "A looming bastion fringed with fire," an image which Basil Willey calls "a powerful symbol of Tennyson's smouldering unrest and sense of impending sorrow."[55] In many other passages of *In Memoriam* Tennyson realizes a complex emotional condition through a setting described with economy, compression, and a minimum of significant details, a feat which Eliot would repeat years later in many of his poems.

In *Maud* Tennyson pushes the technique of symbolic setting to an extreme point. Whereas in *In Memoriam* the descriptions of nature are rather objective and thus indirectly and subtly reveal the emotional state of the protagonist, in *Maud* the speaker himself directly describes scenes which more obviously symbolize the stages of his passion. These descriptions reflect and depict his very soul. The startling opening quatrain is an excellent example, for the speaker's anguished memory of his father's violent death colors the landscape red, and he sees the hollow as a bloody, gaping grave:

> I hate the dreadful hollow behind the little wood;
> Its lips in the field above are dabbled with blood-red heath,
> The red-ribb'd ledges drip with a silent horror of blood,
> And Echo there, whatever is ask'd her, answers 'Death.'

The lines both suggest his morbid obsession with the loss and foreshadow his subsequent disillusionment and his cynical revulsion from life itself. Contrasted to this tortured landscape is Maud's garden, symbol of an earthly paradise of release, serenity, and love. The work can thus be seen as a kind of symbolist poem in which landscape plays a dominant role.

The symbolic use of setting in *Idylls of the King* serves as a final example of Tennyson's artistry. Throughout the poem appropriate seasonal settings "symbolize the moral condition of the realm itself," as Jerome Buckley perceptively points out. The cycle begins with a freshly beautiful Camelot in the spring; then it progresses through scenes of a hot, passionate summer of collapsing ideals and on to "the winter wasteland of Arthur's defeat."[56] The city of Camelot, the forests, and the wasteland function as three highly symbolic landscapes. The city represents man's idealistic endeavors, his godlike aspect, while the "great tracts of wilderness" symbolize his bestial side. Camelot's sun-touched palaces and shining towers suggest a purity not found at Yniol's manor, Doorm's hall, or Pellam's castle, all of which are overgrown with vines or mosses of the wilderness. Yet that purity does not endure, and, as the knights themselves fall into degradation, so also falls Camelot, symbol of their moral condition. It disintegrates into

> heaps of ruin, hornless unicorns,
> Crack'd basilisks, and splinter'd cockatrices,
> And shatter'd talbots, which had left the stones
> Raw that they fell from.

In addition to these two landscapes, the wasteland also serves as symbol, suggesting both emotional and spiritual sterility as well as the frustration and emptiness of selfish desire (a distinct similarity to Eliot's wasteland). Percivale, for example, finds himself "Alone, and in a land of sand and thorns,/And [he] was thirsty even unto death." These lines anticipate the scene of Eliot's protagonist among the sterile mountains of Section V of *The Waste Land*. The city, the forests, and the wasteland thus work as significant symbols for spiritual or emotional states in Tennyson's *Idylls*.

Not only does Tennyson's general method in using landscape seem to have influenced Eliot, but even specific settings and details found in Tennyson reappear in the later poet's work. While some of these shared settings may be conventional and thus indicate no direct influence, the particular ways in which the scenes are used, the special meanings they evoke, and the concrete details they contain seem remarkable, rather than casual, in their similarity. This close similarity suggests that Eliot may indeed have drawn from Tennyson's symbolic landscapes; further, it suggests that the two poets are more alike in sensibility than has generally been recognized.

The most obvious of the Tennysonian settings that may have influenced Eliot is the desert or wasteland. Details of Eliot's wasteland,

> where the sun beats,
> And the dead tree gives no shelter, the cricket no relief,
> And the dry stone no sound of water,

are scattered through Tennyson's poems. The vast emptiness

of the desert is apparent in Mariana's "level waste" with its single tree and in "The Palace of Art" where a solitary figure appears in a sinister surrealist landscape: "One seem'd all dark and red—a tract of sand,/And some one pacing there alone. . . ." In "Morte d'Arthur" a wind shrills "All night in a waste land, where no one comes," and in *Idylls of the King* Guinevere's surrealistic nightmare is "An awful dream, [in which] she seem'd to stand/On some vast plain before a setting sun." These landscapes anticipate the same emptiness and loneliness of Eliot's "I sat upon the shore/Fishing, with the arid plain behind me" as well as the eerie scene described by the hollow men:

> This is the dead land
> This is cactus land
> Here the stone images
> Are raised. . . .
>
> Is it like this
> In death's other kingdom
> Waking alone. . . .

Additional aspects of Eliot's wasteland can be found in Tennyson's poems. The barren mountain rocks, dry rustling grasses, and noisy cicada of *The Waste Land*, I and V, appear in the "stony drought," "knee-deep mountain grass," and "dry cicala" of "Mariana in the South." Similar details are seen in the *Idylls;* for example, Lancelot comes to a "naked shore,/Wide flats, where nothing but coarse grasses grew." And in "Demeter and Persephone," a poem written at the very end of Tennyson's career, Section IV's details of an arid landscape evoke blackness, desolation, and death. Robert G. Stange remarks, "This waste land is both a concrete extension of the mood of the bereaved Demeter and the image of a society without faith or hope. . . ."[57]

Other significant landscape symbols appearing in both Tennyson and Eliot are the garden, the house, and the ocean. For both poets the garden represents a refuge, a place of happiness and serenity, an Eden on earth; and Tennyson's gardens have special qualities which seem to link them specifically to Eliot's garden scenes. Roses and/or apple trees grow in the gardens of both poets, the roses symbolizing human love and the apple trees the innocence and purity of Eden. In Tennyson's "Ode to Memory" is a "garden bower'd close/With plaited alleys of the trailing rose," and "The Hesperides" sings of a garden with a golden apple in a golden tree. A couplet in "Locksley Hall" describes what is surely an apple tree in a richly overgrown island garden: "Droops the heavy-blossom'd bower, hangs the heavy-fruited tree—/Summer isles of Eden lying in dark-purple spheres of sea." And *Maud* has a garden of lilies and roses. Other scenes scattered through Tennyson's poetry anticipate Eliot's rose garden with its children in the apple tree. Another interesting similarity in these garden settings is the emphasis on alleys and walkways, perhaps symbolic of the sense of mystery and wonder existing there. Tennyson's "Long alleys falling down to twilight grots" and Eliot's "empty alley [leading] into the box circle" have clear affinities.

The house is another shared symbol, a dark or decaying house in particular. The symbol in both Tennyson and Eliot is often used to convey the mood of spiritual desolation and moral deterioration. The dark, vacant house of *In Memoriam* perfectly expresses the protagonist's feeling of irreparable loss, aching emptiness, and numbing despair. The transiency of man's life is also suggested. Decaying houses appear even more frequently than dark ones in Tennyson's works: the rotting grange of "Mariana" and the disintegrating buildings of Camelot are two representative examples. Eliot's poetry is filled with similar houses: the decaying rented house of Gerontion, the abandoned chapel in the arid mountains of *The Waste Land*, the crumbling house of "East Coker" with its field mouse behind the wainscot, and the dead, dust-choked house of "Little Gidding."

Finally, the ocean plays a prominent and complex role in the work of the two poets. Both use the sea as an obvious symbol of fertility and renewed life, and both often convey this meaning specifically through references to mermaids and hair. In Tennyson's "The Merman" the speaker exclaims:

> I would sit and sing the whole of the day;
> I would fill the sea-halls with a voice of power;
> But at night I would roam abroad and play
> With the mermaids in and out of the rocks,
> Dressing their hair with the white sea-flower;
> And holding them back by their flowing locks
> I would kiss them often under the sea.

The echoes in "The Love Song of J. Alfred Prufrock" are inescapable:

> I have heard the mermaids singing, each to each.
>
> I do not think that they will sing to me.
>
> I have seen them riding seaward on the waves
> Combing the white hair of the waves blown back
> When the wind blows the water white and black.

The ironic contrast between the virile, assertive speaker of Tennyson's poem and the timid, passive Prufrock renders both poems more meaningful. The sea as a symbol of the creative, life-giving force is thus seen in both poets, but they also use it to represent destruction and the violent side of human emotions. The young man in *Maud* sitting alone in the garden reveals the fury of his surging emotions through a description of the destructive raging of "the tide in its broad-flung ship-wrecking roar,/ . . . the scream of a madden'd beach dragg'd down by the wave." Similarly, in "The Dry Salvages" Eliot's violent sea "tosses up our losses, the torn seine,/The shattered lobsterpot, the broken oar/ . . . an ocean . . . littered with wastage."

Thus, it seems clear that Tennyson did indeed contribute to the poetic craft of T. S. Eliot. The Victorian poet developed to a high degree the use of exterior setting to symbolize complex emotional states, and this landscape technique both in general method and in specific details seems to have exerted a great influence on the modern poet's selection of landscape as a dominant symbol in his poetry.

While Tennyson's influence on Eliot has rarely been recognized, the fact of Baudelaire's great impact on him has been long established. He discovered Baudelaire about 1907 and saw in him "the great master of the nineteenth [century in French literature]."[58] However, it was in the 1920s that the force of Baudelaire's influence was especially intense. Eliot admired him for his sense of his own age as well as for his ability to reveal the essential sameness of man in all ages. He felt a profound kinship with Baudelaire because their basic subject was the conflict of good and evil in the soul of man, the aspiration toward God and the downward pull toward Satan, the struggle between *Spleen* and *Idéal.* Eliot was also impressed with Baudelaire's technical mastery and particularly with his imagery which he raised "to the *first intensity*"[59] by using it as a symbol, as a means of suggesting a spiritual or emotional état d'âme. In this way Baudelaire avoided the direct description upon which Tennyson relied and thus brought an important innovation to modern literature. Eliot was obviously much attracted to this "gift of finding concrete equivalents for intangible feelings."[60]

Although these general debts have been acknowledged, Baudelaire's specific influence on Eliot's use of symbolic setting has received little recognition. Landscape as symbol is one of Baudelaire's major poetic devices, and he achieves two advances in the technique as seen in Tennyson: he makes the important shift from exterior to interior landscape (le paysage intérieur), and he introduces the modern metropolis as a new subject for symbolic landscapes.[61] These two advances are his foremost contributions to Eliot's landscape technique.

Marshall McLuhan brilliantly discusses the first of these in his essay, "Tennyson and Picturesque Poetry." Tennyson, he explains, symbolizes states of mind through great skill in selecting and manipulating *external* landscapes, but he is in effect bound to those external settings. Thus, as symbols they lack immediacy and variety. He brings landscape technique to a high point, but he goes no further. As McLuhan puts it, "if one asks what it was of landscape art that the Romantics and the Victorians did not achieve, it must be replied, *le paysage intérieur* which had to wait for Baudelaire, Laforgue and Rimbaud." By le paysage intérieur McLuhan means psychological landscape, the landscape of the mind, which is composed of widely disparate objects in juxtaposition: "[Interior] landscape is the means of presenting, without the copula of logical enunciation, experiences which are united in existence but not in conceptual thought."[62]

Interior landscape has several advantages over the exterior landscape of Tennyson. First, it avoids what McLuhan calls "the extraneous aids of rhetoric or logical reflection and statement" and thus enables the poet to present the état d'âme directly with a great gain in intensity. The reader finds himself inside, an involved participant, rather than an outside spectator as in Tennyson's picturesque art. Second, it makes possible a higher degree of psychological realism, for the mind itself is evoked in all its complexity. By means of interior landscape Baudelaire can "range across the entire spectrum of the inner life," symbolizing by the diverse objects in the landscape the linkage of disparate experiences in the human mind.[63] Symbolic setting is thus one of the basic devices through which he attained his reputation as "a great *psychological* realist, [who] explored not merely the mind and the emotions, but the nerves of contemporary urban man with an insight which was undreamed of in French poetry before him."[64] Besides permitting the use of any kind of experience and object, le paysage intérieur provides for additional complexity in that it "moves naturally towards the principle of multiple perspectives." As an example, McLuhan cites the opening lines of *The Waste Land* where the Christian Chaucer, Sir James Fraser, and Jessie Weston are "simultaneously present." He also points out that the use of le paysage intérieur insures control over the effect, for "the arrangement of the landscape is the formula of the emotion" and can be adjusted until accurate. This type of manipulation is impossible with Tennyson's external landscapes.[65] Thus, taking up where Tennyson left off, Baudelaire brings the technique of symbolic setting to a high level with the move to psychological landscape.

The second important innovation is the shift from natural to urban landscape. The city is Baudelaire's dominant symbol for the soul of man. In his 1950 lecture, "What Dante Means to

Me," Eliot speaks of the impact which Baudelaire's use of metropolitan setting had on him:

> I think that from Baudelaire I learned first, a precedent for the poetical possibilities, never developed by any poet writing in my own language, of the more sordid aspects of the modern metropolis. . . . From him, as from Laforgue, I learned that the sort of material that I had, the sort of experience that an adolescent had had, in an industrial city in America, could be the material for poetry; and that the source of new poetry might be found in what had been regarded hitherto as the impossible, the sterile, the intractably unpoetic. . . . [H]is significance for me is summed up in the lines:
>
> > Fourmillante Cité, cité pleine de rêves,
> > Où le spectre en plein jour raccroche le passant . . .
>
> I knew what that meant, because I had lived it before I knew that I wanted to turn it into verse on my own account.[66]

Eliot realized that, by adding the city to the subject matter of poetry, the French poet had opened a whole new territory for use as symbolic landscape: "It is not merely in the use of imagery of common life, not merely in the use of imagery of the sordid life of a great metropolis, but in the elevation of such imagery to the *first intensity—presenting it as it is, and yet making it represent something much more than itself*—that Baudelaire has created a mode of release and expression for other men." (The second group of italics is mine.)[67] Baudelaire then uses urban landscape both for itself, its concrete reality, and for its symbolic value, its abstract reality. As Martin Turnell expresses it, "Baudelaire's Paris is not a local affair, a mere emanation of his personal sensibility as to some extent Laforgue's is. Its significance is universal. It is the modern world and it is a sign of Baudelaire's greatness that he manages to present it as a physical—a terrifyingly oppressive physical—reality."[68]

The actual Paris of Baudelaire's own experience makes up this physical reality of the city in his poems. He portrays its every aspect starkly and directly: the dusty streets in the glaring noon sunlight, the dim middle class apartments filled with heavy expensive furniture, the miserable slum hovels of the poor. He sets forth in marked detail all "les plis sinueux"[69] of Paris: "le faubourg secoué par les lourds tombereaux," "[les] sales plafonds [où] un rang de pâles lustres/Et d'énormes quinquets projetent leurs lueurs," "la Seine déserte" in the dawn hours.

But Baudelaire's city is also a complex symbol capable of suggesting a multiplicity of intangible emotions. For example, Paris is often used to symbolize the evil in man, the fact that "chaque jour vers l'Enfer nous descendons d'un pas." In "Le Crépuscule du Soir," the streets themselves are seen as ant hills swarming with prostitutes: "La prostitution s'allume dans les rues;/Comme une fourmillière elle ouvre ses issues." Paris itself is a kind of Inferno. The modern city also symbolizes impermanence; in a passage which anticipates the opening of "East Coker," the poet cries, "Paris change! . . . palais neufs, échafaudages, blocs,/Vieux faubourgs." Connected with this feeling of transience are those of exile, rootlessness, loss of direction, and confusion. The indiscriminate mixture of old suburbs and nouveaux riches palaces, the mazelike streets ("les plis sinueux"), the sterile dry concrete ("le pavé sec")—all these aspects of the Paris landscape symbolize man's fragmented, empty existence. Eliot uses many of these details in his early poems especially, symbolic winding streets, vacant lots, pretentious palaces, and crumbling brothels.[70] Finally, Baudelaire's city conveys the horror of modern life, haunted by real ghosts of guilt, anguish, and apathy: "Fourmillante cité, cité pleine de rêves,/Où le spectre en plein jour raccroche le passant!"

The mastery with which Baudelaire uses the techniques of interior landscape and symbolic urban settings can best be realized by a brief study of several poems. The resulting influence on Eliot can then be seen more specifically.

"Invitation au Voyage" evokes a mental landscape to suggest the emotion of "luxe, calme, et volupté," serenity and wellbeing in love. This paysage intérieur is filled with brilliant colors, light, and warmth, and it contains both natural and art objects. The first scene is an indoor one, its stylized contents suggesting the richness and ease of complete love:

Des meubles luisants,
Polis par des ans,
Décoreraient notre chambre;
  Les plus rares fleurs
  Mêlant leurs odeurs
Aux vagues senteurs de l'ambre,
  Les riches plafonds,
  Les miroirs profonds,
La splendeur orientale. . . .

The room of the lovers has a decorative ceiling and contains shining marbles and elaborate mirrors; the air is permeated with the rich smells of rare flowers and perfumes while an Oriental magnificence characterizes the whole. Many of these details appear in the room of the anti-Cleopatra in *The Waste Land*, II, although there they have a quite different connotation.

The second scene, which is juxtaposed to the first by its outdoor setting, conveys the same état d'âme through natural objects. Here a sunset bathes canals, light boats, a village, and neighboring fields in shimmering colors of blue and gold:

—Les soleils couchants
Revêtent les champs,
Les canaux, la ville entière,
  D'hyacinthe et d'or;
  Le monde s'endort
Dans une chaude lumière.

The concept of the earthly paradise with its purity, happiness, and security of love is perfectly symbolized by this quiet landscape which sets the speaker's mind immediately before the reader and allows him to enter it. In Eliot a similar use of paysage intérieur to suggest aspects of paradise can be seen especially in "Marina," where the misty firs, the lapping water, and the grey rocks constitute the emotional state of Pericles.

A second important poem is "Le Cygne" where Baudelaire's ability to symbolize an état d'âme through urban landscape is clearly seen. The city scenes here convey the feeling of exile and loss in modern man. The first setting is one of decay and disintegration, a collection of fragments:

Ces tas de chapiteaux ébauchés et de fûts,
Les herbes, les gros blocs verdis par l'eau des flaques,
Et, brillant aux carreaux, le bric-à-brac confus.

The lines suggest the fragmented nature of modern man's life, as do the later "crowd of twisted things" and "heap of broken images" in Eliot. The second scene portrays an escaped swan wandering among the mazelike, dry stones searching for water; the "pavé sec" and the "ruisseau sans eau" suggest an arid desert, symbolizing physical and emotional sterility. Again echoes are heard in Eliot's *The Waste Land*, especially in Section V. The final scene of Baudelaire's poem presents a changing, indifferent city suburb on a muddy, foggy day. "La muraille immense du brouillard" in particular conveys a sense of isolation, of being irrevocably lost or imprisoned. This symbol of city fog is seen again and again in Eliot, from "Prufrock" and "Morning at the Window" through *The Waste Land* to *Four Quartets*. The city, then, in the work of both poets functions as an effective symbol of man's confused, sterile, and desolate state.

Two final examples of Baudelaire's symbolic landscapes are found in "Les Sept Vieillards" and "Un Voyage à Cythère," both of which seem to have greatly influenced Eliot's *The Waste Land*. In "Les Sept Vieillards" the setting is another foggy morning in the slum area of the "Fourmillante cité." The protagonist stands on a muddy street where the dirty yellow fog has distorted the height of the houses to nightmarish proportions:

Un matin, cependant que dans la triste rue
Les maisons, dont la brume allongeait la hauteur,
Simulaient les deux quais d'une rivière accrue,
Et que, décor semblable à l'âme de l'acteur,

Un brouillard sale et jaune inondait tout l'espace,
Je suivais . . .
Le faubourg. . . .

In this scene symbolizing the sordid corruptibility of man appear seven disgusting old men. They are, if not specifically the Seven Deadly Sins, at least sin or evil in general, which lurks furtively in the dark recesses of the city. Sister M. Cecilia Carey in her article, "Baudelaire's Influence in *The Waste Land*," has noted that the landscape's quality of eerie unreality particularly influenced Eliot, whose "interest in the phantasmagoric" developed from this type of setting and atmosphere and found "expression in surrealistic scenes stressing the unreal."[71]

If the air of unreality is impressive in "Les Sept Vieillards," it is the stark reality of the landscape in "Un Voyage à Cythère" which stands out. The raw descriptions of the desert isle where the sins of lust are punished are echoed in the "stony rubbish" of *The Waste Land*. The land in Baudelaire's poem is dry and barren, "une pauvre terre," "un terrain des plus maigres,/Un désert rocailleux troublé par des cris aigres." Here the lustful are punished for their sexual rapacity by being hanged on "un gibet à trois branches,/Du ciel se détachant en noir, comme un cyprès." When their bodies have rotted, they are attacked by ferocious birds. The entire setting is symbolic of the corrupting downward pull of the flesh; it is the mind of the protagonist gnawed by the voracious lusts of the body. Eliot's desert has many of the same qualities, although, as Sister Cecilia Carey points out, in Baudelaire's wasteland sexual sins are punished whereas in Eliot's they are committed.[72]

Thus the settings of city and desert form a major part of Baudelaire's landscape symbolism, but the garden and sea are also Baudelairean symbols from which Eliot may have drawn. The garden is for Baudelaire an Eden of childlike purity, removed from the lustful experience of the adult. In *"Moesta et Errabunda"* the paradisal garden is specifically childlike, and the emphasis again and again falls on the purity of love there:

> Comme vous êtes loin, paradis parfumé,
> Où sous un clair azur tout n'est qu'amour et joie,
> Où tout ce que l'on aime est digne d'être aimé,
> Où dans la volupté pure le coeur se noie! . . .
>
> Mais le vert paradis des amours enfantines . . .
> L'innocent paradis, plein de plaisirs furtifs. . . .

Similarly, in the opening poem of *Tableaux parisiens,* the poet speaks of escaping to a dreamland

> des horizons bleuâtres,
> Des jardins, des jets d'eau pleurant dans les albâtres,
> Des baisers, des oiseaux chantant soir et matin,
> Et tout ce que l'Idylle a de plus enfantin.

These lines seem to anticipate the garden of "Ash Wednesday," IV, as well as the rose garden of *Four Quartets.* Again the innocence of love is suggested by the garden isle, which forms a startling contrast to the barren Cythera in "Un Voyage à Cythère":

> Belle île aux myrtes verts, pleine de fleurs écloses,
> Vénérée à jamais par toute nation,
> Où les soupirs des coeurs en adoration
> Roulent comme l'encens sur un jardin de roses. . . .

It seems quite plausible that Eliot drew at least partially from Baudelaire his complex symbol of the rose garden.

Baudelaire's many-faceted symbol of the ocean may also have influenced Eliot. In Baudelaire the restless tossing of the sea suggests man's own anguish ("Je te hais, Océan! tes bonds et tes tumultes,/Mon esprit les retrouve en lui"); its powerful sweeping waves symbolize the force of passion ("Fortes tresses, soyez la houle qui m'enlève!/Tu contiens, mer d'ébène, un éblouissant rêve"); its depth and width convey the mystery of man's soul as in "L'Homme et la Mer," and finally the inscrutable and unfathomable newness of the ocean represents man's quest for "le nouveau" ("Plonger . . ./Au fond de l'Inconnu pour trouver du *nouveau!*").

Baudelaire, then, as well as Tennyson, offered Eliot a highly developed technique of symbolic landscape. In what is clearly a case of the interaction of poetic tradition and the individual talent, the twentieth century poet took what he needed from these predecessors and then made three refinements. First, and most important, he attained that objectivity lacking in Tennyson and Baudelaire, both of whom use landscape to express personal emotion. Eliot's landscape technique effects a change "from personal to impersonal manipulation of experience."[73] As Denis Donoghue notes in *The Ordinary Universe*, "If we look ahead from Tennyson to Eliot, with an agreed glance at the French Symbolists, we see that the state of mind is more and more deeply secreted in the landscape, the 'scene'; and the withdrawal of comment and reflection. We also see, as part of the same fact, a movement toward the embodiment of meaning, rather than its 'expression.' "[74] Furthermore, Eliot's landscapes are composites of actual scenes from his own life and real or imagined settings from many literatures. Thus they possess greater complexity than those of Tennyson and Baudelaire, whose landscapes are basically limited to their own immediate environments. A final degree of refinement lies in Eliot's method of choosing the bare minimum of scenic details, but details which immediately and clearly evoke the total landscape. While Tennyson glories in minute, prolonged descriptions of his settings, Baudelaire begins the shift to selection of significant details. It is Eliot, however, who brings concise evocation of symbolic landscape to a high point.

Thus, although Eliot is usually thought a modernist poet employing techniques largely new and original, an important element of his poetic technique, the use of landscape as symbol, derives from one of the oldest of poetic traditions. Further, the generally accepted view that he received inspiration only from the French Symbolists of the nineteenth century, and virtually none at all from English poets of that period, is not entirely correct, for he has drawn from Tennyson as well as Baudelaire in creating his symbolic landscapes. Building upon the tradition as developed by these two artists, Eliot added his own individual talent to forge a cluster of landscape symbols which recur in his poetry again and again with ever increasing significance and power of communication. With a knowledge of the background of these particular symbols, we can now turn to a close study of them as they work within the context of the poems themselves, developing and deepening as Eliot searches for and finds the meaning behind human experience.

II · The Early Poetry

In his early poetry through *The Waste Land,* Eliot presents life as an empty and meaningless experience, a sequence of trivia, a nightmare of boredom. The poet uses urban landscape as a major means of conveying this contemporary condition of ennui or spiritual torpor, for, as Baudelaire taught him, the industrial city is a highly effective symbol for the complexities of modern existence. Basically, Eliot relies on two types of urban settings to symbolize this general futility. The crude squalor of backstreet slum scenes suggests the sterility and hopelessness of lower class life. And the elegantly furnished rooms of such people as the Lady, Mrs. Phlaccus, and the anti-Cleopatra of *The Waste Land,* II, reveal the same emptiness in the lives of the refined upper class. The outward scenes then are symbols through which Eliot expresses the quality of the modern way of life, or, perhaps more correctly, of the modern way of death.

The poet uses four cities from his own experience as sources for these urban settings: St. Louis, Boston, Paris, and London. However, as Hugh Kenner points out in "The Urban Apocalypse," in most of the poems prior to *The Waste Land* the city is vague and unspecified so that we do not know precisely which city we are in.[1] In some works, for example "Prufrock," there are aspects of several cities; in other works, such as "Rhapsody on a Windy Night," the setting may give us the *feeling* of a certain city without identifying it specifically; and in yet other poems, such as "Gerontion," we may have no particular sense of any one specific city but simply of *a* city in general. With the exceptions of "The *Boston Evening Transcript*" and "Burbank with a Baedeker," not until *The Waste Land* does Eliot firmly ground a work in such a clearly identifiable metropolis as London.

Four of the early short poems—"Preludes," "Rhapsody on a Windy Night," "Morning at the Window," and "Sweeney Erect"—render their meanings with striking directness through the symbolic landscape of the city slum. "Preludes" conveys the boredom, meaninglessness, and sordidness of human life in the twentieth century through four urban scenes, two set in the evening (I and IV) and two set in the morning (II and III). Sections I, II, and IV were written in Boston, while Section III was written in Paris; these locations are certainly reflected in the poem's settings, though not specifically. The title itself evokes a bitter irony, for each of the four sections is a prelude to nothing except further emptiness, and each separate scene reveals beneath its surface essentially the same futility.

Section I presents a city slum area at 6 P.M., the dying time of the day: "The burnt-out ends of smoky days." As Elizabeth Drew points out, this is not just the city dusk but "the twilight of an epoch."[2] A sense of rootlessness and corruption is manifested in

> And now a gusty shower wraps
> The grimy scraps
> Of withered leaves about your feet
> And newspapers from vacant lots. . . .

The "broken blinds" and "lonely cab-horse" serve to intensify man's isolation and his imprisonment in the sordid.

The second section stresses the monotony of city life and the downtrodden souls of those who dwell there through a morning scene in which the street is trampled by the muddy feet of people hurrying to choke down coffee, to drown the stale vapors of last evening's beer. The street is, of course, symbolic of the soul. The last three lines emphasize the homelessness of modern man, who lives only in rented rooms, and the futility with which he begins each day:

> One thinks of all the hands
> That are raising dingy shades
> In a thousand furnished rooms.

In Section III the poet exposes one of these rooms and its occupant, probably a prostitute. The physical aspects of the room, the sagging unclean bed, the shadowy ceiling, the dark enclosing shutters, suggest the sordidness of her tarnished soul. Grover Smith notes that Eliot's subject here came from Philippe's *Bubu de Montparnasse:*

> The principal passage from which Eliot took imagery for his poem reads, in Laurence Vail's translation, as follows:
> "At noon, in the hotel room of the rue Chanoinesse, a grey and dirty light filtered through the grey curtains and dirty panes of the window . . . and there was the unmade bed where the two bodies had left their impress of brownish sweat upon the worn sheets— this bed of hotel rooms, *where the bodies are dirty and the souls as well.*
> Berthe, in her chemise, had just got up. With her narrow shoulders, her grey shirt and her unclean feet, *she too seemed, in her pale yellowish slimness, to have no light.* With her puffy eyes and scraggly hair, in the disorder of this room, *she too was in disorder* and her thoughts lay heaped confusedly in her head. These awakenings at midday are heavy and sticky like the life of the night before with its love-making, its alcohol, and its torpid sleep" (italics mine).[3]

Eliot reveals extreme skill in reducing the essence of these two paragraphs to fifteen lines of poetry which symbolize rather than explain directly, as Philippe has done in the parts italicized, the correspondences between the room and the soul of the prostitute.

The final section comes full circle, returning to an evening scene. The circular structure reemphasizes the meaninglessness and the boredom of modern man's life, for the poem ends where it began. The soul of the street, of the city, of man is tortured on the rack, "stretched tight across the skies," or trampled to death by the monotony of the daily repetition symbolized by the "insistent feet/At four and five and six o'clock." In the midst of this depressing urban scene, the protagonist suddenly feels that life must be more than this;

perhaps there is another emotional state, love, or compassion, or even pity:

> I am moved by fancies that are curled
> Around these images, and cling:
> The notion of some infinitely gentle
> Infinitely suffering thing.

However, with a gesture of cynical disillusionment, the speaker dismisses "The notion" in the face of the cruel reality of meaninglessness symbolized by the return to the image of the vacant lot:

> Wipe your hand across your mouth, and laugh;
> The worlds revolve like ancient women
> Gathering fuel in vacant lots.

The universe turns without direction or purpose: "Men and bits of paper, whirled by the cold wind. . . ." Thus the run-down city landscape of dirty streets, dingy rooms, and wasted vacant lots serves as a highly effective objective correlative for the degraded hollow soul of modern man.

A similar slum landscape serves as a major symbol in another early poem, "Rhapsody on a Windy Night," composed while Eliot was in Paris. Here concrete urban scenes impinge on a man's consciousness as he wanders through the mazelike city at night, on a nocturnal odyssey surely suggested by Baudelaire's *Tableaux parisiens.* These scenes and the subsequent thoughts which they evoke symbolize the imprisonment of time and flesh, the corruption of the soul, in short the boredom and horror of the human condition.

The nightmare journey begins at midnight. There is, as Grover Smith points out, a "dissolution of orderly thought into an irrational, almost surrealistic collage of discontinuous mental impressions. . . ."[4] These mental impressions are the protagonist's responses to several disconnected visual images seen in the course of his nocturnal wandering. The first scene is simply of the street with its monotonous and identical rows of street lamps, suggesting the anonymity, the lack of individuality, of the city man's soul. An atmosphere of irrationality and vacancy is evoked by the simile of the madman shaking his dead geranium.

The second scene occurs at 1:30 A.M. when the speaker sees a prostitute leering at him from a lighted doorway:

> The street-lamp said, "Regard that woman
> Who hesitates toward you in the light of the door
> Which opens on her like a grin.
> You see the border of her dress
> Is torn and stained with sand,
> And you see the corner of her eye
> Twists like a crooked pin."

The setting and the woman with her twisted eye symbolize the degradation, the distortion, of the human being in the modern city. They also evoke in the man's consciousness a memory of two other symbols of degradation, one a seaside and the other an urban landscape. The "twisted branch upon the beach" has been severed from its life source, the tree, and as a result is "stiff and white." It thus suggests the dismembered, fragmentary, and isolated aspect of modern man's existence as well as its pervasive deadness. The other symbolic landscape is a factory yard in the industrial, mechanical city, where a broken, rusted spring lies brittle and useless on the ground. The yard itself suggests the ugliness of the human soul in the city, while the broken spring conveys man's loss of vitality, warmth, and indeed of life itself. These "twisted things" convey moral as well as material corruption.

At half-past two the protagonist encounters the third scene; in the gutter of a slum street a hungry cat "devours a morsel of rancid butter." The moral degradation symbolized here again evokes memories of similar scenes: a child without moral values, without a soul ("I could see nothing behind that child's eye"), stealing a toy; a peeping tom peering through shutters; a crab clinging by sheer animal instinct to a stick. The three are identical because ruled by animalistic urges rather than by human, moral ones. Eliot's use here of bodily members such as the tongue, the eye, and the hand not only depersonalizes and objectifies, but also suggests the fragmented, subhuman quality of modern man.

The fourth landscape focuses on the moon, personified as an old diseased woman who is alone with the faded memoirs of a long-dead love (although she could also be interpreted as an old prostitute):

> "A washed-out smallpox cracks her face,
> Her hand twists a paper rose,
> That smells of dust and eau de Cologne,
> She is alone. . . ."

The feeble eye, the loss of memory, the smiling into corners, and the twisting of the paper flower suggest that she is either senile or insane. The "moonscape" is thus a striking symbol for the futility, the loss, the "dead end" of human life. Again the present scene evokes in the protagonist memories of past urban scenes conveying similar ideas of death, degradation, and triviality:

> The reminiscence comes
> Of sunless dry geraniums
> And dust in crevices,
> Smells of chestnuts in the streets,
> And female smells in shuttered rooms,
> And cigarettes in corridors
> And cocktail smells in bars.

The last setting is the most ironic and terrifying of all. On the street he has seen images of degradation and ennui which, even though they evoked corresponding memories from his own experience, seemed somehow outside him. Yet when he returns to his own door, "he steps out of one horror into a worse horror,"[5] for the same things make up his own existence:

> "Here is the number on the door.
> Memory!

> You have the key,
> The little lamp spreads a ring on the stair.
> Mount.
> The bed is open; the tooth-brush hangs on the wall,
> Put your shoes at the door, sleep, prepare for life."

The setting of the crowded apartment house, of dim dingy stairs, unmade bed, toothbrush hanging in its place symbolizes his own entrapment in the meaningless, monotonous routine of empty life and empty death. This realization then is the "last twist of the knife." The exterior urban landscape thus reflects with particular sensitivity the psychological landscape of the protagonist.

"Morning at the Window" is a short poem, again using the lower class section of the city (here probably London) to symbolize the ugliness, the emptiness, the imprisonment of the human soul. The speaker of the poem seems to be looking down on the street from an upper window, observing the futile activities of the morning. The "rattling breakfast plates in basement kitchens" skillfully catch up the dreary routine and subterranean quality of slum existence, and again the symbol of the trampled street is used to convey the downtrodden, tortured aspects of this sordid way of life. The Baudelairean brown fog and muddy streets described with ocean imagery suggest that the passersby, metaphorically walking on the bottom of the ocean, are drowning in a sea of squalor, agony, and vacancy: "The brown waves of fog toss up to me/Twisted faces from the bottom of the street. . . ." Thus even the short poem relies heavily on urban landscape as symbol.

Finally, the corrupt brothel setting of "Sweeney Erect" serves as a symbol of the corruption of passionate, sexual love in the modern world. Sweeney's world is a place of degraded sex, loveless lust, empty and sterile physical gratification. What better symbol could Eliot have chosen than a brothel in a slum? The poem opens in the ancient mythological world, not because that world was beautiful and glorious but because its people had a meaningful relationship with some cosmic order. In Sweeney's world no meaningful bond exists between man and woman, much less between man and God. This contrast reemphasizes the modern emptiness and isolation.

The poem begins with a landscape of the desolate Grecian shore:

> Paint me a cavernous waste shore
> Cast in the unstilled Cyclades,
> Paint me the bold anfractuous rocks
> Faced by the snarled and yelping seas.

The scene, set by the life-giving sea, is rugged, even violent, but vitally alive, and it catches up the passionate meaningful relationship of Theseus and Ariadne, the goddess of vegetation and spring, symbol of fertility and life. Their love relationship was filled with ecstasy and agony, with vibrant emotional involvement:

> Display me Aeolus above
> Reviewing the insurgent gales
> Which tangle Ariadne's hair
> And swell with haste the perjured sails.

As Theseus's ship sails away from Ariadne, so Sweeney abandons his "lover" on the bed in the setting of the brothel. In contrast to the fertility of the mythological pair, this coupling is loveless and sterile, like the mating of beasts. The corruption of sexuality is mirrored in the contrast between Ariadne's wildly blowing hair and the woman's "withered root of knots of hair." Further, the bestiality of this passionless sexual pleasure is reflected in the animal imagery, "Gesture of orang-outang" and "clawing at the pillow slip," and its brutality is seen in the violence of the verbs "Slitted," "gashed," and "cropped out." Sweeney is concerned only with himself; as Smidt points out, he has "no sense of immorality or perversion, lacking knowledge of Good and Evil."[6] The setting of the rented room, sparsely furnished with a bed and sink, conveys the moral vacancy of its occupants as skillfully as do their actions. The poem ends with a view of the corridor of the brothel, where the other "ladies" have gathered excitedly at the door hoping to satisfy their morbid curiosities. They have neither compassion nor understanding; the madam has only mercenary interests: "Mrs. Turner intimates/It does the house no sort of good." Doris alone brings aid, but in the form of stimulants for the body while it is the soul which so desperately needs help. The brothel setting therefore functions as a highly significant symbol of the degradation of man's capacity for meaningful human love.

The common urban scene then in all its physical ugliness and grime symbolizes a correspondent spiritual ugliness and grime in the souls of those who live there. Having revealed this pervading sterility in the lower class areas with their "grimy scraps/Of withered leaves," their "broken blinds and chimney pots," their "thousand furnished rooms" and "sunless dry geraniums," Eliot also exposes the same boredom and horror beneath the surface beauty of middle and particularly upper class society. Beneath the bric-à-brac and flower vases, the teacups and Dresden clocks lies the same emptiness found in the slum tenements.

"A Cooking Egg" is the only one of the early poems whose symbolic décor could be termed middle class. In this work of devastating disillusionment and dullness, the bourgeois "landscape" reflects the monotony and flatness of a middle-aged married couple's life together. Their apartment is cluttered with symbols of their stale existence: the knitting, *Views of the Oxford Colleges*, the "Daguerreotypes and silhouettes" of the ancestors. They sit quietly in chairs "Some distance" apart both physically and emotionally. The dullness is further stressed by contrast with the husband's glorious dreams of honor, wealth, position, and exotic companionship. His anguished disillusionment and despair are most fully expressed in the third section, where references to specific places have symbolic overtones. The penny world of illusion, magic, enchantment which he bought "To eat with Pipit behind the screen" has been devoured by "The red-eyed scavengers . . ./From Kentish Town and Golder's Green." These monsters from the suburbs of London I take to be the monotony of daily, quotidian existence, or, to use Baudelaire's word, ennui. The eagles and trumpets of an exciting life are "Buried beneath some snow-deep Alps," and real life is only boredom. For the loss of all their dreams and for their resigned acceptance of the dullness, multitudes weep in "a hundred A.B.C.'s." These tea rooms, patronized by the middle class, are used here as symbols of the daily, inescapable routine. Thus, although the speaker has presented his own particular plight of disillusionment, the ending of the poem extends his experience into a universal one shared by "Weeping, weeping multitudes."

On the upper level of society, meaningful emotion has been "refined" into empty form, and the elegant settings of the rich reveal the same hollowness as do the sordid settings of the poor. "Portrait of a Lady," relying on the décor for much of its symbolic content, explores the sterile relationship between a young man and an older woman. The woman, according to Conrad Aiken, was patterned upon an actual person whom Eliot knew: "Our dear deplorable friend, Miss X, the *précieuse ridicule* to end all preciosity, serving tea so exquisitely among her bric-à-brac, was to be pinned like a butterfly to a page in *Portrait of a Lady.*"[7]

The poem opens with a drawing room scene which symbolizes the emotional relationship of the woman and the young man:

> Among the smoke and fog of a December afternoon
> You have the scene arrange itself . . .
> And four wax candles in the darkened room,
> Four rings of light upon the ceiling overhead,
> An atmosphere of Juliet's tomb. . . .

The references to "the scene," to Shakespeare's play *Romeo and Juliet,* to the theatrical darkness and light point out the superficiality of their liaison. The fact that it is December, the dying time of the year, in the late afternoon, the dying time of the day, increases the significance of the darkened room that resembles a vault of the dead. The initial impression created by the décor is reinforced by the remainder of Section I. The woman reaches out to the young man as another way, in addition to the teas and concerts, by which to fill her empty existence: "Without these friendships—life, what *cauchemar!*" The futility and boredom of her life are mirrored in her speech with its hesitations, fragments, repetitions, and monotonous rhythm:

> "You do not know how much they mean to me, my friends,
> And how, how rare and strange it is, to find
> In a life composed so much, so much of odds and ends,
> [For indeed I do not love it . . . you knew? you are not blind!
> How keen you are!]
> To find a friend who has these qualities. . . ."

The young man, however, retreats from this too-demanding emotional attachment, finding escape in external trivialities:

> —Let us take the air, in a tobacco trance,
> Admire the monuments,
> Discuss the late events,
> Correct our watches by the public clocks.
> Then sit for half an hour and drink our bocks.

In Section II, setting again plays an important symbolic role. The scene is the same room, filled now with the glow of a spring sunset, and a bowl of lilacs replaces the flickering candles. The light and the flowers hint at a hope of rebirth as the woman pleads indirectly with the young man to become more emotionally involved:

> "I am always sure that you understand
> My feelings, always sure that you feel,
> Sure that across the gulf you reach your hand."

Yet the light of sunset fades into darkness, and the life is twisted out of the lilacs. Similarly, the young man retains his self-possession and rejects more intimate attachment. He does confess, however, that the hyacinths of the park garden make him conscious of some potential deeper meaning in human relationships. The garden, of course, is one of Eliot's dominant landscape symbols, suggesting both human and divine love, and the hyacinths, as in Section I of *The Waste Land*, are traditional symbols of fertility. But the meaningful relationship symbolized by the garden is something quite beyond him.

With the failure of the spring, the deadliness of winter once again approaches, and the young man returns to the room to seek his release. The surroundings reflect his emotional state; the dark stairs suggest his humiliation and emotional clumsiness, while the bric-à-brac among which his "smile falls heavily" conveys his nervousness and embarrassment as he awkwardly wriggles out of the trap. The lady of course pretends to be unhurt, assuming the mask so necessary to modern man:

> "You will write, at any rate.
> Perhaps it is not too late.
> I shall sit here, serving tea to friends."

The poem ends with a projected future scene, the young man sitting at a desk in a foreign hotel room on a late winter afternoon:

> Well! and what if she should die some afternoon,
> Afternoon grey and smoky, evening yellow and rose;
> Should die and leave me sitting pen in hand
> With the smoke coming down above the housetops. . . ?

The foreign location and the impersonal desk implied in the lines suggest his detachment, his emotional apathy. At this funereal time of day, he questions the meaning of her death and of their sterile relationship and finds it to lie in the realm of mercenary values. What has it cost him? Devoid of all real feeling, he probes not the heart, but the mind. Thus the futility, boredom, and emotional sterility of upper class existence is symbolized to a great extent by the setting in "Portrait of a Lady."

In the short Bostonian poems, landscape has the same function. "The *Boston Evening Transcript*" lifts the veil from the genteel tradition to reveal the emptiness of proper Bostonian lives. The scene is the front steps of an imposing home on a Boston street at evening. Behind the door wait deadened people whose high point of life is the arrival of the evening paper: "I mount the steps and ring the bell, . . ./And I say, 'Cousin Harriet, here is the *Boston Evening Transcript.'* " While the setting in this poem helps to symbolize the emptiness of *life,* in "Aunt Helen" it reflects the emptiness and futility of *death.* Aunt Helen's meaningless decease creates no vacuum, no real loss. The "small house near a fashionable square" remains, with its dogs and its Dresden clock, which still ticks on the mantelpiece. The only real change is the subsequent trivial death of the parrot and the disrespectful actions of the servants, expressed in their disregard of the dining room furniture:

> And the footman sat upon the dining-table
> Holding the second housemaid on his knees—
> Who had always been so careful while her mistress lived.

Symbolic landscape is an even more outstanding element in the three major poems of Eliot's early work, "The Love Song of J. Alfred Prufrock," "Gerontion," and *The Waste Land.* Indeed, these poems use both upper and lower class urban landscape to symbolize the pervading sterility and lack of meaning or purpose in the souls of modern men.

The structure of "Prufrock," as Leonard Unger has pointed out, is analogous to a series of slides, each of which presents a landscape or scene symbolizing a facet of the protagonist's soul: "All the scenery of the poem, indoor and outdoor, is finally the psychological landscape of Prufrock himself. The streets, rooms, people, and fancies of the poem all register on Prufrock's consciousness, and thus they are his consciousness, the man himself."[8] The dominant motif of the poem, and of Prufrock's inner self, is the realization of life's emptiness. The sense of boredom and futility so oppresses the sensitive protagonist that he is led to an overwhelming question which he dares not ask: What is the meaning of this life? He realizes the sterile monotony of his "works and days," and he senses that a more fruitful and meaningful life must exist. However, he cannot break out of his enclosed physical and mental landscape and is doomed to run the inescapable treadmill of a life which combines the futility of the Lady's and of Sweeney's worlds.

While the poem *is* like a series of slides, it is not a random or haphazard collection but one which is very carefully and, I think, tightly ordered. The poem can be seen as falling into four parts. Part I (ll. 1–69) shows Prufrock's approach to the question and gives a good deal of background information about his life and personality. Part II (ll. 70–74) is the climax of the poem in which Prufrock reveals his inability to ask the question and his agonized frustration at this failure. Part III (ll. 75–119) contains justifications for his rejection of the question, the rejection itself being stated directly only at the end of this section. Part IV (ll. 120–131) reveals the emptiness of his future, as the consequence of his failure to ask the question and act on it. The structure also has a time scheme as complex as those of Faulkner and Proust, with verb tenses extremely important throughout the work. Being set in the mind of the protagonist, the poem is constantly operating in the present tense with shifts both backward and forward. In Part I the present shifts into the past to reveal the quality of Prufrock's existence up to this point ("For I have known them all already, known them all:—/Have known the evenings, mornings, afternoons") and into the future to explore tentatively the possibility of asking the question ("And indeed there will be time/To wonder, 'Do I dare?' and, 'Do I dare?' "). Part II begins with an imaginary near-future in which Prufrock tries to phrase the question ("Shall I say, I have gone at dusk . . . ?") and ends with the agony of his realization in the *present* that he will be unable to succeed. Part III opens in the present but slips immediately into a near-future in which the protagonist looks back at the now *past* moment of the present and imagines that he had asked the question unsuccessfully ("And would it have been worth it, after all . . . ?/It is impossible to say just what I mean!"). The section ends with an abrupt and violent return to the present ("No! I am not Prince Hamlet, nor was meant to be"). In Part IV past, present, and future are intermingled, with the sterile future ironically juxtaposed to the fertile but now past possibilities of a richer life, and the poem closes with the image of drowning in the present.

The complexity of the structure is matched by the complexity of the settings, which are both real and imaginary. Of the former, the dominant one is a rather fashionable house in the city, although the urban slums are glimpsed at the beginning of the poem. The city itself is not clearly identified and yet has aspects of at least three specific places, as Hugh Kenner notes in his essay "The Urban Apocalypse": "If we tend to suppose that Prufrock treads the streets of Boston, still his surname and his yellow fogs are from St. Louis, and the Paris of Laforgue has left its impress."[9] The imagined settings, beside or below the sea, are as significant as the real ones. They all have symbolic meanings, as we shall see from a close analysis of the poem.

Prufrock begins by inviting his double self, the public Prufrock and the private one, to go to a social gathering, an early evening cocktail party or a high tea:

> Let us go then, you and I,
> When the evening is spread out against the sky
> Like a patient etherised upon a table. . . .

He projects his own complex feelings of helplessness and inadequacy, of spiritual disease and numbness, into the atmosphere of the evening urban landscape with a simile that recalls the agony of the rack in "Preludes" and symbolizes the living death of Prufrock's existence. From this skyscape his view turns to the route he is following on the way to his destination. It leads through Sweeney's world of the slums, a world of

> certain half-deserted streets,
> The muttering retreats
> Of restless nights in one-night cheap hotels
> And sawdust restaurants with oyster-shells. . . .

These desolate backstreets suggest the emptiness of slum life, while the cheap hotels and low-class restaurants are not just reminders of the transient life of a metropolis but, as Drew remarks, symbols of "the homelessness of the human soul."[10] The mazelike, dirty streets paralleling the twisting and turning avenues of Prufrock's mind lead him to recognize the same sterility in his own life:

Summer surprised us, coming over the Starnbergersee
With a shower of rain. . . .
THE WASTE LAND, 11. 8-9.

The Starnbergersee, near Munich.

[W]e stopped in the colonnade,
And went on in sunlight, into the Hofgarten,
And drank coffee, and talked for an hour.
THE WASTE LAND, 11. 9-11.

The Hofgarten, Munich.

The Hofgarten, Munich. The colonnade can be seen in the background.

A crowd flowed over London Bridge, so many,
I had not thought death had undone so many.
THE WASTE LAND, 11. 62-3.

London Bridge, about 1920.

King William Street, London.

Flowed up the hill and down King William Street,
To where Saint Mary Woolnoth kept the hours
With a dead sound on the final stroke of nine.
THE WASTE LAND, 11. 66-8.

Saint Mary Woolnoth, Lombard Street, London.

By the waters of Leman I sat down and wept . . .
THE WASTE LAND, 1. 182.

Lake Leman,
Lausanne.

Mr. Eugenides. . .
Asked me in demotic French
To luncheon at the Cannon Street Hotel
Followed by a weekend at the Metropole.
THE WASTE LAND, 11. 209, 211-14.

The Promenade, Brighton. The Metropole Hotel is the building
in the center of the photograph.

St. Magnus Martyr,
Lower Thames Street,
London, about 1921.

> . . . where the walls
> Of Magnus Martyr hold
> Inexplicable splendour of Ionian white and gold.
> THE WASTE LAND, 11. 263-5.

The interior of St. Magnus Martyr, Lower Thames Street, London.

The river sweats
Oil and tar
The barges drift
With the turning tide. . . .
THE WASTE LAND, 11. 266-9.

The Thames River, looking east from London Bridge, about 1921.

Southwest wind
Carried down stream
The peal of bells
White towers. . . .
THE WASTE LAND, 11. 286-9.

The Tower of London, seen from the Thames River.

Kew Gardens, near London.

'Trams and dusty trees.
Highbury bore me. Richmond and Kew
Undid me.'
THE WASTE LAND, 11. 292-4.

'On Margate Sands.
I can connect
Nothing with nothing.'
THE WASTE LAND, 11. 300-2.

Margate Sands, Kent.

> Streets that follow like a tedious argument
> Of insidious intent
> To lead you to an overwhelming question. . . .

This overwhelming question is: What value does life have? Is it only futile vacancy? Is nothing meaningful?[11] Yet Prufrock fears the question and retreats into the safety of the social gathering in a refined drawing room of an elegant house, only to discover that the question haunts him there. The room itself catches up the monotony of well-bred life, for its bored and boring women talk tediously and ignorantly of Michelangelo, whose great activity and passionate grasp on life contrast painfully with Prufrock's passivity.

Through the windows Prufrock sees a yellow fog which partially obscures the outer landscape of sooty chimneys and clogged drains filled with stagnant water.[12] This "yellow fog that rubs its back upon the window-panes,/The yellow smoke that rubs its muzzle on the window-panes" is symbolic of what Drew calls "the creeping, choking atmosphere of spiritual miasma,"[13] which exists in the souls of Prufrock and his fellowmen. It is that numbing spiritual torpor which Baudelaire calls ennui and Christians call acedia, an inescapable apathy which, creeping into every corner, draws Prufrock hypnotically into its passionless spell. The fog is similar in symbolic function to the ether of the first lines, which also suggests the drugged quality of Prufrock's existence.

In a frantic, though ultimately futile, attempt to escape the numbness represented by the fog-enclosed drawing room, Prufrock considers "disturbing the universe" by asking his question: " 'Do I dare?' and 'Do I dare?' " But even his timid deliberations suggest failure; he is too afraid to ask: "And time yet for a hundred indecisions,/And for a hundred visions and revisions. . . ." Significantly, his negative or at least tentative approach to the daring act is symbolized by an element of setting, a staircase. Mounting a stairway in Eliot's poetry often signifies making a spiritual effort; that Prufrock is constantly aware that he can (and will) "turn back and descend the stair" conveys his implicit rejection of that effort.

The next section, a re-view of the boredom and futility of his life and of the lives of those who would not understand the question had he the courage to ask it, contains no landscape symbols. Rather it uses trivial objects such as coffee spoons and cigarette butts to suggest the triviality of his existence:

> For I have known them all already, known them all:—
> Have known the evenings, mornings, afternoons,
> I have measured out my life with coffee spoons;. . .
> Then how should I begin
> To spit out all the butt-ends of my days and ways?

Prufrock realizes that, if he began to talk of the meaninglessness which is his every minute, he would be dissected by the cruel and impersonal eyes of the women who do not want their patterned lives disturbed. Seeing himself as an insignificant insect, he shrinks in terror at imagining their penetrating stares:

> And I have known the eyes already, known them all—
> The eyes that fix you in a formulated phrase,
> And when I am formulated, sprawling on a pin,
> When I am pinned and wriggling on the wall, . . .
> . . . how should I presume?

Abruptly, Prufrock and the poem reach the crisis, and Eliot uses two symbolic landscapes brilliantly here at the heart of the work. Prufrock imagines how he might present the question if he could gather the moral courage to ask it. He would begin by explaining that the barren slum area through which he passed on his way to the party had forced him to recognize the same sterility in his own life. The urban scene of transient, lonely, sordid men leaning from the windows of the "one-night cheap hotels" gathers up all the negative qualities of his own existence:

> Shall I say, I have gone at dusk through narrow streets
> And watched the smoke that rises from the pipes
> Of lonely men in shirt-sleeves, leaning out of windows? . . .

Yet Prufrock's attempt at explanation trails off into nothingness as he realizes that he would never be able to communicate successfully. He explodes with terror and frustration at his inadequacies, and again a landscape is used to symbolize his feelings. It is an undersea scene in which Prufrock sees himself as an anonymous clawed creature, without identity, companionship, or human significance: "I should have been a pair of ragged claws/Scuttling across the floors of silent seas." The quiet sea floor is symbolic here, not of fertility and life, but of sterility and death-in-life. As Helen Gardner remarks, there is an overwhelming "sense of meaninglessness . . . blended with acute self-disgust and sheer panic in . . . [this] haunting image. . . ."[14]

The irony is that Prufrock does not and will not express aloud his vision of emptiness and the universal question which it provokes. Instead he sinks back into the numbing dullness of the yellow fog and the triviality of the drawing room:

> And the afternoon, the evening, sleeps so peacefully!
> Smoothed by long fingers,
> Asleep . . . tired . . . or it malingers,
> Stretched on the floor, here beside you and me.
> Should I, after tea and cakes and ices,
> Have the strength to force the moment to its crisis?

The implicit answer is no, and Prufrock goes on to compile a list of excuses: he is not great; he would have been misunderstood, ridiculed, rebuffed; he would have been exposed and defenseless "as if a magic lantern threw the nerves in patterns on a screen." The refined drawing room in the background serves as a subtle understated symbol of the triviality of the externals to which he is bound. The details of the porcelain, the cups, the sofa pillows, as well as the literal servants implied by the reference to the "eternal Footman," all fuse to create the symbolic setting. Finally, with an explicit and emphatic "No!" Prufrock assures himself that he is not the man to be concerned with universal questions. He is not a Prince Hamlet, but rather a Polonius who has a minor and even ludicrous role; he is "At times, indeed, almost ridiculous—/Almost, at times, the Fool." In the future, he will concern himself only with trivial questions, "Shall I part my hair behind? Do I dare to eat a peach?"

The poem ends with a return to the symbol of the sea, here signifying both life and death. Prufrock has had a visionary insight into the paradisal world of meaningful existence, symbolized by the sea and its life-rhythms of creation, destruction, and re-creation:

> I have seen them riding seaward on the waves
> Combing the white hair of the waves blown back
> When the wind blows the water white and black.

As mentioned earlier, there is a startling resemblance between this use of symbolic seascape and Tennyson's in "The Merman." Both poets also employ hair, in addition to the sea, to suggest fertility. Prufrock's agony lies in his awareness of the meaning life can have, "I have heard the mermaids singing, each to each," and his realization that he himself cannot partake of that fertility, "I do not think that they will sing to me." Thus, he sinks down into the sterile sea of his meaningless drawing-room world, there to drown of spiritual torpor:

> We have lingered in the chambers of the sea
> By sea-girls wreathed with seaweed red and brown
> Till human voices wake us, and we drown.

The outer landscape is thus a highly significant symbol of the inner landscape of Prufrock's being. The actual drawing room suggests the superficial values of Prufrock's own sterile existence composed of cultured social gatherings, while the slum setting represents the sordid reality of emptiness, veiled by the elegant trivia of an upper class existence. In addition to these literal urban settings are the ocean settings that exist within Prufrock's mind. These communicate ironically (1) the destructive sterility of the life he leads and (2) the fulfillment of a creative existence that he is unable to attain.

In "Gerontion," too, symbolic setting plays an important role in conveying the essence of Gerontion's state of mind. Philip Headings has remarked that "Gerontion" is perhaps the least understood of Eliot's major poems,[15] and, before considering the use of landscape here, an interpretation of this elusive work is presented. Eliot himself furnishes what seems to me a significant clue to its basic theme in his essay "Thoughts After Lambeth." There he says: "The World is trying the experiment of attempting to form a civilized but non-Christian mentality. The experiment will fail; but we must be very patient in awaiting its collapse; meanwhile redeeming the time: so that the Faith may be preserved alive through the dark ages before us; to renew and rebuild civilization, and save the World from suicide."[16] In addition, two lines in "Choruses from 'The Rock' " seem to be an exact, and revealing, description of the poem's protagonist: "But you, have you built well, that you now sit helpless in a ruined house?/Where many are born to idleness, to frittered lives and squalid deaths, embittered scorn in honey-hives . . ." (II, ll. 4–5). Through the persona of Gerontion, Eliot portrays a nightmare vision of this spiritually diseased, nonChristian world on its way to extinction. Gerontion, an infirm, impotent, and somewhat senile old man who has rejected Christ in favor of self-possession and material goods,[17] symbolizes contemporary civilization in all its spiritual sterility and decay. Thus the contents of Gerontion's soul are also the contents of that civilization's soul, and both are suggested largely through landscape. However, the landscape symbols in "Gerontion" are far more general than those in the other early poems. While the details themselves are specific, it is difficult, if not impossible, to tell whether the setting is in the city or the countryside. Eliot, it seems, has consciously chosen an abstract landscape, for the poem as a whole is more obviously universal than the private tragedies of the Lady, the wanderer of "Rhapsody on a Windy Night," and Prufrock.

In the opening lines Gerontion reveals his sterile situation:

"Here I am, an old man in a dry month,/Being read to by a boy, waiting for rain." He and his civilization suffer from a blindness which is moral and spiritual as well as physical. The blankness of his world is heightened by the contrast evoked by the first three words, "Here I am." They awaken echoes of ancient Biblical men who answered "Here am I" to God's call (Genesis 22:1 and Exodus 3:4). These men did not reject Him, but submitted their wills to His Will. Thus their lives were rich and fulfilled through a meaningful relationship with God. Gerontion, on the other hand, has never given of himself in any way; his words are a statement of self-possession rather than a humble response of self-surrender. The three symbolic wartime landscapes suggest through contrast his refusal to commit himself:

> I was neither at the hot gates
> Nor fought in the warm rain
> Nor knee deep in the salt marsh, heaving a cutlass,
> Bitten by flies, fought.

Each landscape symbolizes active involvement: the passionate hot gates of Thermopylae, the life-renewing warm rain on the battleground, and the soldier-filled salt marsh, which might possibly be the Thames estuary where invasions of Britain were countered in the past. All of these settings are in a very real sense "foreign" to Gerontion.

Having defined himself through the negative method of describing landscapes in which he did *not* appear, Gerontion then delineates his immediate environment. Whereas the battlefield scenes pulsate with life and energy, Gerontion's surroundings are deathlike and enervated. He lives in a rotting house rented from a Jewish landlord:

> My house is a decayed house,
> And the jew squats on the window sill, the owner,
> Spawned in some estaminet of Antwerp,
> Blistered in Brussels, patched and peeled in London.

The symbol of the house works on several levels. It suggests the actual crumbling building in which Gerontion lives. Further, it indicates the decay of his body, which has lost "sight, smell, hearing, taste and touch," and of his soul, which has shrunken through rejection of Christ. Finally, it symbolizes the moral and spiritual corruption of his civilization which worships material gods.

The exact location of the house is difficult to ascertain. The references to the Jew's background of Antwerp, Brussels, and London may indicate an urban slum setting, although they may function only as symbols of his commercial and corrupt character. (Antwerp, one of the largest seaports in the world, has historically been a great industrial and financial center with a large number of Jewish residents. Indeed, its Stock Exchange served as a model for the London Stock Exchange. Brussels and London are both capital cities serving as international economic complexes.)

There are two possible interpretations of the lines, "The goat coughs at night in the field overhead;/Rocks, moss, stonecrop, iron, merds." The more common view that "the field overhead" is the sky and "the goat" is the constellation Capricorn sets the time as winter, appropriate as the season of death and ironically of the birth of the now neglected Christ. However, an alternate reading, considering landscape, takes into account the second line, integrally linked to the first line by the semicolon but ignored by the first reading, as well as the literal meanings of "field" and "goat." The alternate reading is further substantiated by lines 31–32, "An old man in a draughty house/*Under a windy knob*" (italics mine), "knob" meaning a prominent rounded hill or mountain. In this second reading the "field overhead" is a barren, littered pasture (if the country) or a vacant lot (if the city) on a hill above and behind the house. There a lone goat, once a symbol of passion, wanders weak and unhealthy: "The goat coughs at night. . . ." The sterile rocks, funguslike growths, rusted springs or tin cans, and animal excrement filling the field convey the sordid corruption and ugliness of Gerontion and his world. John Crowe Ransom sees an additional irony in this drab landscape: "The words 'Rocks, moss, stonecrop' make just such a series of detail as Wordsworth might have employed lovingly in one of his listings of the features of a fair landscape. But the landscape in question is only 'the field overhead,' where the goat ranges. . . . We may take the 'iron' to mean the scrap-iron of used-up metal gadgets tossed from the passing cars, and composing not a landscape but a litter; and merds are merds. There could not be terms terser and more euphemistic at the same time, but they have their savagery."[18] While in reality Gerontion's house is below this windswept, littered hill, the implication of a reversed and chaotic world is clear. Overhead is the infertile field rather than the richly meaningful sky. Gerontion's civilization is smothered beneath a filthy covering that is like the dirt over a grave.

Having described the highly symbolic exterior landscape, Gerontion then exposes the interior of the house. It catches up all the meaningless routine of an empty life. The anonymous woman passes heavily and mechanically through the trivial, ordinary motions of a day: "The woman keeps the kitchen, makes tea,/Sneezes at evening, poking the peevish gutter." As in "Morning at the Window," the kitchen setting suggests monotonous imprisonment in daily routine, and the sputtering flame in the fireplace, "the peevish gutter," mirrors the listlessness and nervous irritability of trapped humanity.

The final summary sigh of the passage moves from this drab earthly landscape out into the vast and empty nothingness of interstellar space: "I an old man,/A dull head among windy spaces." The limitless vista is a striking symbol of man's terrifying condition of utter loneliness, and the image of the head blown aimlessly about in the void with neither direction nor goal foreshadows a line from "Burnt Norton," "Men and bits of paper, whirled by the cold wind."

From this cosmic "landscape" of helpless passivity and utter desolation, there is an abrupt transition to the fiery intensity of Christ the Tiger, Christ the Avenger come to punish Gerontion's civilization for its rejection of Him. This depraved civilization is represented by four people in symbolic room settings. Each of the four has chosen something other than Christ as his god. For Mr. Silvero it is a monetary and sensual love of the Limoges enamels. That he walks all night in what is surely a rented hotel room suggests his restlessness and rootlessness, his lack of purpose and of absolute values. Hakagawa is no doubt in a museum, where he manifests a perversion of the Communion service by worshipping Titian's paintings in a mock religious ceremony of bowing. Madame de Tornquist, whose dim room is symbolic of the darkness of her soul, is a medium who assumes the role of priestess "shifting the candles." The word "shifting" also suggests a sense of restlessness. Fräulein von Kulp pauses in a dingy corridor either before entering or after leaving a hotel room, probably for illicit sex. Hugh Kenner calls this arrested moment in the hall "an epiphany of guilty terror."[19] Each enclosed setting functions as a subtle symbol for the emptiness and degradation of the lives of these sterile people. The section ends with two devastating and powerful symbols summarizing Gerontion's sterile condition; "Vacant shuttles/Weave the wind" conveys utter futility as does the setting in "An old man in a draughty house/Under a windy knob." Gerontion, like his house, is an empty and decayed husk swept through by the wind.

Having defined himself and his civilization, particularly through the use of symbolic landscape, Gerontion now attempts to defend himself from blame in having rejected Christ. However, in his very defense, he reveals that he is, as Kenner notes, "aware of his guilt, of his own acedia, of the process of his life and civilization drawing to a close."[20] Perhaps because these two passages are a direct confrontation with Christ, there is no use of landscape symbolism except for the oblique allusion to a labyrinthine house of horrors and the direct reference to Gerontion's rented house. In the passage on history, the structure of which reflects the chaos of a life without direction, Gerontion asserts that life or human history is to blame because it gives belief too soon into young, weak hands incapable of understanding it or too late into aged, tired hands incapable of acting on it. In the second passage, with even more terror and urgency in his voice, Gerontion desperately tries to evade the empty death which he has chosen in rejecting Christ:

> Think at last
> We have not reached conclusion, when I
> Stiffen in a rented house.

He makes a final attempt at self-vindication, crying,

> I that was near your heart was removed therefrom
> To lose beauty in terror, terror in inquisition.
> I have lost my passion. . . .

He uses the passive "was removed" to escape blame when actually he removed himself; he was the active agent in his "withering away from God."[21] As a result, he is now rotten in both body and soul: "I have lost my sight, smell, hearing, taste and touch. . . ."

In the last section, there is a return to symbolic landscape in Gerontion's vision of the final annihilation of his civilization. However, it is no longer the landscape of the house, the field, and the rooms; it is a cosmic setting which suggests the total destruction of Gerontion's civilization as it is blasted in fragments into outer space:

> De Bailhache, Fresca, Mrs. Cammel, whirled
> Beyond the circuit of the shuddering Bear
> In fractured atoms. Gull against the wind, in the windy straits
> Of Belle Isle, or running on the Horn.

The full and awful significance of Gerontion's earlier words, "A dull head among windy spaces," is now revealed. The ruin is complete, from the "windy straits" of Belle Isle in Labrador to the stormy Cape Horn in South America. The Gulf into which Gerontion's civilization is whirled is, as Rajan puts it, "more than geographical."[22] It is the gulf of utter obliteration, death without resurrection. This is the end which awaits those who reject Christ.

Gerontion's vision, perceived in stark horror, is one of physical and spiritual sterility and ennui climaxed by inevitable doom. It is a portrait of the nonChristian world on its way to suicide, a portrait which is communicated to a great extent through the use of symbolic landscape. The final lines return again to the dominant symbol of the house: "Tenants of the house,/Thoughts of a dry brain in a dry season." The infertile tenants of this rented civilization, the futile thoughts of this decaying mind, these wither for lack of the life-renewing rain which they have rejected. The abyss awaits them.

While "The Love Song of J. Alfred Prufrock" and "Gerontion" are, without question, major works, *The Waste Land* is the apex of Eliot's early poetry. Significantly, the technique of using urban landscape as symbol reaches its high point here. In the poem Eliot presents the full horror of a civilization that has rejected both human and divine love and that consequently is physically, emotionally, and spiritually sterile. Eliot's first choice for the epigraph was the agonized death cry of Joseph Conrad's Kurtz, " 'The horror! The horror!,' " and this cry echoes and reechoes in every terrifying scene in *The Waste Land*.

Landscape is a major element in the communication of this vision of horror. The poem consists of a collage of symbolic urban and desert settings, each of which reveals one or more aspects of the sickness of man's soul in this modern Inferno. They are thus complex symbols which, as Brooks points out, "resist complete equation with a simple meaning."[23] Suggested to a great extent by Baudelaire, the two symbols of the city and the desert dominate the poem as they dissolve in and out of one another. They represent the inner landscape of the soul: a sordid, chaotic, barren hell.

The urban setting has also taken on a new specificity, as Hugh Kenner suggests. Whereas in the earlier poems the locale is "a city we cannot name,"[24] in *The Waste Land* the metropolis is London with concrete streets, buildings, and suburbs which actually exist. A greater sense of reality as well as a greater sense of terror thus infuses the poem. To see an actual, perhaps familiar, location dissolve into a desert of boredom and terror before one's eyes has far more impact than if the setting were unspecified and general, and I think that this is one of the major reasons for the shock generated by the poem when it appeared in 1922.

Section I, "The Burial of the Dead," presents a panoramic

view of the wasteland which reveals the general characteristics of its barren terrain and the major themes of the poem as a whole. The land and the human soul are shown to be locked in the grip of a death-in-life without hope of resurrection. The poem begins in an anguished tension between life and death, for the deadened, apathetic inhabitants of *The Waste Land* resist the stirring of new life:

> April is the cruellest month, breeding
> Lilacs out of the dead land, mixing
> Memory and desire, stirring
> Dull roots with spring rain.

These lines recall the people of past poems—the Lady, twisting life out of the lilacs; Prufrock, overflowing with "memory and desire" but incapable of attaining either; Gerontion, "dull roots," "a dull head among windy spaces," waiting for spring rain. The people of the wasteland want only "a little life"; they fear the anguish of passionate action, "breeding," "mixing," "stirring," and cling to the passive inertia of winter, "covering" and "feeding."

After this general introduction, Eliot turns to his first symbolic setting in and near Munich. The Starnbergersee[25] is a beautiful lake just south of Munich. Eliot himself visited there in 1911, at which time it was a fashionable resort catering to an international, cosmopolitan, and well-to-do clientele. The Hofgarten, a public park in the heart of Munich, is bordered on two sides by buildings with a white colonnade. Between the colonnade and the park is a tree-shaded area of outdoor cafes. In the poem the shower of rain comes over the lake, but most of the action takes place in the surroundings of the Hofgarten, as the speaker shelters from the rain under the colonnade, goes out into the garden when the sun reappears, and drinks coffee and talks in one of the outdoor cafes. The female speaker, a wealthy tourist, one of the rootless travellers, is modelled on Countess Marie Larish, whom Eliot met in Munich and whose book of memoirs entitled *My Past* (1913) is a source for lines 8–17. The fragmentary quality of the speaker's life is revealed by the snatches of her conversation:

> Summer surprised us, coming over the Starnbergersee
> With a shower of rain; we stopped in the colonnade,
> And went on in sunlight, into the Hofgarten,
> And drank coffee, and talked for an hour.

The shower of rain over the lake is not symbolic of rebirth or fertility but is only another monotonous, even annoying, event in her sophisticated but trivial life. The colonnade and the sun-touched Hofgarten are not representative of beauty or happiness but suggest only portions of "a routine by which horror is evaded."[26] This is one of the few scenes in Eliot's poetry where the garden is not a symbol for either an actually or potentially meaningful experience, but rather the reverse.

As the speaker relates a childhood experience of terror and ecstasy, she describes a contrasting landscape of high, snow-covered mountains symbolic of intense emotion:

> And when we were children, staying at the archduke's,
> My cousin's, he took me out on a sled,
> And I was frightened. He said, Marie,
> Marie, hold on tight. And down we went.
> In the mountains, there you feel free.

This experience was not encrusted with the fashionable boredom and indifference to which she is now bound in her desire to escape meaningful emotions. Significantly, this first scene closes with a return to the empty and frivolous life symbolized by the setting. Her confession, "I read, much of the night," suggests sleepless, restless hours in her lonely hotel room and echoes the description of "Gerontion's" Mr. Silvero. And her final words stress again the rootless existence of the world traveller continually on the move: "[I] go south in the winter."

With a brilliant gift for significant juxtaposition, the poet moves abruptly from the German landscape to the desert of the wasteland. It is a sterile plain of "stony rubbish" where

the sun beats,
And the dead tree gives no shelter, the cricket no relief,
And the dry stone no sound of water.

The parched land, at least partially suggested by Baudelaire's Cythera and by Tennyson's wildernesses, of course symbolizes the barren soul of man, incapable of emotional commitment to other human beings or to God. It is, indeed, the landscape of Hell. Being an extremely complex symbol, it also carries connotations of isolation, desolation, and death of the spirit.

Looming up out of the level waste is a red rock, an ambivalent symbol which has teased many critics out of thought. Most commentators have seen it as something malign and sinister, and it does certainly have these qualities as a part of the desert landscape. The scorching red color evokes the fires of the Inferno, the searing heat of the desert, and the blood of violent death in contrast to the later cool and serene blue rocks of "Ash Wednesday."[27] Yet it also carries connotations of stability and protection. The rock's shadow provides the only refuge from the hot sun: "Only/There is shadow under this red rock. . . ." Going outside the poem, Philip Wheelwright points to several Biblical quotations which suggest this quality of Eliot's rock. Psalms 89:20 speaks of "the rock of salvation"; Isaiah 17:10 calls God "the rock of thy strength"; and in the New Testament Peter is referred to as a rock. However, Wheelwright finds an even more specific passage in Isaiah 32:2 where the prophet foretells the blessing of Christ: "And a man [Christ] shall be as an hiding place from the wind, and a covert from the tempest; as rivers of water in a dry place, *as the shadow of a great rock in a weary land*" (italics mine).[28] Further, in Eliot's juvenilia is a Yeatsian poem entitled "The Death of Saint Narcissus," in which the speaker invites a "you" to "Come in under the shadow of this grey rock."[29] There he reveals a vision of the life of Saint Narcissus, who gave up worldly pleasures and "became a dancer to God." The wasteland rock thus can stand as a symbol, however ambiguous, of some kind of refuge, even some hope for salvation. Beneath its shadow will be revealed the wretched condition of man's soul in the modern wasteland

("I will show you fear in a handful of dust") with the hope that this terrifying vision will move the protagonist (and the reader) to see himself there, to amend his life, and thus to have some possibility of rebirth.

The desert landscape with its complex symbolic rock gives way to a garden setting, framed by two allusions to the sea from Wagner's "Tristan and Isolde." The first quotation is a song of love and longing sung by a young sailor in Act I. Here the sea symbolizes the potential for fertility and fulfillment in a fully realized love. In the second quotation, from the opera's last act, the sea has become empty and barren, *"Oed' und leer das Meer,"* suggesting the failure of love. These two views of the sea sum up the meaning of the scene in the hyacinth garden, where the failure of love in the wasteland is revealed. An archetypal symbol of fertility and rebirth, the hyacinth garden seems at first to offer some meaning in the wasteland. The girl whose arms are full of flowers and whose hair is wet with dew serves as a type of grailbearer bringing redemption from impotence. Yet the protagonist feels only terror before her demand for meaningful emotional involvement, for surrender of self, and he rejects it:

> [W]hen we came back, late, from the Hyacinth garden,
> Your arms full, and your hair wet, I could not
> Speak, and my eyes failed, I was neither
> Living nor dead, and I knew nothing,
> Looking into the heart of light, the silence.

He is like many of the numbed characters of the early poems who cannot or will not commit themselves: Prufrock, the young man in "Portrait of a Lady," Gerontion. The four negatives, "not," "neither," "nor," "nothing," serve to intensify his inability to respond. The potentially fertile garden setting has become as *"Oed' und leer"* as the sea of the second Wagner quotation.

Having revealed the degeneration of love through garden and sea symbols, Eliot now shows the degeneration of religious belief through the symbol of the fortune teller. Man relies on superstition and magic in place of the faith in Christ which he has denied. Although no actual setting is described, the dimly-lighted, eerie room of Mme. Sosostris is implicit in the depiction of her activities and suggests perhaps the twilight of civilization. Significantly, each of her cards reveals destructive and meaningless death for the inhabitants of the wasteland:

> Here, said she,
> Is your card, the drowned Phoenician Sailor, . . .
> Fear death by water.

Section I ends with a terrifying vision of the Inferno of modern life revealed through a London landscape. The specific setting is the City, the financial district of London. This area is composed of grey streets and grey stone buildings, without any green or natural thing in sight. It is filled with people and choking car fumes and is in a very literal sense stifling and sterile:

> Unreal City,
> Under the brown fog of a winter dawn,
> A crowd flowed over London Bridge, so many,
> I had not thought death had undone so many.
> Sighs, short and infrequent, were exhaled,
> And each man fixed his eyes before his feet.

It is a nightmare scene, suggested by Baudelaire's lines, "Fourmillante cité, cité pleine de rêves,/Où le spectre en plein jour raccroche le passant," and by Dante's *Inferno*, Cantos III and IV in particular. The atmosphere is choked with a brown fog similar to Baudelaire's "brouillard sale et jaune [qui] inondait tout l'espace." It gives the City a spectral appearance, but, as Robert Day reminds us, it is a decidedly real aspect of winter-time London at 9 A.M.[30] At the same time, the dirty fog is symbolic of the drabness and dreariness of the life of a City worker, the anonymity and solitude of his existence, and the numbing spiritual miasma which deadens his soul with apathy.[31] Further, "under" suggests that these people are buried beneath the fog and that this is in a very real sense a burial of

the dead. Northrop Frye's comment that the setting is "spiritually subterranean"[32] is quite perceptive.

The crowd flowing over London Bridge works on a realistic
as well as a symbolic level. It is a literal account of the masses
on their way to work in the offices of the City. Eliot's own copy
of the 1908 edition of Baedeker's guide to London contains the
following description of London Bridge: "[This most important
bridge] connects the City, the central point of business, with
the Borough. . . . It is estimated that 22,000 vehicles and about
110,000 pedestrians cross London Bridge daily, a fact which
may give the stranger some idea of the prodigious traffic carried on in this part of the City. Newcomers should pay a visit to
London Bridge on a week-day during business hours to see
and hear the steady stream of noisy traffic."[33] John Hayward's
notes for the French translation of *The Waste Land* further illus-
trate the literal aspects of the description: "The crowd is the
morning crowd of commuters coming into the City from the
suburbs on the south side of the Thames, businessmen, clerks,
typists, etc. . . . A typical London scene during the morning
'crush hours.' "[34] Finally, Day comments on the terrifyingly
realistic details of the crowd: "The density of such crowds is
typical of the urban rush hour; 'death' is their fate, a living
death in the Hell of the City; 'sighs, short and infrequent' may
owe as much to smog as to Dante; and 'each man,' if he does
not keep 'his eyes fixed before his feet,' may be pushed off the
pavement or transfixed by an umbrella ferule. 'Fourmillante' is
appropriate enough to any modern metropolis, but nowhere
does the adjective become so cruelly exact as in London's City
at rush hour, when the identically black-clad hordes, pince-nez
agleam and umbrellas brandished like antennae, pour into or
out of Underground tunnels and the vast anthills of banks."[35]
The City is a world as savage, brutal, and animalistic as any
African jungle. As Eliot says in "Choruses from 'The Rock,' "

> The desert is not remote in southern tropics,
> The desert is not only around the corner,
> The desert is squeezed in the tube-train next to you,
> The desert is in the heart of your brother.

On the symbolic level, the crowd flowing over the bridge is as stagnant, grey, and polluted as the commercial Thames which flows under it. That each man walks with his eyes downcast sums up the dull despair and monotony of his daily existence. These nameless millions imprisoned in dull office routines are as dead as the lost souls in Dante's *Inferno*. Their apathetic indifference links them to the souls inhabiting the Vestibule of Hell, and their lack of faith in Christ recalls the first circle of Hell whose occupants, although cut off from God for eternity, still desire that union but have no hope of ever attaining it.[36] Cleanth Brooks's remarks on Eliot's use of Dante here are particularly perceptive: "The echo of *The Divine Comedy* is not merely a flourish or an attempt to touch up the modern scene by giving it literary overtones. What connects the modern scene with Dante's *Inferno* is the poet's insight into the nature of hell. The man who sees the crowds flowing over London Bridge as damned souls, if challenged for putting them thus into hell, might justify his observation by paraphrasing a line from Christopher Marlow: 'Why, this is hell, nor are they out of it.' "[37]

But Eliot has not yet finished. Calling upon two specific London landmarks, he symbolizes the infernal deadness even further:

> A crowd flowed over London Bridge. . . .
> Flowed up the hill and down King William Street,
> To where Saint Mary Woolnoth kept the hours
> With a dead sound on the final stroke of nine.

King William Street, ironically lined with life insurance offices, is a broad, imposing street that leads into the heart of the City. The church of St. Mary Woolnoth is located on the corner of King William Street and Lombard Street, directly across from Lloyd's Bank where Eliot worked from 1917–1925. Lombard Street is called the street of the bankers, having inherited its name from the Lombard money dealers of Venice and Genoa. It is an appropriate symbol for the corrupt commercial aspect of modern life.[38] The dominant characteristics of the church of St.

Mary Woolnoth, built from 1716–27 by Hawksmoor, a pupil of Wren, are heaviness, squareness, and mathematical symmetry. It is located directly over an Underground station, and an exit sign mars the front view. In the poem its clock heavily clangs out the hour of 9 A.M.,[39] marking the moment of man's daily burial in the deadness of office routine. The church in the modern world has been transformed from a symbol of the timeless to a symbol of man's imprisonment in time, and it is indeed a significant landmark of London and its "timekept City," as Eliot calls it in "Choruses from 'The Rock' ":

> I journeyed to London, to the timekept City,
> Where the River flows, with foreign flotations.
> There I was told: we have too many churches,
> And too few chop-houses. There I was told:
> Let the vicars retire. Men do not need the Church
> In the place where they work, but where they spend their
>   Sundays.
> In the City, we need no bells. . . .

Yet St. Mary Woolnoth is an extremely complex landscape symbol. Being located in the midst of the financial district, she is a commercial church as is also implied by the "wool" of her name. Day explains this aspect of the symbolism more fully: "St. Mary Woolnoth is the bankers' church *par excellence* . . . kept open at unusual hours so that the members of the financial community may be refreshed in any spiritual dryness that may visit them. But it is 'up the hill,' far from water, and surrounded by banks, with the Bank Station of the Underground system disgorging directly beneath it."[40] The church and the area it represents are thus "evil, commercial, sterile, unfruitful, anti-religious," and Day concludes that St. Mary Woolnoth stands in direct contrast to St. Magnus Martyr, the fishermen's church of Section III.[41] In this passage of eight and one-half lines, Eliot has brilliantly used urban landscape as a symbol of the withered soul of modern man.

In the closing lines of Section I, the protagonist suddenly sees one he knows in the swarming rush-hour crowd and questions him about the corpse he buried in his garden. Is the corpse like the fertility gods Osiris and Adonis or the Christian Jesus, all of whom rose again? Or does the undercurrent of horror suggest that the fertility gods and Christ are actual corpses incapable of rebirth, having been murdered by the rejection of the secular world? Is not this a planting without hopes of harvest, a true burial of the dead gods? As in the passage on the hyacinth girl, the garden is a symbol of potential fertility that fails to be realized. With sudden intensity, Eliot directly involves the reader by echoing Baudelaire's lines from "Au Lecteur": " 'You! hypocrite lecteur!—mon semblable,—mon frère!' "

In Section II, entitled "A Game of Chess" from Middleton's *Women Beware Women*, Eliot shows the degeneration of meaningful human love into indifference or animalistic sex through the sterility of the marriage relationship in the upper and lower levels of society. In the former he uses direct and detailed description of setting to reveal the emptiness, while in the latter he only implies the nature of the surroundings.

The section begins in the richly-furnished boudoir of a wealthy woman. The room itself is described in minute detail, conveying to the reader a sense of extravagant abundance. It has a coffered ceiling and a fireplace in which a fire blazes. Above the mantel is a painting of the metamorphosis of Philomela, and other similar paintings hang on the walls. The woman herself is seated in an elaborately gilded chair before a marble-topped dressing table, brushing her hair. On the table is a mirror with a gold rococo frame of vines and cupids surrounded by a clutter of satin cases overflowing with jewelry and "vials of ivory and coloured glass" containing perfume of every description. A seven-branched candelabra is reflected in the mirror, and these candles, along with the fire, provide a flickering light which plays over the setting.

This detailed description of the room works on a symbolic as well as a realistic level. In addition to depicting an environment of wealth and culture, the description suggests by contrast the quality of the woman's existence. Described ironically in terms recalling the passionate Cleopatra of Shakespeare's *Antony and*

Cleopatra, "The Chair she sat in, like a burnished throne,/ Glowed on the marble," this woman is actually her opposite. While Cleopatra's barge was surrounded by life-giving water, the woman's chair is in the midst of sterile fire and hard marble. The heavy sensuality of the profuse imagery conveys the fertility of a type of human love which is beyond her: the "fruited vines," the "golden Cupidon," the "laquearia" suggesting Dido, the painting of the "change of Philomel." The miraculous change of Philomela is impossible, and consequently meaningless, in the modern world. Thus the myths portrayed by the paintings in the room cannot communicate because their stories are no longer understood: they are merely "other withered stumps of time." Eliot's metaphor here is particularly brilliant, recalling the stump of Philomela's tongue left after Tereus destroyed it[42] and thereby suggesting the inability of the old fertility myths to speak to the modern world. Even the dolphin, ancient symbol of fertility, is frozen into lifelessness, carved immovable in the stone of the fireplace:

> Huge sea-wood fed with copper
> Burned green and orange, framed by the coloured stone,
> In which sad light a carvèd dolphin swam.

The flickering flames of the fire and the candles symbolize lust, while the synthetic perfumes and glittering jewels indicate artificiality and materialism. The chaotic abundance of the room perhaps suggests also a parallel chaos in the woman's life. The images of fertility in the setting work then basically by contrast to convey the sterility of her existence, for they have no meaning in the modern context except as ornaments.

Having established the woman's état d'âme through symbolic setting, Eliot dramatizes a scene between her and her husband (or perhaps her lover), revealing the enormous gulf that separates them. The woman's shrill, rasping voice betrays her tension, as she frantically questions him: "What are you thinking of? What thinking? What?" In contrast to this abrupt and nervous barrage of words are the husband's slow, melancholy thoughts, mourning a meaningless death: "I think we are in rats' alley/Where the dead men lost their bones." Suddenly unable to evade the horror of the emptiness, the woman screams in hysteria,

> "What shall I do now? What shall I do?"
> "I shall rush out as I am, and walk the street
> "With my hair down, so. What shall we do to-morrow?
> "What shall we ever do?"

Yet the husband's thoughts reveal that she, like Prufrock, will slip back into the safety of the monotonous daily routine, in which water means not rebirth, but a morning bath or a rainy afternoon: "The hot water at ten./And if it rains, a closed car at four."

Beneath the surface beauty of the lady's dressing room the poet has found horror and emptiness frantically veiled with boredom. Now beneath the ugliness of a lower class pub he sees them again. In this vulgar setting, symbolic of the sordidness of life in the slums, we overhear a woman relating an earlier conversation with her friend, Lil. Over her beer, she reveals the degradation and emptiness of a marriage based solely on sexual gratification. The key symbols are infidelity, "he wants a good time,/And if you don't give it him, there's others will," and abortion, expressive of the sterility of such a loveless union:

> It's them pills I took, to bring it off, she said. . . .
> Well, if Albert won't leave you alone, there it is, I said,
> What you get married for if you don't want children?

The sacredness and beauty of a meaningful sexual relationship in love have degenerated into the public ugliness of vulgar tavern gossip. This sordid tale of meaningless, grotesque marriage is interrupted again and again by an insistent and urgent warning, "HURRY UP PLEASE ITS TIME," signaling not only the closing of the pub but also the closing of a civilization. It is a warning that this perverted way of life can only lead to destruction. As the imbibers lurch into the street, their drunken good-byes recall those of Ophelia who met death by water. The implication of a similar end for these inhabitants of the wasteland is too strong to miss.

As the two urban settings in Section II helped to symbolize the degeneration of human love and of sex within marriage, the nine urban scenes of Section III serve to reveal the sterility of love and sex in other human relationships. Sex without love, sex stripped of meaning, is portrayed in all its perversions. Indifference alternates with horror until the end of the section where a hope for redemption through purgation appears briefly.

The section opens with a landscape of London in early winter:

> The river's tent is broken; the last fingers of leaf
> Clutch and sink into the wet bank. The wind
> Crosses the brown land, unheard.

It is a bleak, entirely realistic scene. The Thames is grey and empty in the clammy mist of a chilly London morning, and along its muddy, brown banks rise bare, leafless trees. The setting is symbolic of a complex état d'âme. The naked trees and "brown land" suggest sterility, while the utter solitude and pervading silence express a sense of desolation and loneliness. The dominant feeling, however, is that of despair and death, conveyed by Eliot's description of "the leaves as drowning fingers clutching at the bank. . . ."[43] This landscape of the deserted wintry Thames reveals then a desperate suicidal state of mind. By using a "flashback" landscape of the summer-time Thames, Eliot rounds out his depiction of the river and deepens its symbolic import. In the summer it was covered by a romantic canopy of green leaves, but ironically its waters were polluted by "empty bottles, sandwich papers,/Silk handkerchiefs, cardboard boxes, cigarette ends." The summer Thames thus symbolizes the general corruption of contemporary civilization, the specific vice of illicit sex being represented by the contraceptive silk handkerchiefs and cardboard boxes.[44] Two allusions, one literary and the other Biblical, reinforce the theme of the desolate state of man's soul. The refrain from Spenser's marriage song, "Sweet Thames, run softly, till I end my song," heightens by contrast the pollution of the modern Thames, for it ironically evokes the river in springtime freshness and purity as nymphs joyfully prepare for a bridal. The Biblical echo, "By the waters of Leman I sat down and wept," adds a sense of exile and sorrow to that of decay and desecration. The substitution of the word "Leman" for "Babylon" is significant in two ways; *leman* is an old word for lover and suggests the profanation of its earlier rich connotations, and, of biographical interest, Leman is the lake at Lausanne where Eliot went in November, 1921 to consult Dr. Roger Vittoz and where he wrote part of *The Waste Land*.

The second urban landscape is the seedy gashouse district. In the darkness of a winter evening, the protagonist is "fishing in the dull canal" of stagnant water. Around him are the garrets and tenements of the lower class area, and behind him a slum rat creeps "softly through the vegetation/Dragging its slimy belly on the bank." In this grimy setting, the repulsive rodent, terrifyingly real and physical, symbolizes the degradation of the body, as do Sweeney and the prostitute Mrs. Porter. In lines parodying Day's *Parliament of Bees*, the protagonist hears not the hunting horns and hounds of Acteon approaching the naked Diana but the "sound of horns and motors, which shall bring/Sweeney to Mrs. Porter in the spring." These are, as Williamson remarks, "the sounds of the city, . . . in a familiar pursuit. They are the modern sounds of hunting, of lust."[45]

The protagonist encounters yet another perversion of sexuality in "Mr. Eugenides, the Smyrna merchant/Unshaven, with a pocket full of currants." Again the urban setting is highly symbolic. Eliot reminds us that we are in the nightmarish City district, now under the brown, suffocating fog of a winter *noon*. The commercial businessman invites the protagonist to a homosexual liaison symbolized by the Cannon Street Hotel and the Metropole. The Cannon Street Hotel was located in the heart of the business district near the Bank and the Cannon Street Station.[46] According to Hayward, it "was at this period a common and convenient meeting place for foreign businessmen and their British colleagues, being . . . at the terminus of one of the routes to the continent."[47] Eliot himself must certainly have frequented it, especially since his position at Lloyd's was in the Foreign Department, and he uses the commercial hotel to symbolize the hollowness, sordidness, and amorality of the businessman in general and of Mr. Eugenides in particular. The invitation to a weekend at the Metropole in Brighton implies that Mr. Eugenides participates in homosexuality.[48] The Metropole had at the time a notorious reputation as a licentious pleasure spot for wealthy businessmen. John Hayward recalls a music hall song which suggests its particular character:

> Now Henry VIII was a wag in his day
> He had several wives and was very gay
> He founded the Metropole, Brighton, they say . . .
> Really! Yes, would you believe it![49]

Thus the Metropole represents the debasement and perversion of sex.

From this symbolic noonday setting in the City, the protagonist turns to the "violet hour" in the squalid flat of a typist. The scene is certainly one of the most horrifying in *The Waste Land;* Elizabeth Drew calls it "a ghastly parody of the fertility ritual," and Allen Tate labels it "one of our most terrible insights into Western civilization."[50] The typist's apartment suggests the boredom, chaos, and sordidness that comprise her existence. The monotony of her daily routine is presented in the details of the dirty breakfast dishes, the gas stove, the food in tin cans, the drying laundry. The messy tangle of "stockings, slippers, camisoles, and stays" piled on the couch reflects the chaos and disorder of her soul. All these together, especially the unwashed dishes, the sofa-bed, and the underclothes, express the sordidness of her life. Having with Tiresias "perceived the scene," we should be prepared for the following episode of mechanical, apathetic copulation. Northrop Frye points out perceptively, but none too prettily, that the typist "lets her body be used like a public urinal. . . ."[51] To point up the debasement of love, Eliot ironically describes the passionless sex act itself in the sonnet form,[52] a form traditionally used to express passionate, meaningful love. However, these fourteen lines disclose only indifference, bestiality, and emptiness:

> Flushed and decided, he assaults at once;
> Exploring hands encounter no defence;
> His vanity requires no response,
> And makes a welcome of indifference.

The dark stairs down which the young man gropes his way upon departing are also symbolic, suggesting the blackness and vacancy of his soul as it descends into moral and spiritual blindness. This use of stairs can be found throughout Eliot's poetry; ascending a stair connotes positive spiritual effort, while descending a stair indicates spiritual weakness, cowardice, and/or failure.

From the typist's apartment, the protagonist heads east "along the Strand, [then] up Queen Victoria Street." These two major streets leading into the City are lined with shops and the offices of commercial firms. Instead of going on into the City, however, he turns down toward the river, to a fishermen's bar on Lower Thames Street. This street is in the poor dock district and runs alongside the river past the Billingsgate Fish Market. Here in this setting he catches for a moment a vision of a fruitful, productive life. The fishermen are associated with fish, a pagan symbol of sexual fertility and a Christian symbol of spiritual fertility. They have a meaningful relationship with one another, "a clatter and a chatter from within," and with God, "the walls/Of Magnus Martyr hold/Inexplicable splendour of Ionian white and gold." The church of St. Magnus Martyr, located on Lower Thames Street between London Bridge and the Billingsgate Fish Market, was built in the years 1671–87 by Christopher Wren, and its stone tower was a "welcome to the City for people coming over old London Bridge before the new bridge was built in 1831."[53] Surrounded by commercial buildings such as ice-storage warehouses, its exterior is dull and unspectacular. However, its interior is breathtakingly beautiful; one's first impression is of brilliance and light. Dark rich wood is contrasted by white walls and barrel-vaulted ceiling, bright white-and-gold fluted Ionic columns, and a white cupola giving a sense of airiness and light. The decorations, including candle brackets, sword-rests, and shrines, are numerous, and many are of gold. Eliot himself in his notes to *The Waste Land* remarks, "The interior of St. Magnus Martyr is to my mind one of the finest among Wren's interiors,"[54] and it is interesting for the visitor to note Eliot's own lines from the poem quoted on a plaque in the church.

The church is a complex symbol of the significant, fulfilled life in Christ, in opposition to the commercial St. Mary Woolnoth. Its name, St. Magnus Martyr, suggests immediately the concepts of surrender to God, of dying to gain life, of meaningful existence in Christianity. Further, its location on Lower Thames Street links it with life-giving water. Finally, its brilliant interior with dazzling white cupola and columns of white and gold fills the poem with its first real light. Commenting that white and gold are the liturgical colors of Easter and of rejoicing, Day concludes that "all this pomp is the physical expression of a spiritual reality."[55] Thus this dock district with its shining church stands as one of the few symbols of glory and life in the poem.

Immediately, however, the protagonist turns from this vision of the river as living water to an opposing view of it as a dirty "conveyor of commerce" which "sweats/Oil and tar." In this passage he journeys east down the industrial Thames from the heart of London to Greenwich, describing in the first part the present-day aspect of the setting. This section of the river is literally polluted by the red-sailed commercial barges which leave a film of oil on the water. In addition, smoke from factories fills the air, and débris and garbage float in the water:

> The river sweats
> Oil and tar
> The barges drift
> With the turning tide
> Red sails
> Wide

To leeward, swing on the heavy spar.
The barges wash
Drifting logs
Down Greenwich reach
Past the Isle of Dogs.

The Isle of Dogs is a poor dock district about midway between London and Greenwich. The area is indeed ugly and barren, totally dominated by industrialism.

The second half of the passage forms a contrast by presenting the river in an earlier, purer state. The references to Elizabeth and Leicester, "A gilded shell/Red and gold" (in direct contrast to the ugly, heavy barges), a fresh wind, pealing bells, and brilliant white towers all suggest a freshness and lightness in painful juxtaposition to the modern river. (Eliot uses the same technique at the beginning of "The Fire Sermon.") The white towers are part of the Tower of London, just downstream of London Bridge and clearly visible from the Thames. Built of white Caen stone in 1078 by William the Conqueror, they are passed by the protagonist on his journey toward Greenwich and seem to symbolize beauty and purity. In Eliot's time they would have been a dingy grey, suggesting directly the pollution by the modern commercial world. With his usual skill in creating many-faceted symbols, Eliot has used the river setting to convey again the horrifying, corrupting powers of modern materialism.

The final three landscapes are scenes of meaningless seductions. Two of them take place on or near water which has no cleansing power. The first Thames daughter, from the middle class district of Highbury, is violated on a river excursion to Richmond and Kew Gardens, large parks on the Thames a few miles upstream of London. Both are famous for the natural beauty of their riverbank settings, especially Kew's Botanical Gardens which "extend to the bank of the river, and along it, in sylvan vistas and avenues."[56] Ironically, this idyllic, Edenlike landscape symbolizes lust and sterility rather than innocent love and fertility. Skillfully, Eliot marks the progression of the summer seduction, not by the traditional gestures of love, but by the areas of London's environs being passed at each stage of the assault. The trip begins in the hot, dry city with its "Trams and dusty trees" signifying the mechanical, parched, and infertile nature of the approaching sex act. As the couple's canoe passes Kew Gardens, their lust increases, so that "By Richmond [two miles upstream] I raised my knees/Supine on the floor of a narrow canoe." The girl's cold, objective description of her violation in terms of landmarks perfectly communicates the emptiness of sex in the wasteland.

The second daughter is also indifferent to her "rape," the violation itself being so meaningless and the idea of a new start so futile that she feels neither remorse nor resentment:

> "My feet are at Moorgate, and my heart
> Under my feet. After the event
> He wept. He promised 'a new start.'
> I made no comment. What should I resent?"

Ironically, it is the man who weeps while the girl is unfeeling: her heart is no longer in its traditional place, but trampled beneath her feet; she uses the neutral word "event" to describe her seduction; and she makes the coldly impersonal statement, "I made no comment." Moorgate, the scene of the act, designates a slum area and is also a major street leading into the heart of the City district. Significantly, Moorgate is the name of the Underground station which Eliot himself used while working at Lloyd's Bank. This urban area suggests again the ugly sordidness of city life, drained of meaningful emotion.

The third daughter expresses the final moral state of complete degradation in fragmented, aimless lines which reflect the quality of her existence:

> "On Margate Sands.
> I can connect
> Nothing with nothing.
> The broken fingernails of dirty hands.
> My people humble people who expect
> Nothing."

The scene of her violation is Margate Sands, a popular commercialized beach resort in Kent where many London workers spend their two-week vacation at the end of the summer. Eliot himself knew this area well and indeed wrote part of *The Waste Land* while living at Margate from mid-October to mid-November, 1921.[57] Ironically, although we have left the metropolitan area, the sea here is as *"Oed' und leer"* as in Section I and the seaside setting as sterile as the urban one. The beach is edged with cheap eating establishments, trinket shops, and amusement areas. The sand itself is dirty and littered with paper, empty bottles, and other débris. It is an appropriate setting for the degraded meaningless seduction of which the speaker remembers only "The broken fingernails of [the] dirty hands" of her seducer.

As if coming into the middle of a conversation, the reader overhears first the girl's fragmentary statement of the setting and then an expression of the meaningless quality of the seduction itself (and by implication of her life in general). The following physical description of broken fingernails on dirty hands works on several levels. A typical Eliotean device is to use a part of the human body rather than the whole to suggest the fragmented nature of the modern human being, and, while he has used the device in the other two daughters' songs, it has its greatest force here in the third. Further, the hands are those of her seducer and tell us something about him and about the seduction. The description implies that their sex act was completely physical (even animalistic), meaningless, impersonal, and fragmented or "broken." This small but significant concrete detail is all the girl remembers of the act itself. The hands of the seducer then seem to remind her of those of her own family; they too are poor lower class people who have broken fingernails and dirty hands. Their lives are empty and meaningless, and the repetition of the key word "nothing" at the end of her speech emphasizes the situation: "My people humble people who expect/Nothing." These few lines reveal Eliot's technique of rich compactness at its best.

At the bottom of the abyss suddenly flare up the fires of lust mixed with the fires of purgation, as we are transported from modern London to Augustine's Carthage: "To Carthage then I came/Burning burning burning burning." Pagan Carthage was a city of licentiousness where Augustine indulged his lusts of the flesh; thus, it is intimately connected to contemporary London. However, implicit in the very mention of Carthage is Augustine's subsequent conversion to the love of God and his turning away from the fires of lust: "O Lord Thou pluckest me out [of the burning]."[58] Carthage then also suggests salvation from the flaming fires of lust through the flaming fires of refinement. It stands for self-love sacrificed upon the altar of the love of God and functions therefore as a symbol of possible redemption in the wasteland.

While several settings of Section III were on or beside river or sea, Section IV takes place far beneath the ocean's surface where a corpse slowly disintegrates:

> Phlebas the Phoenician, a fortnight dead,
> Forgot the cry of gulls, and the deep sea swell
> And the profit and loss.
> A current under sea
> Picked his bones in whispers.

Many critics have interpreted this passage as redemptive, seeing in it "a symbol of surrender," a "suggestion of an ineffable peace," a process of purification, "a natural or pagan salvation," and even a "baptism, the process by which men signify entrance into the world of the spirit."[59] However, it seems to me from the content as well as from the context that this undersea landscape symbolizes a death as empty and meaningless as the commercial life of "profit and loss" seen in the wasteland city. It is the absolute and terrifying end for those who are consumed in the fires of self-love, for death is portrayed as physical dissolution and nothingness.

The title, "Death by Water," recalls the warning of Section I, "Fear death by water," and suggests that water here functions only in its negative capacity as a destructive agent; the description of the drowned body is particularly sinister, with the ocean current, like a predatory bird, picking the remaining meat off the bones in eerie whispers. The corpse has no control over its movement (as it lacked control in life) but is washed about by the sea and ultimately drawn into the whirlpool:

> As he rose and fell
> He passed the stages of his age and youth
> Entering the whirlpool.

The whirlpool, being an irresistible force of destruction, seems to me symbolic of final and total annihilation through death.

This gruesome description of a meaningless death is followed immediately by a warning to the people of the wasteland and to the reader, for the protagonist turns to the reader and addresses him directly:

> Gentile or Jew
> O you who turn the wheel and look to windward,
> Consider Phlebas, who was once handsome and tall as you.

The meaning is simply this: Phlebas was once as alive and strong and handsome as you are. But, as you have seen, he is now a decomposing corpse, and death for him is the absolute end. Consider that your fate will be the same if you continue in your empty life. Section IV is a powerful direct statement of Eliot's theme that a meaningless life leads only to an equally meaningless death.

"What the Thunder Said," the final section, is composed mainly of a complex nightmare landscape revealing a vision of the ultimate chaos and disintegration of the spirit. The poem itself, however, ends with a hint of salvation, a hope for rebirth.

The opening passage is a composite landscape, symbolic of events surrounding Christ's crucifixion:

> After the torchlight red on sweaty faces
> After the frosty silence in the gardens
> After the agony in stony places
> The shouting and the crying
> Prison and palace and reverberation
> Of thunder of spring over distant mountains. . . .

The torchlight and chilly gardens suggest Christ's night of prayer and subsequent arrest in Gethsemane, while the stony places, prison, and palace with their shouting and crying evoke the imprisonment, trial, Golgotha itself, and the resurrection. After undergoing the agony of the Cross in order to save man, Christ, and his gift of rebirth, is rejected by the modern world. As a result, its inhabitants are dying spiritually and emotionally: "He who was living is now dead/We who were living are now dying. . . ."

This spiritual/emotional sterility is forcefully symbolized by a return to the landscape of the wasteland. Here, as Gardner notes, "The mountains . . . are merged with the images of rock and desert in a landscape of horror and drought."[60] This rocky, waterless region is the landscape of the protagonist's soul, and his physical anguish, especially his thirst, parallels his parched spiritual condition: "Here is no water but only rock/Rock and no water and the sandy road. . . ." In addition to the rock, sand, and singing grass of the desert setting, there are also hostile, sinister barbarians who suggest some vague unspecified evil: "red sullen faces sneer and snarl/From doors of mudcracked houses. . . ."

After an unnerving, hallucinatory vision in which an indistinct figure "Gliding wrapt in a brown mantle, hooded" appears, as the risen Christ did to the disciples on the road to Emmaus, the protagonist climbs higher on the mountain road so that he has a panoramic view of the surrounding landscape. He perceives the horror of final ruin as civilization falls into chaos, echoing the destructive vision of Gerontion. Looking down, he sees "hooded hordes swarming/Over endless plains, stumbling in cracked earth." The hordes and the flat plains of cracked mud suggest the horror of civilization's regression to violent barbarism and bestiality, completely devoid of spirituality. Looking up, he sees a city exploding in the violet air:

> What is the city over the mountains
> Cracks and reforms and bursts in the violet air
> Falling towers
> Jerusalem Athens Alexandria
> Vienna London
> Unreal. . . .

Eliot uses the first four cities as symbols, linking them closely with London to suggest inescapable and terrifying similarities. Most critics go no further than remarking that the five are important centers of Western culture. However, Warren French in *The Twenties: Fiction, Poetry, Drama* reveals that "What the first four cities listed share is that each played some specially important role in the intellectual and spiritual development of Western man—in the emergence of the Western consciousness—and each was subsequently in some fashion destroyed."[61] I would like to take French's theory a bit further and point out that each city was destroyed or partially destroyed by a force considered at the time to be *barbarian*, and thus brutalizing and bestializing. Jerusalem, a great center of learning and religion as well as political power, was sacked numerous times in the period prior to Christ's birth, but more important its Great Golden Age from the fourth to the seventh centuries was ended by a Persian invasion in 614. It was again taken by barbarian forces in the eleventh century by the Turks, in the thirteenth century by the Tatars, and in the sixteenth century by the Turks. Athens was the Greek capital and center of Western Civilization, possessing culture, philosophy, power, and wealth. The prospering city was captured and largely destroyed by the Persians in 480 B.C. An equally devastating invasion by the Henli, a Germanic people, occurred in A.D.267, and the city was taken by the Turks in 1456. Indeed, for almost two thousand years Athens was in bondage to outside forces. The third city, Alexandria, was the capital of Egypt from its founding in 332 B.C. by Alexander the Great to its capture by the Arabs in A.D. 642. During this period it was a center of commerce, culture, and learning with a great library and museum, both of which were destroyed. The city was also taken in 1517 by the Turks. Finally, Vienna with its musical and political preeminence was attacked by Turks in 1529 and again in 1683. Although she resisted long seiges both times, much of the city was destroyed.[62] The four cities thus are symbols of the destruction of man's spiritual and cultural nature by barbarism. By including London in the list, Eliot suggests—and indeed warns—that this modern city and the civilization which she represents are heading for a similar destruction of cultural, moral, and spiritual attainments, not by literal barbarians as in the past but by the barbarian attitudes (materialism, selfishness, physical lust) of contemporary man as revealed in the poem.

Eliot further links London to these four cities by the reference to "Falling Towers," an obvious symbol of destruction. (The Tarot pack, for example, contains a card on which a tower is struck by lightning.) In each of the four cities was a tower or towerlike structure, which subsequently was either partially or totally destroyed; Vienna, for example, was surrounded in the thirteenth century by city walls with six fortified gates and nineteen towers. The connection with the Tower of London, symbol of England's power and glory, as well as with the bell towers of many London churches is obvious. The nightmarish and terrifying quality of this vision of ruin is emphasized by the word "Unreal" at the end of the list. As it recalls the phrase "Unreal City" used to describe London in Section I (l. 60) and in Section III (l. 207), this final word links London once more, and irrevocably, with the fates of the preceding cities.

The following passage describes the ruins of the destroyed cities, where everything is upside down, the bats, the towers, the bells still trying to keep the hours of the monotonous daily routine:

> And upside down in air were towers
> Tolling reminiscent bells, that kept the hours
> And voices singing out of empty cisterns and exhausted wells.

The modern city whose sterility and sordidness are exposed through the entire poem is totally destroyed,[63] and the whole world becomes a gaping grave of chaos and death. Yet even here Eliot may intimate a possible hope for redemption; for the bells, though upside down, are still tolling, and voices, though coming from "empty cisterns and exhausted wells," are still singing. One may justifiably feel that the tolling is loud and discordant and that the disembodied voices are eerie and sinister, and thus interpret them as symbols of disorder, fragmentation, and terror. However, if these sounds are *music,* and music that issues from and continues in difficult circumstances, then they might express the possibility of salvation even in this landscape of chaos and ruin. The ambiguity of the lines is such, I think, as to allow both interpretations.

As the nightmare vision fades, the protagonist finds himself at his destination, the chapel. In medieval legend the chapel housed the Holy Grail, and the knight who could make his way there would find salvation and fulfillment. However, Eliot has used the chapel ironically to suggest the nadir of despair rather than the zenith of attainment, for in *The Waste Land* the chapel is deserted and in ruins, its door swinging on broken hinges in the wind, its windows broken out, its gravestones overturned:

> In this decayed hole among the mountains
> In the faint moonlight, the grass is singing
> Over the tumbled graves, about the chapel
> There is the empty chapel, only the wind's home.
> It has no windows, and the door swings. . . .

It forcefully conveys the anguish of utmost despair, of total sterility.

Yet at this moment of utter futility appear three symbols of hope: the cock, symbol of dawn; the lightning, signaling the approach of life-giving rain; and the commands of the thunder. For these commands the protagonist is transported to the foothills of the Himalayas:

> Ganga was sunken, and the limp leaves
> Waited for rain, while the black clouds
> Gathered far distant, over Himavant.

The steamy jungle landscape suggests an anguished waiting for rain. Finally, the thunder speaks and here also Eliot has relied to some extent on symbolic settings. In the first command the "empty rooms" represent the empty lives and deaths of their transient inhabitants; in the second command Ugolino's tower prison of course stands for the prison of self; and the seascape of the third command (taken in all probability from Eliot's boyhood memories of sailing off the Massachusetts coast) symbolizes the freedom and joy of an ordered, fulfilled life.

By no means does the poem end where it began,[64] for the protagonist has moved toward a restoration of fertility although he has not yet attained it. This progression is symbolized to a great extent through the landscape; the wasteland is now behind the Fisher King who is still fishing in what are hopefully more fertile waters: "I sat upon the shore/Fishing, with the arid plain behind me." He has passed through the desert and is on its far side, though still within its borders. He has decided to attempt an ordering of his own life despite the chaotic, crumbling background where "London Bridge is falling down falling down falling down." The reference to *"Le Prince d'Aquitaine à la tour abolie"* recalls the "Falling towers" of line 374 and Ugolino's death tower implied in lines 412–13. These two negative quotations, both of which suggest decay and destruction, frame two positive quotations which hold the keys to rebirth. The first contains the words of Arnaut Daniel who "hid him in the fire which refines them." He is a symbol of willing and joyful purgation of sin. The second expresses the desire for regeneration: "When shall I be as the swallow?" The swallow is a bird of spring, the bird of consolation,[65] and the bird of renewed life as seen in the Procne-Philomel legend. These ideas give strength to the protagonist who will use them to keep his own life from falling into ruins: "These fragments I have shored against my ruins. . . ." However, they seem like utter madness to the world. The poem ends with the three repeated commands and a benediction of peace, "Shantih shantih shantih." Thus, *The Waste Land* projects a hope for rebirth through the symbols of the hyacinth garden, the fishermen's bar, the church of Saint Magnus Martyr, the refining fires, the commands of the thunder, and the fragments at the end of the poem. However, what dominate the work are, in Helen Gardner's words, "its visions [revealing] man's incapacity to achieve satisfaction, the boredom of his quotidian existence, and the horror of his ignobility."[66] And these striking visions are for the most part revealed through symbolic urban/desert settings.

In Eliot's early poetry through *The Waste Land*, then, urban landscape serves as a highly effective symbol for the sterility and degradation of the modern human soul. Influenced to a great extent by Baudelaire's use of city settings, Eliot has skillfully created a system of urban symbols which evoke the complexities of existence in the contemporary world. Rented rooms, dirty winding streets, vacant lots, dimly-lit stairs, raucous pubs, Underground stations, urban churches, the financial district constitute the core of the city symbolism. Based upon real landmarks of Boston, St. Louis, Paris, and London, these symbols possess a haunting reality that heightens their power of communication. And what they communicate with a violent impact is Eliot's harsh vision of the modern soul stripped of all significance.

III · The Middle Poetry

In his early poetry Eliot reveals the emptiness of the human soul without God. Urban landscape with its dingy streets, sooty buildings, and brown fog forms a major symbolic cluster in the rendering of this terrifying vision and provides a brilliant objective correlative for the grime and sterility of the modern soul. As an integral element of Eliot's symbolic code, this setting appears throughout the body of his poetry. However, it never again plays the dominant, encompassing role it has in the early poetry through *The Waste Land,* and the reason is easily found.

The middle poetry, which includes "The Hollow Men," "Ash Wednesday," and the Ariel poems, marks a transitional period in Eliot's work. It does not signal a sharp break or an extreme about-face in relation to the early poetry; rather, it is a development out of what went before. Having in the early works exposed the horrifying lack of meaning in human life, Eliot in these middle poems moves toward a recognition of what *can* give significance to human existence, of what *can* restore the lost fertility and purity of the soul. The closing lines of *The Waste Land* clearly point the way out of the Inferno and toward a kind of Purgatory. The middle works are then a positive movement toward rebirth and renewal.

This evolution of content, this shift of emphasis, requires a corresponding shift in symbolism, for the highly charged urban landscape already has a definite, though infinitely complex, function in Eliot's symbolic system. Thus, Eliot creates what Elizabeth Drew calls "a new symbolic *centre,*"[1] in which natural, rather than urban, landscape is dominant. Gardens, flowers, trees, and fountains rather than slum areas, street lamps, and tube stations now form the symbolic landscapes, and the literary affinities move from Baudelaire toward Tennyson.

However, as in the case of Eliot's subject, the change in the landscape symbolism is not a rejection of the earlier symbolism but a development from it and an integration of it, "An easy commerce of the old and the new." Some of the landscape symbols found in the early poetry, often in minor roles, retain their meanings as they move to major roles in the middle poems. For example, the garden which appeared quietly at least six times in the early poetry,[2] keeps its meaning of perfection and joy in the middle and late works where it plays a dominant part. Other symbols, however, are altered somewhat from their early meanings. The rocky desert of *The Waste Land* conveys sterility, anguish, and death, while in "Ash Wednesday" it takes on its New Testament significance as a place of fasting and preparation; hence, it symbolizes a kind of spiritual purification. The dimly-lit stairs that suggest spiritual blindness in the early poems become, like Dante's Mount, symbolic of spiritual aspiration toward God. And water, almost totally destructive earlier, regains its traditional meaning of rebirth. The established landscape symbols are thus integrated into the new symbolic center. As Elizabeth Drew puts it, "Some of the old symbols remain, but their emotional quality is subtly changed and shifted by the appearance of new ones which combine with them."[3]

What are these new symbols created from rural landscape? They are, as one would expect, a mixture of the traditional and the personal. Many are archetypal symbols with long-established meanings, the rose, the fountain, and the yew. Blended with these are such symbolic landscapes from Eliot's own experience as the New England coast of "Ash Wednesday" and "Marina."[4] While many critics feel, as does Helen Gardner, that these newer symbols lack "the sharp precision as well as the realism of the earlier [ones],"[5] I would strongly disagree. Although the outlines are sometimes vague, as if obscured by that New England mist of "Marina," the details of the landscapes are as clear-cut and precise as any of the urban symbols. For example, in "Ash Wednesday" a seascape with "white sails still fly[ing] seaward" is presented, and in "Journey of the Magi" a tavern is described with significant concrete details. Even the shadowy landscape of "The Hollow Men" contains definite landmarks: a swollen river flowing through a hollow valley, cactus, broken stone. The symbolic landscape of the middle poetry (as well as that of the late works) is then a mixture of old and new, a development and enrichment of the symbolic system established in the early works. Centering on the countryside rather than the city, it suggests the new hope for the rebirth of the human soul.

The first of the middle poems, "The Hollow Men," is a transitional poem in the truest sense of the word, for it belongs partially both to the early poems and to the middle poems and wholly to neither. In subject matter and tone, it echoes the early works in that it presents a shocking picture of the empty soul after death, the final stage of the dead body described in Section IV of *The Waste Land*. Yet, some could well argue that the poem portrays what is properly the beginning of any movement to redemption, a recognition of the utter nullity of man by himself, of man in total exile from God; thus, its content also mirrors that of the more positive middle poems. Its landscape technique, too, is transitional, belonging to both periods and to neither. Eliot departs from his usual practice and uses a basically literary landscape that is technically neither urban nor rural.[6] Thus, in its landscape symbolism, the poem is unique.

The work, as mentioned above, presents a vision of the soul completely separated from God. What better symbol could Eliot choose than the shadowy surrealist landscape of the Dantean Vestibule of Hell? In the *Inferno* the souls of the opportunists, of those who were wholly self-interested, are placed in a position of total separation in the Vestibule:

> Here sighs and cries and wails coiled and recoiled
> on the starless air, spilling my soul to tears. . . .

> And I,
> holding my head in horror, cried: "Sweet Spirit,

> what souls are these who run through this black haze?"
> And he to me: "These are the nearly soulless
> whose lives concluded neither blame nor praise.
>
> They are mixed here with that despicable corps
> of angels who were neither for God nor Satan,
> but only for themselves. The High Creator
>
> scourged them from Heaven for its perfect beauty,
> and Hell will not receive them since the wicked
> might feel some glory over them."[7]

They are cut off not only from God and from other men, but also from Satan; they do not even belong to Hell. Eliot sees the same condition in modern man's soul; its physical, emotional, and spiritual isolation is skillfully expressed through the grey, fragmented landscape of a no-man's land, aspects of which were perhaps also suggested by some of Tennyson's nightmare scenes. One of the paintings in "The Palace of Art" conveys a sense of eeriness and desolation through a dimly-lit desert landscape:

> One seem'd all dark and red—a tract of sand,
>   And some one pacing there *alone*,
> Who paced forever in a *glimmering land*,
>   Lit with a low large moon (italics mine).

In addition, the surrealistic waste of Guinevere's dream suggests isolation and the semi-darkness of dusk: "she seem'd to stand/On some vast plain before a setting sun." And finally Joseph Conrad's *Heart of Darkness* can be seen as a source for both the tone and the landscape details in the poem. Regarding the former, Helen Gardner suggests that "The Hollow Men" exhibits the "feeling of total meaninglessness, the extremity of skepticism which Marlow said he felt on the brink of death: 'a vision of grayness without form filled with physical pain, and a careless contempt for the evanescence of all things. . . .' "[8] Further, the locale of death's dream kingdom, like Conrad's Africa, is "a place of darkness," and its stagnant, unregenerative "tumid river" has clear affinities with the Congo river of the story: "An empty stream, a great silence. . . . The air was warm, thick, heavy, sluggish. . . . The long stretches of the waterway ran on, deserted, into the gloom of over-shadowed distances. . . . And this stillness of life did not in the least resemble a peace."[9] Eliot's desert, then, with its overtones of the Dantean Vestibule, of Tennysonian wastes, and of the Conradian jungle, is a brilliant symbol for the desolation of the apathetic soul. [10]

In Section I the speaker identifies himself as one of the hollow men: "Shape without form, shade without colour,/ Paralysed force, gesture without motion. . . ." Two minor landscape symbols are used here, both conveying the emptiness of selfish past lives:

> Our dried voices, when
> We whisper together
> Are quiet and meaningless
> As wind in dry grass
> Or rats' feet over broken glass
> In our dry cellar.

The rustling dry grass suggests the sterile desert landscape of *The Waste Land*, V, and the arid cellar with its broken glass recalls the slum setting of *The Waste Land*, III. These familiar details from the earlier work efficiently suggest the negative quality of the lives of the hollow men: the wind, futility and emptiness; the dry grass, sterility; the rats, physical repulsiveness and dirtiness; the broken glass, fragmentation; and the dry cellar, the subterranean aspect of their previous existence. These scenes are remembered from the past lives of the speaker and his companions; the speaker has not yet described their present environment.

However, in Section II he describes it in negative terms; it is not like death's other kingdom. [11] There, in the other kingdom,

> the eyes are
> Sunlight on a broken column
> There, is a tree swinging
> And voices are

> In the wind's singing
> More distant and more solemn
> Than a fading star.

The swinging tree, the sunlight, the voices, and above all the eyes of that landscape suggest the innocence, light, and joy of Paradise. By implication, "the twilight kingdom" in which the speaker finds himself possesses none of these but rather their opposites, guilt, darkness, and sorrow.

The third section contains the first direct description of the speaker's surroundings:

> This is the dead land
> This is cactus land
> Here the stone images
> Are raised, here they receive
> The supplication of a dead man's hand
> Under the twinkle of a fading star.

The desert landscape is the landscape of his soul: the dead land which can grow only cactus plants symbolizes its sterility; the broken stone suggests its shattered, fragmentary nature; and the dim halflight of the fading stars conveys its darkness and apathy. The soul is totally alone in this deserted waste, its only activity being futile prayers to stone fragments.

Section IV further describes the geography of Eliot's surrealistic vestibule of Hell. It is a "hollow valley" of "dying stars." The valley carries connotations of imprisonment, of dejection, of Psalm twenty-three's "valley of the shadow of death," while the dying stars suggest again the eerie halflight and echo the "starless air," the dirty "black haze," the "infected light" of Dante's "twilight country."[12] Further, in the valley is a swollen river on whose banks the indifferent gather:

> In this last of meeting places
> We grope together
> And avoid speech
> Gathered on this beach of the tumid river.

The fact that the river is tumid suggests disease and infection, indicating that its water is far from life-giving. The place recalls "the joyless beach of Acheron"[13] which forms the dividing line between Dante's Vestibule and the circles of Hell proper (III, 74). Thus this nightmare landscape symbolizes the état d'âme of total despair. The hollow men can only hope futilely for the bliss of God forever denied them:

> the perpetual star
> Multifoliate rose
> Of death's twilight kingdom
> The hope *only*
> Of empty men (italics mine).

The star of God's realm, in contrast to the dying stars of the vestibule, is eternal, and the glorious rose with its connotations of beauty, fertility, and life opposes the cactus, symbolic of ugliness, drought, and death.

Significantly, the last glimpse of the landscape, given in the opening quatrain of Section V, is focused on the cactus, specifically the prickly pear:

> *Here we go round the prickly pear*
> *Prickly pear prickly pear*
> *Here we go round the prickly pear*
> *At five o'clock in the morning.*

The nonsensical nursery rhyme catches up the utter futility and devastating emptiness of the souls of modern human beings as the hollow men tramp endlessly around the desert plant in the dim hours of an eternal early morning without a dawn.

"The Hollow Men" is, then, as Bradbrook points out, "the dead center in Eliot's poetry, [for] it records the experience of utter destitution. . . ."[14] Landscape again assumes a dominant role in the communication of this experience, giving the reader an insight into a soul rendered sterile and void through commitment to nothing beyond self.

In "Ash Wednesday" Eliot portrays the soul attempting to turn from self, to make a commitment to God, to find meaning for the human experience of life and death. In short, the soul in

"Ash Wednesday" affirms something beyond self in opposition to the souls of the early poems.[15] The title signifies the first day of Lent, "a day of fasting, contrition, and self-denial in which the [Christian] tries to renounce all other things and turn toward the things of God."[16] The poem's structure reflects the difficulty of this action as the six sections alternate between views of struggle and visions of attainment. The last section summarizes with poignant intensity the final conflict of flesh and spirit and suggests the ultimate victory of spirit. This poem of spiritual struggle is the major work of what might well be called Eliot's Purgatorio.

Rural landscape as symbol is an integral element of the poem, appearing in each of the six sections. It is skillfully manipulated and highly complex. Eliot uses *personal* settings to suggest what the protagonist hopes to reject, thereby giving immediacy and intimacy to the agony of renunciation. On the other hand, his use of *traditional* settings to convey what the protagonist hopes to affirm communicates the universality and stability associated with spiritual fulfillment. The result is a brilliant, though subtle, rendering of theme through symbol.

In setting up the framework of the poem in Section I, Eliot uses symbolism very sparingly in favor of a direct approach. However, the one reference to landscape is highly evocative. In this first section the unidentified protagonist, presumably an old man, states that he is attempting to turn away from all the things of this world, even the best things, in order to embrace the spiritual world. The hesitations and repetitions in the verse indicate the difficulty of such a renunciation. In the opening passage the speaker rejects earthly success and fame, and he refuses to mourn for his vanished youth or his approaching death:

> Because I do not hope to turn again
> Because I do not hope
> Because I do not hope to turn
> *Desiring this man's gift and that man's scope*
> I no longer strive to strive towards such things
> (Why should the agèd eagle stretch its wings?)
> Why should I mourn
> The *vanished power of the usual reign?* (italics mine).

The second passage is an elaboration on the loss of youthful, perhaps sexual, powers. As ecstatic as some youthful experiences are, they are only transitory:

Because I do not hope to know again
The *infirm* glory of the positive hour. . .
The one veritable *transitory* power
Because I cannot drink
There, where trees flower, and springs flow, for
there is nothing again (italics mine).

Youthful, sexual love, symbolized by the fertile garden with its blossoming fruit trees and life-giving spring waters,[17] is the highest good this world has to offer; yet it is not eternal and must thus be rejected in favor of a higher, divine love.[18] Thus, in the third passage the speaker renounces his earthly beloved[19] and turns toward God:

Because I know that time is always time
And place is always and only place
And what is actual is actual only for one time
And only for one place
I rejoice that things are as they are and
I renounce the blessèd face
And renounce the voice
Because I cannot hope to turn again. . . .

The extreme difficulty of this act is emphasized in the last eighteen lines of the section where he asks God for help:

Teach us to care and not to care
Teach us to sit still.

Pray for us sinners now and at the hour of our death
Pray for us now and at the hour of our death.

Section II employs a highly symbolic desert-garden landscape to suggest the serene peace and harmony of union with God. The desert here is quite different from the desert of *The Waste Land* and the cactus land of "The Hollow Men," although some critics assert that the three are the same and carry similar meanings.[20] This desert is also a place of death, but it is a death of the body and of the self; as E. E. Duncan-Jones notes, there is "a dying to self, which from the spiritual point of view (and here no other is relevant) is seen as wholly gain."[21] Thus the desert setting takes on its Biblical meaning of a place for fasting, prayer, preparation, a place for cleansing the soul. It is like the wilderness in which John the Baptist fasted and the one in which Christ spent his forty days of preparation. In opposition to those of *The Waste Land* desert, the details of this arid landscape suggest serenity and peace. Instead of the scorching heat of noon, it is the "cool of the day." The "quiet of the desert" connotes not isolation and loneliness but tranquillity. In place of a "dead tree [which] gives no shelter" is a living, evergreen juniper tree in whose shade the bones repose. And finally the sand itself, no longer barren and unproductive, is a "blessing." In the midst of this meaningful desert of purgation, the white bones, symbolic here of a return to purity, sing of Christ as a rose garden that gives significance to human existence:

> The single Rose
> Is now the Garden
> Where all loves end. . . .

Addressing themselves to Mary, the bones thank her for the gift of her Son:

> Grace to the Mother
> For the Garden
> Where all love ends.

The symbolic garden landscape is used here with its traditional meaning; it suggests a place of security, fulfillment, and joyous perfection. In this context particularly, it recalls the Garden of Eden where human and divine love were united. Thus it is an appropriate symbol for the love of Christ, which gives significance both to man's life and to his death, to what would otherwise be an "endless/Journey to no end." With this knowledge of divine love, the protagonist ends the section with a tone of serenity and assurance.

The two symbolic settings of Section III return to the agony and frustration of the spiritual effort. Here the protagonist does battle with fear (or despair) and with a temptation of the flesh. The dominant symbol is the stair, an element of setting that appears often in the early poems as a sign of spiritual descent or vacuity.[22] In this poem, however, it is symbolic of the difficulty of spiritual ascent. It is, as Duncan-Jones remarks, Eliot's "own version of the usual image of spiritual progress."[23]

As a symbol here, the stair is both traditional and personal, both universal and particular. Traditionally, it partakes of Dante's purgatorial mountain with its "rock-walls sheer,"[24] its narrow cornices, and its treacherous, winding path:

> Meanwhile, we'd reached the mountain's foot—and dead
> Upright it rose, a cliff so steep and sheer,
> 'Twould make the nimblest legs seem dull as lead.
>
> The craggiest way, the most remote and drear. . .
> (Purgatory, III, 46–69).

The levels themselves resemble a huge staircase, and, even more important, a winding stair cut into the face of the rock connects each of these levels:

> We'd gained the stair-head, where, the second time,
> A cutting comes to break that mountain-flank
> Which sets us free from evil as we climb . . . (Purgatory, XIII, 1–3).

Further, each stair has two turns.[25] Thus, while mounting, one would have two opportunities to stop and look back. This point helps to clarify Eliot's description of "the first turning of the second stair," "the second turning of the second stair," and "the first turning of the third stair." These Dantean overtones contribute in two ways to Eliot's symbol. First, they convey the extreme difficulty of the spiritual climb in physical terms. Second, as Matthiessen so clearly points out, they serve as "a reminder that the stages of the soul which Eliot is depicting correspond also to a completely developed pattern of philosophic and religious thought . . . and . . . thus enable [the experience] to possess a more universal significance."[26]

Another source for the traditional aspects of Eliot's stair can be found in Tennyson's "The Holy Grail," where the stair symbolizes the difficulty of the spiritual ascent to purity. Lancelot recounts his agonizing search for the Holy Grail, the final approach to which is made by climbing a towering stair:

> "I heard the shingle grinding in the surge,
> And felt the boat shock earth, and looking up,
> Behold, the enchanted towers of Carbonek,
> A castle like a rock upon a rock,
> With chasm-like portals open to the sea,
> And steps that met the breaker! . . .
> Then from the boat I leapt, and up the stairs,
> There drew my sword. . . .
> Up I climb'd a thousand steps
> With pain; as in a dream I seem'd to climb
> For ever. . . ."

While the stair symbol has traditional and universal overtones, it is also Eliot's own creation, being particular, concrete, and realistic. Stephenson's suggestion that it is the dark winding stair of an old castle with the fetid smell associated with artillery towers[27] is a fascinating one, which notes the Tennysonian echoes. However, most of these towers do not have banisters, and their slotted windows are narrow rather than rounded; thus the exact location of the stairs is still ambiguous. Wherever they are specifically located, their details are precise enough. The second staircase with its two turns strikingly represents the soul's terrifying battle with fear and despair. In the dark, stinking, close atmosphere, the protagonist looks back and relives his immediate experience of battling "the devil of the stairs" who had twisted him against the banister in an attempt to throw him back down:

> I turned and saw below
> The same shape twisted on the banister
> Under the vapour in the fetid air
> Struggling with the devil of the stairs. . . .

After the second turning he is no longer able to see the two figures, and faces the fear of total destruction and death, symbolized by a treacherous, dark, and clammy stair described in terms of two aged mouths:

> At the second turning of the second stair
> I left them twisting, turning below;
> There were no more faces and the stair was dark,
> Damp, jaggèd, like an old man's mouth drivelling, beyond repair,
> Or the toothed gullet of an agèd shark.

On the third stair the protagonist has to struggle, not with fear and terror, but with the temptation of earthly, sexual beauty represented by a springtime country landscape seen through a slotted window. The shape of the window itself, "bellied like the fig's fruit," immediately evokes overtones of fertility and sensuality. The landscape may have been suggested to Eliot by one of the tapestries described in Tennyson's "The Palace of Art":

> For some were hung with arras green and blue,
>   Showing a gaudy summer-morn,
> Where with puff'd cheek the belted hunter blew
>   His wreathed bugle-horn.

Eliot's setting conveys the same fresh, sensuously charming atmosphere. His landscape is a flowery meadow filled with objects to delight the senses: the eye-appealing colors of white, blue, green, lilac, and soft brown; the sound of flute music; the smell of hawthorn and lilac; the feel of hair blown by a gentle breeze; and even the taste of that fragrant hair "over the mouth blown." The ambiguous figure playing the flute seems to be a mixture of the fertility god Pan and of a seductive brown-haired maiden clothed in blue and green. It is a setting altogether enchanting to the flesh:

> At the first turning of the third stair
> Was a slotted window bellied like the fig's fruit
> And beyond the hawthorn blossom and a pasture scene

The broadbacked figure drest in blue and green
Enchanted the maytime with an antique flute.
Blown hair is sweet, brown hair over the mouth blown,
Lilac and brown hair. . . .

Yet this beauty is a distraction of the world, a temptation to
leave the difficult struggle of spiritual ascent and descend to the
easy pleasures of the earth. It is "distraction, music of the flute,
stops and steps of the mind over the third stair." However,
the protagonist overcomes the temptation, continues to climb,
and the landscape fades in the distance. With a God-given
"strength beyond hope and despair," he goes on "climbing the
third stair." The section ends with a fragment from the liturgy
of the Mass, spoken just prior to the taking of the Sacrament;
these words seem quietly to indicate the soul's movement
toward the condition of purity. Thus, the settings of the dark
stair and the pastoral meadow suggest the arduousness of
spiritual ascent.

Section IV, like Section II, presents a vision of the higher
dream of the soul's surroundings upon attaining purification.
The setting is a serene garden with fountains and springs of
living water, with yew trees (traditionally symbolic of everlasting life), with singing birds and quiet pathways. It recalls the
innocence of the Biblical Garden of Eden and the bliss of
Dante's Earthly Paradise into which the soul enters after climbing the purgatorial Mount. Dorothy Sayers's description of the
latter in her introduction to Dante's *Purgatory* points up the
similarities: "Green and cool and fragrant with flowers, mur-
murous with birdsong and bubbling brook and tree-tops rustling in the wind that moves with the turning worlds, holding
fast its secret of repatriation and renewal, this is the place that
all mankind remembers."[28] The whole scene, elusive and
barely tangible like things of the spirit, catches up the essence
of beatitude and spiritual joy.

With abrupt suddenness, the protagonist turns in Section V
to the secular world, which contains two types of lost souls:
those who totally reject the higher dream of beatitude and
those whose wills are too weak for the spiritual effort necessary

to attain it. The first two passages describe the former, using landscape only in the broadest terms. These souls cannot hear the word of Christ because of the great noise:

> Where shall the word be found, where will the word
> Resound? Not here, there is not enough silence
> Not on *the sea* or on *the islands,* not
> On the *mainland,* in the *desert* or the *rain land* . . . (italics mine).

They live in spiritual blindness, having denied Christ:

> No place of grace for those who avoid the face
> No time to rejoice for those who walk among noise
> and deny the voice. . . .

These lines recall many of the sterile figures who people the early poems: Prufrock, the young man of "Portrait of a Lady," Gerontion, and all the inhabitants of *The Waste Land.* In the last two passages of the section, the protagonist requests Mary to pray for those of weak will:

> Will the veiled sister pray for
> Those who walk in darkness, who chose thee and oppose thee, . . .
> And are terrified and cannot surrender
> And affirm before the world and deny between the rocks
> In the last desert between the last blue rocks
> The desert in the garden the garden in the desert
> Of drouth, spitting from the mouth the withered apple-seed.

Here Eliot again makes use of the symbolic garden-desert setting to suggest the closeness and yet the extreme distance between spiritual death (desert) and spiritual rebirth (garden). Those souls standing at the gates of the garden are yet in the desert of spiritual drought. If they cannot make the final spiritual effort, if they cannot become fully purged, "spitting from the mouth the withered apple-seed" of sin, then they will remain in the desert.

Section VI summarizes with extreme poignancy the agonizing conflict between the worlds of spirit and flesh, for once again the beauty of the earth enchants the protagonist against his will: "(Bless me father) though I do not wish to wish these things. . . ." Eliot here, I think, is attempting to show the earth at its most beautiful, as something extremely difficult to give up. Its renunciation must be seen as anguishing to attest to the even greater beauty of that for which it is being renounced. As lovely as the earth is, Paradise is infinitely more beautiful. Thus, Eliot chooses for his setting the coast of New England; it is neither sinister nor seductive but fresh and innocent, suggesting the best the natural world has to offer:

> From the wide window towards the granite shore
> The white sails still fly seaward, seaward flying
> Unbroken wings
>
> And the lost heart stiffens and rejoices
> In the lost lilac and the lost sea voices
> And the weak spirit quickens to rebel
> For the bent golden-rod and the lost sea smell
> Quickens to recover
> The cry of quail and the whirling plover
> And the blind eye creates
> The empty forms between the ivory gates
> And smell renews the salt savour of the sandy earth. . . .

The majority of the scenic details are from Eliot's reminiscences of the New England shore, "the fir trees, the bay and golden-rod, the song-sparrows, the red granite and the blue sea of Massachusetts."[29] The white sails recall both the boats that one could see from the windows of the Eliot house at Gloucester and the boats that Eliot himself sailed in the waters off Cape Ann. The lilac, fragrant in early summer, still grows on the grounds of the Eliot house, and goldenrod, bent by the ocean wind, is in great evidence along the rocky coast. In addition to the striking visual images are the equally realistic aural and olfactory ones, the cries of birds and the distinctive smells of salt and sand.[30]

While the details of the setting are mainly personal, there is at least one significant literary echo: "white sails" flying seaward recall a similar detail from Tennyson's *Idylls of the King*:

"Men saw the goodly hills of Somerset,/And white sails flying on the yellow sea. . . ." Both landscapes suggest the exuberant yet fragile beauty of the earth. The speaker's reaction to this beauty is a complex one of both attraction and renunciation, operating simultaneously (although the victory of renunciation is implied in the closing passage). On one level, the lost heart (lost to paradise if it turns to the earth) stiffens against the loss of physical beauty, rejoices in that beauty, and longs to return to it. The powerful concrete images of the sight and smell of lilac and the sounds of the sea create for the reader a tangible physical beauty. The adjective "lost" that modifies the lilac and the sea voices implies that they are lost to the protagonist if he has indeed definitely chosen the difficult way of spiritual discipline. The weak spirit (see Section V) both comes to life and hurries, "quickens," to rebel against its ascetic choice and to return to the aesthetic ("the bent golden-rod and the lost sea smell"), to take back, "recover," what it has given up (the sounds of quail and plover, the smell of "the salt savour of the sandy earth"). All the senses tempt the protagonist to return to the physical world. Yet, coexisting with this feeling of attraction is an equally powerful one of rejection. In "Ash Wednesday" union with God is worth the agonizing renunciation, and the lost heart (lost to the world in a spiritual, and positive, sense) stiffens or steels itself against the pain of the loss and rejoices in that loss, having attained a greater good. Thus this is "the time of tension between dying and birth," between dying to the world and being born to God.[31]

The poem ends with a rocky, solitary landscape, symbolic of the stark discipline, the bare humility, and the continuing difficulty of the spiritual effort:

> The place of solitude where three dreams cross
> Between blue rocks. . .
> Teach us to sit still
> Even among these rocks. . . .

The landscape is neither sterile nor terrifying, but rather serene and reposeful. It almost certainly suggests a tranquillity of mind arising from the protagonist's final surrender to God's will: "Our peace in His will. . . ."

Thus the natural landscape in "Ash Wednesday" plays an unquestionably significant role in symbolizing the arduousness of the spiritual ascent as well as the final joy that awaits the determined soul. The poem is perhaps one of Eliot's most brilliant, though certainly less recognized, achievements in the use of symbolism.

The Ariel poems, published separately from 1927 to 1930, contain four short poems; two of these, "Journey of the Magi" and "Marina," make use of natural landscape as symbol. In "Journey of the Magi" Eliot presents a starkly realistic view of the story of the wise men. One of the kings recalls in his old age the visit to the Christ Child and tries to determine its significance. In describing the journey itself, he uses three different settings. The first two catch up the quality of the "old dispensation," of the pagan world without Christ, while the third suggests the new life offered by God's Son.

The magus begins in stanza one by re-creating the wintry landscape of the journey. The snow was either piled in drifts that clogged the roads, the "ways deep," or was melting on the muddy ground; and the air was "sharp" and icy. In short, it was the "very dead of winter," a phrase suggesting the death of the old way of life. As the wise men travelled, they encountered other difficulties symbolized by urban settings: "the cities hostile and the towns unfriendly/And the villages dirty and charging high prices. . . ." The whole secular world, from the cursing camel men to the greedy innkeepers and lazy camels, seemed determined to impede their progress and often caused them to wish for their distant kingdoms:

> There were times we regretted
> The summer palaces on slopes, the terraces,
> And the silken girls bringing sherbet.

This landscape of palaces and terraces evokes the essence of the pagan life of ease and sensual pleasure, a man-centered existence based on the philosophy of hedonism. Thus the settings of Stanza I suggest a way of life before the coming of Christ.

In opposition, Stanza II presents a country landscape evocative of the rebirth and fertility brought by Christ's entrance into man's world. At the time of day symbolic of renewed life, the entourage descended into a valley:

> Then at dawn we came down to a temperate valley,
> Wet, below the snow line, smelling of vegetation;
> With a running stream and a water-mill beating the darkness,
> And three trees on the low sky,
> And an old white horse galloped away in the meadow.

Every detail of the valley's geography sets it in contrast to the cold, deathlike landscape in which the kings had been travelling. The temperature hinted of the approach of spring. Further, this warmth had melted the snow so that the valley had life-giving water and odors of growing plants, symbolic of fertility. The "running stream" of water differed from the frozen lakes and ponds the magi must have seen on their way. This moving water also functions as a contrast to all the stagnant waters of the early poems.[32] The water-mill that beat the darkness is seen by Elizabeth Drew as a vital force symbolic of "throbbing, driving life."[33] Silhouetted against the "low sky" are three trees, quite clearly standing for the three crosses of Calvary. Finally, in a meadow an old white horse galloped away. The meaning of the horse is ambiguous. Being old, it perhaps represents the old dispensation that will fade away with Christ's birth. However, it could be an additional portent of Calvary, for a white horse seen in a dream was a traditional English and German symbol of death.[34] In any case, the valley as a whole conveys the significance of Christ's appearance in man's world and is indeed at a far remove from the "hollow valley" of "The Hollow Men."

After describing the valley, the old king says,

> Then we came to a tavern with vine-leaves over the lintel,
> Six hands at an open door dicing for pieces of silver,
> And feet kicking the empty wine-skins.

The realistic details of this symbolic setting, as Eliot notes in *The Use of Poetry and the Use of Criticism,* came from his own experience: "six ruffians seen through an open window playing cards at night at a small French railway junction where there was a water-mill. . . ."[35] As in the early poetry, the tavern or bar is symbolic of the human soul that either has never known or has rejected Christ. The pieces of silver evoke the betrayer Judas as well as the soldiers gambling for Christ's robe at the foot of the cross, while the "empty wine-skins" suggest not only drunkenness but also the emptiness of the old way of life. Even the use of hands and feet rather than the whole person conveys the fragmented quality of the old order in which Christ was unknown and/or the new order in which He is denied. The tavern is a complex symbol pointing to the spiritual void of the old dispensation as well as that of the secular modern age.

Finally, the king recounts their arrival at the stable, and significantly he does not describe the scene at all:

> and so we continued
> And arrived at evening, not a moment too soon
> Finding the place; it was (you may say) satisfactory.

It simply does not stand out in his memory, for it was a disappointment and a mystery he has not yet understood: "this Birth was/Hard and bitter agony for us, like Death, our death." He is no longer able to live in the old pagan way, but neither can he live in the new Christian way. Therefore, he says in a voice heavy with weariness and resignation, "I should be glad of another death," meaning his own.

The landscapes in the poem function as clear symbols of the two orders of existence between which the old magus is hopelessly caught: the summer palaces, the dirty villages, the tavern on the one hand and on the other the temperate valley with its meadow, green plants, and running water. Indeed, these settings communicate the very essence of the poem's meaning: the agony of the magus's irresolvable dilemma.

"Marina" is a striking work in many ways. It is certainly, as Bradbrook says, "one of the most beautiful and moving [poems] that Eliot has written,"[36] and it is perhaps, to quote

Elizabeth Drew, his "only purely joyous poem."[37] Its dominant symbol is the landscape of the New England coast and specifically of Rogue Island at the tip of Sebascodeagan Island in Maine's Casco Bay.[38] This remote, isolated setting is precisely drawn in the poem. Rogue Island is a tiny island of grey rock ("what grey rocks," "what granite islands") with a cluster of tall pine trees at one end. A thick pine forest covers the larger island from which one can reach Rogue Island, and a light mist drifts in and out of the trees continually. The songs of birds fill the air, along with the cry of gulls and the sound of waves washing against the rock shore; otherwise, there is silence. In the poem Eliot stresses four aspects of the literal scene: the grey rocks, the fog, the song of the woodthrush, and the scent of the pine trees. The fragile beauty of this setting suggests first the joy of Pericles's rediscovery of his daughter, with overtones of Lear's awakening scene. On a deeper level, however, the landscape conveys the ecstasy of rebirth of the soul, of reunion with the Divine.

The poem opens with a description of the setting, as Pericles's boat nears the shore:

What seas what shores what grey rocks and what islands
What water lapping the bow
And scent of pine and the woodthrush singing through the fog. . . .

All the details of the landscape suggest the innocence, beauty, and tranquillity of an earthly paradise: the lulling sound of the lapping water, the quiet grey of the rocks, the fragrant scent of the towering pines, and the song of the woodthrush. And the delicate mist somewhat obscuring the whole scene conveys the sense of mystery and awe associated with Eden. The coastal setting is a perfect symbol for the joy of regained and renewed life through purification of the spirit. In the next two passages, the "wind,/[the] breath of pine, and the woodsong fog" of the setting emphasize the victory of the spiritual world over the temporal: "By this grace dissolved in place. . . ."

The middle section of the poem concerns Pericles's growing awareness of the reality of Marina. At first, he has difficulty in accepting what his own aged eyes see and what his own aged hands touch, as she seems to fade and then to reappear:

> What is this face, less clear and clearer
> The pulse in the arm, less strong and stronger—
> Given or lent? more distant than stars and nearer than the eye. . . .

But two memories serve to ascertain the truth of her being. The first, in lines anticipating "New Hampshire" and "Burnt Norton," recalls her childhood, "Whispers and small laughter between leaves and hurrying feet/Under sleep," while the second evokes the time in which she was conceived and born and the boat built:

> I made this, I have forgotten
> And remember.
> The rigging weak and the canvas rotten
> Between one June and another September.
> Made this unknowing, half conscious, unknown, my own.

In the last section of the poem, Pericles reaches finally a full awareness of Marina's existence and its significance:

> This form, this face, this life
> Living to live in a world of time beyond me; let me
> Resign my life for this life, my speech for that unspoken,
> The awakened, lips parted, the hope, the new ships.

She is an extension of his own life, renewed hope, rebirth of the soul. The coastal setting, reappearing in the final lines of the poem, therefore catches up the totality of this intense experience of recognition and regeneration, of a life fulfilled and invested with meaning:

> What seas what shores what granite islands towards my timbers
> And woodthrush calling through the fog
> My daughter.

Like the myth of the Fisher King in *The Waste Land*, the Pericles-Marina story is a framework. It is a parable of the lost soul suddenly given life through the miraculous appearance of a meaningful figure; it is, in short, a parallel to Christ's gift of salvation to the secular world. Thus the coastal landscape symbolizes more than just Pericles's rebirth; it conveys the regeneration of the human soul.

In Eliot's middle poetry, then, the dominant landscape is natural and Tennysonian rather than urban and Baudelairean. In place of the streets, hotels, Underground stations, there are valleys, gardens, meadows, pine trees, and sea coasts as Eliot moves from depictions of the emptiness and degradation of the soul to visions of its fulfillment and purification.

IV · "Landscapes"

After completing what we have called the middle poetry, Eliot wrote "Landscapes" (1934–35), a series of five short poems devoted entirely to symbolic natural landscapes and bearing as titles for the first time, if we exclude *The Waste Land*, the names of their settings. The works have excited very little critical comment; the "Landscapes" in general and their symbolism in particular have been largely ignored. George Williamson in *A Reader's Guide to T. S. Eliot* begins on an exciting note: "The 'Landscapes' . . . are experiments . . . in a symbolism that is used in *Four Quartets*. From each place he distils an essence which concentrates a state of mind and thus becomes accessible to a spiritual history." However, he goes no further and leaves the tantalized reader with these ambiguous statements. Grover Smith in *T.S. Eliot's Poetry and Plays: A Study in Sources and Meaning* points out in a short discussion the relationship between the "Landscapes" and *Four Quartets*. He gives a brief analysis of "New Hampshire" and notes that "Usk" and "Rannoch, by Glencoe" exhibit "mild but exact symbolism." Like Williamson, however, he never explains what the symbolism is or what it means. Helen Gardner, in her article "The Landscapes of Eliot's Poetry," mentions the poems in one paragraph, and Father Genesius Jones makes some interesting suggestions in *Approach to the Purpose: A Study of the Poetry of T. S. Eliot* but does not place them in a unified context. Other major critics such as Matthiessen, Drew, and Kenner barely touch on the poems or do not bring them up at all. The only exception to this general neglect is an illuminating article by E. A. Hansen who explores "the musicality of the 'Landscapes,' " concentrating mainly on Eliot's use of syntax and rhythm.[1]

112

Yet though they are little known, seldom discussed, and relegated to a place among Eliot's minor works, these poems share many of the outstanding qualities of his more widely read works; indeed, they are minor only in their length. Like Eliot's major poems, they are concerned with the meaning of human existence. Furthermore, their rhythms are as appropriate and original and their settings as highly symbolic as those in the best known of Eliot's works. While the landscapes are extremely personal and somewhat obscure (especially "Usk"), they have their foundations in traditional settings with traditional meanings; as personal as they may seem, they are integrally linked with the universal.

While the "Landscapes" are important in their own right, they are perhaps even more worthy of attention as experiments in preparation for *Four Quartets.* (Indeed, Eliot was working on "Burnt Norton" during the same time, in the early 1930s.) They foreshadow some of the landscape techniques that he employs in this masterpiece, and they reveal several significant changes from his previous methods. First, landscape takes on an even greater symbolic function than it had in the early and middle poems. In the majority of the poetic works through "Marina," he uses a persona, a kind of central intelligence, as the major means of symbolizing emotional, moral, and/or spiritual states, with landscape as a secondary, though highly important, symbol. The titles themselves indicate this reliance on symbolic characters: "The Love Song of J. Alfred Prufrock," "Portrait of a Lady," "Gerontion," "Sweeney Erect," "The Hollow Men," and "Marina," to mention a few. However, in the "Landscapes" and later in *Four Quartets* he turns to landscape as the *foremost* means of objectifying the emotional/spiritual content, so that a particular landscape becomes the central symbol in each of the individual poems. Second, a corresponding change in the kinds of titles he uses marks the shift in symbolism; the settings themselves provide the titles of "Landscapes" and *Four Quartets.* Third, he chooses as these major symbols highly personal landscapes from his own experience, either from his childhood in America ("New Hampshire," "Cape Ann," "The Dry Salvages") or from visits made as an adult, largely in the

British Isles ("Usk," "Rannoch, by Glencoe," "Burnt Norton," "East Coker," "Little Gidding," "Virginia"). Fourth, although the settings derive from his personal experience, they bear universal meanings in that they are linked to traditional, or archetypal, symbols. The garden is the conventional symbol underlying the personal landscapes in "New Hampshire," "Cape Ann," and "Burnt Norton," as are the river in "Virginia" and "The Dry Salvages," the chapel in "Usk" and "Little Gidding," and the earth (closely associated with human history) in "Rannoch, by Glencoe" and "East Coker." These experimental aspects of "Landscapes" are closely linked with the kinds of uses he makes of landscape in *Four Quartets*. There are also, however, important ways in which he later alters these techniques for the *Quartets*, and these will be discussed at the end of the chapter, following a close analysis of the five poems which make up "Landscapes."

The "Landscapes" originally appeared as separate poems in this order: "New Hampshire" and "Virginia" in *The Virginia Quarterly Review* in April, 1934; "Rannoch, by Glencoe" in *The New English Weekly* in October, 1935; and "Usk" and "Cape Ann" were privately distributed in December, 1935. However, they were published together and in their present order in *The Collected Poems*, 1936; it seems clear that they were intended then to be considered as a unified group. When the poems are read as a cycle, as a single entity, their thematic and artistic significance is readily apparent. On a literal level, they follow a seasonal sequence, beginning and ending with spring. On a symbolic level, they trace the movement of human life from innocence through experience to the moment when life must be relinquished, the seasonal pattern suggesting the passage from childhood purity to the purity of spiritual rebirth in the adult. Thus, they are a "spiritual history," to use Williamson's expression. Each landscape symbolizes an elusive state of the soul, and the poems alternate between positive and negative spiritual conditions: "New Hampshire" is positive; "Virginia," negative; "Usk," positive; "Rannoch, by Glencoe," negative; and "Cape Ann," positive. The speaker's remark, "The palaver is finished," in the concluding line of the final poem applies to

This is the dead land
This is cactus land. . . .
"THE HOLLOW MEN," 11. 39-40.

The desert of the American Southwest.

What seas what shores what grey rocks and what islands
What water lapping the bow
And scent of pine and the woodthrush singing through the fog. . . .
"MARINA," 11. 1-3.

Rogue Island, Casco Bay, Maine.

Rogue Island, Casco Bay, Maine.

Children's voices in the orchard
Between the blossom- and the fruit-time. . . .
"NEW HAMPSHIRE," 11. 1-2.

Professor Sheffield, T. S. Eliot, Ada Eliot Sheffield, Marian Eliot, and
Theresa Eliot on a picnic near Randolph, New Hampshire, about 1933.

Red river, red river,
Slow flow heat is silence. . . .
"VIRGINIA," 11. 1-2.

The Rivanna River, Charlottesville, Virginia.

Gitchell's St

Do not suddenly break the branch, or
Hope to find
The white hart behind the white well.
"USK," 11. 1-3.

The castle ruins, Usk, Wales.

Seek only there
Where the grey light meets the green air
The hermit's chapel, the pilgrim's prayer.
"USK," 11. 9-11.

The chapel in the castle ruins, Usk, Wales.

Shadow of pride is long, in the long pass
No concurrence of bone.
"RANNOCH, BY GLENCOE," 11. 11-12.

The Pass of Glencoe, Scotland, site of the MacDonald Massacre of 1692.

Listlessness of ancient war,
Languor of broken steel,
Clamour of confused wrong, apt
In silence. Memory is strong
Beyond the bone.
"RANNOCH, BY GLENCOE," 11. 6-10.

The Celtic Cross at Glencoe, Scotland, erected to the memory of the
MacDonald Massacre of 1692.

O quick quick quick, quick hear the song-sparrow,
Swamp-sparrow, fox-sparrow, vesper-sparrow
At dawn and dusk.
"CAPE ANN," ll. 1-3.

Jerry K

The Eliot house, Cape Ann, Massachusetts.

the whole series and not just to "Cape Ann." When approached from this point of view, the poetic sequence takes on considerable importance in the canon of Eliot's work.

The first poem, "New Hampshire," describes an apple orchard in spring, "Between the blossom- and the fruit-time." The description of the New Hampshire orchard is grounded in Eliot's personal experience, for he visited this state numerous times both as a child and as an adult. In the collection of the Houghton Library of Harvard University are several photographs of Eliot taken in the 1930s and 1940s in the New Hampshire locations of Dublin, Randolph, and Mt. Monadnock. One of these (dated 1933) is of particular interest, for it shows Eliot and four companions on a picnic in a country setting. Eliot is sitting on a low stone wall, behind which is an orchard of small trees.

In the poem the trees are filled with children playing happily among the tree branches:

> Children's voices in the orchard
> Between the blossom- and the fruit-time:
> Golden head, crimson head,
> Between the green tip and the root.

Birds fly, singing, through the air over the trees: "Black wing, brown wing, hover over." The golden hair of the child, the green of the tree, and the season of spring are all traditional symbols of fertility and innocence.[2] Thus the orchard setting is symbolic of the purity and joy of Eden, of the beginning of human life both with Adam and Eve and with every child born into the world. However, the reference to the brown and the black wings of the birds, with their traditional connotations of the passage of time, death, and mourning, lends an ominous note to the scene, as does the sense of heaviness and impending doom implied by the word "hover." The fact that the orchard is filled with apple trees, "Swing up into the apple-tree," increases the poignance of this childhood innocence so soon to be lost. Not only is it traditional that the apple tree symbolizes Adam and Eve's loss of innocence in the garden of

Eden, but also many writers have used the *mature autumn* apple tree loaded with fruit as a symbol of *old* age. (See, for example, Robert Frost's "After Apple-Picking.")

Indeed, in the brief middle section of the poem the speaker, a mature adult, considers with sorrow the inevitable passing of youth and his own future death:

> Twenty years and the spring is over;
> To-day grieves, to-morrow grieves,
> Cover me over, light-in-leaves. . . .

The phrase "light-in-leaves" projects the future dying of the apple tree's leaves in autumn and thereby evokes the sense of inescapable decay and death both of nature and of man, a striking similarity to G. M. Hopkins's "Spring and Fall: To a Young Child." However, the phrase also suggests the speaker's desire to escape from this harsh reality by returning to the happy, timeless world of the youngsters among the sun-lit leaves of the trees.[3]

With this transitional link the poem shifts back to the present orchard landscape where the season is still spring and innocence is alive and precious. The short lilting rhythms of nursery rhyme as well as the sharp juxtaposition of the "Golden head" and the "black wing" are symbolic of this transient purity:

> Golden head, black wing,
> Cling, swing,
> Spring, sing,
> Swing up into the apple-tree.

The two universal symbols, golden hair and spring (used here both as verb and as noun), combine with Eliot's personal symbols, the swinging (freedom) and the singing (joy) of the children in the apple orchard, to create one of his most meaningful landscapes. The poem is not a simple description but a symbolic expression of the poignant beauty and brevity of youth and innocence on man's earth.

"New Hampshire" has affinities particularly with "Burnt

Norton," but also with portions of "East Coker" and "Little Gidding," in that all make similar use of gardenlike settings to suggest joyous innocence and purity. In the garden of "Burnt Norton," where an ecstatic moment is experienced, "the leaves were full of children,/Hidden excitedly, containing laughter," and at the end of the poem is a second reference to "the hidden laughter/Of children in the foliage." In addition, in Part II a tree filled with summer sunlight is described:

> Ascend to summer in the tree
> We move above the moving tree
> In light upon the figured leaf.

"East Coker," III, contains a symbolic allusion to "The laughter in the garden, echoed ecstasy," as does "Little Gidding," V, "And the children in the apple-tree/Not known, because not looked for."

In the spring of 1933 Eliot went to the University of Virginia in Charlottesville to give the Page-Barbour Lectures, printed in 1934 as *After Strange Gods: A Primer of Modern Heresy*. While there he viewed the landscape which he was to transform into a symbol for his second poem of the series, entitled "Virginia." The poem moves into the realm of experience, as Eliot symbolizes through landscape the death-in-life of spiritual apathy and paralysis of the will. This état d'âme is at the opposite pole from the affirmative spiritual effort of "Ash Wednesday." Indeed the poem is closely linked with "The Hollow Men" in its portrayal of spiritual vacuity and in its use of a sluggish river in a barren landscape. Further, it anticipates the muddy, brown river of "The Dry Salvages" with its negative connotations.

To convey the deathlike immobility of the soul, Eliot uses the Virginia setting in the dead-heat of summer, when the heavy, scorching air has smothered sound and paralysed movement. The poem opens with the slow, plodding rhythm of "Red river, red river,/Slow flow heat is silence." The slowly moving river is certainly based on the muddy Rivanna river at Charlottesville, but it may also have been suggested to Eliot by a painting described in Tennyson's "The Palace of Art":

And one, a full-fed river winding slow
By herds upon an endless plain,
The ragged rims of thunder brooding low,
With shadow-streaks of rain.

In any case, the red river is a complex symbol containing numerous layers of meaning. Its water is far from life-giving; it is stagnant, warm, barely moving, choked with dust, and clogged with heavy red mud. (Mud as a symbol of both degradation and the flesh appears in several other poems, including "Preludes," "Morning at the Window," *The Waste Land*, V, and "Burnt Norton," II.) The river is in direct contrast to fertile and cool water, such as the "running stream" of "Journey of the Magi." Further, the fact that the river is red connotes blood as well as heat and mud. Red suggests sin generally and violence specifically, being associated not only with Dante's river of blood in *Inferno*, XIII, but also with the flooding Mississippi River with "its cargo of dead Negroes, cows, and chicken coops" mentioned in "The Dry Salvages." Finally, the heat and blood called forth by the color red suggest the fever and infection of disease, thereby linking the Virginia river with the "tumid river" of "The Hollow Men." Hence this still river symbolizes the lack of will to undertake the spiritual effort toward meaningful existence: "No will is still as a river/Still."

Brooding over the river and surrounding landscape is a heavy silence in contrast to the children's voices and the birds' songs of "New Hampshire," which connoted fertility and exuberant life. The single trill of the mocking bird is virtually the only sound in the poem, and, as the schoolgirl Diana Steward notes,[4] the sudden noise brings out more forcefully the silence, loneliness, and ugliness of the landscape:

Will heat move
Only through the mocking-bird
Heard once?

In addition, the thrice-repeated "still" is used to suggest not only lack of movement but also absence of sound.[5] This silence then symbolizes the sterility, emptiness, and isolation of the hollow soul.

In line six, Eliot introduces the motif of waiting through a view of the landscape surrounding the stagnant river:

> Still hills
> Wait. Gates wait. Purple trees,
> White trees, wait, wait,
> Delay, decay.

Each element of the landscape expresses the silent, interminable waiting in the dry heat, recalling Gerontion, "Here I am, an old man in a dry month,/Being read to by a boy, waiting for rain," as well as the inhabitants of *The Waste Land:*

> Ganga was sunken, and the limp leaves
> Waited for rain, while the black clouds
> Gathered far distant, over Himavant.

The hills are quiet and immovable. The gates suggest the entrance to a garden, which throughout Eliot's poetry symbolizes original or regained innocence and purity; for example, in "Burnt Norton," one goes into the rose garden "Through the first *gate,*/Into our first world," and in "Little Gidding" one reenters the Garden of Eden through "the unknown remembered *gate.*" Here, however, the gates wait hopelessly, for they will never be touched by those with dead souls. Thirdly, the sinister and unreal purple and white trees are decaying and sterile, "without the life of the green leaves."[6] In this static landscape they, like the paralysed soul, are simply existing rather than acting: "Living, living,/Never moving."

Suddenly, the speaker makes his presence known:

> Ever moving
> Iron thoughts came with me
> And go with me. . . .

These iron thoughts seem similar to Gerontion's "Thoughts of a dry brain in a dry season," in that they are as futile, hard, and sterile as the soul that possesses them. The poem ends where it began, "Red river, river, river." Here, however, the rhythm of the repetitious "river, river, river" fading away into nothingness is even more dulling and monotonous than in the first line. Thus the whole lifeless landscape, and the red river in particular, represents the soul numbed and deadened by spiritual torpor.

The third poem, "Usk," is without doubt the most elusive of the series. Usk is the name of a town and river in Southeast Wales; the landscape contains the ruins of Roman walls as well as an early twelfth-century castle partially destroyed in Owen Glendower's revolt of 1402.[7] The castle ruins at present are privately owned and closed to the public. Although the grounds are not kept up, the site is fascinating. It sits on a high hill overlooking the town and the river. The walls and several towers remain standing, and the location of a chapel is quite evident. Faded and decaying markers, as well as information in an old guidebook, indicate that it was once a tourist attraction, and Eliot may have visited it as he made several trips to Wales. He had already been there by 1935, for he wrote in a report prepared for the twenty-fifth reunion of Harvard's Class of 1910, "I have travelled a little in foreign parts, such as California, Scotland, and Wales. . . ." The original draft of the poem, then titled "Usk Valley. Breton," is written in longhand on the back of a copy of his poem "Mr. Pugstyles," which may suggest that he composed it on the spot using the only paper he had with him.[8] This information about the actual location contributes to an understanding of the poem, especially when it is considered in combination with two additional clues.

One clue to the poem's meaning is furnished by *Four Quartets*. As "New Hampshire" corresponds in both theme and garden symbol to "Burnt Norton" and "Virginia" is linked by its river symbol to "The Dry Salvages," so "Usk" is similar to "Little Gidding" in its use of the chapel symbol. "Little Gidding" with its isolated chapel and its grey late-afternoon light seems to share not only its setting but also its theme with "Usk." Both describe a pilgrimage to a place of prayer, and the counsel to the pilgrim at Little Gidding applies equally to the visitor to Usk:

> [Y]ou would have to put off
> Sense and notion. You are not here to verify,
> Instruct yourself, or inform curiosity
> Or carry report. You are here to kneel
> Where prayer has been valid.

Thus, "Usk" portrays an état d'âme in direct opposition to that of "Virginia." Like "Ash Wednesday" and "Little Gidding," it symbolizes through landscape the effort of the soul to attain spiritual discipline.

Further, according to Mrs. Eliot, Eliot used to say that "an understanding of 'Usk' depends partly on the immediate evocation of the scenery in *The Mabinogion.*"[9] *The Mabinogion,* a collection of eleven medieval Welsh tales based on folklore and mythology, contains some early examples of Arthurian romances which tell of the adventures of Arthur and his knights as they do battle with giants, witches, and other formidable foes. One of the tales, entitled "Peredur," is an early version of the legend of Percival, hero of the Holy Grail stories. The central setting of the Arthurian stories is Arthur's castle at Usk: "Arthur was accustomed to hold his Court at Caerlleon upon Usk, . . . for Caerlleon was the place most easy of access in his dominions both by sea and by land." And the Welsh countryside of valleys, hills, and meadows provides the setting for many of the adventures of the various heros: "The next day, Peredur went forth by the high road, along a mountain ridge, and he saw a valley of a circular form, the confines of which were rocky and wooded. And the flat part of the valley was in meadows, and there were fields betwixt the meadows and the wood."[10] In addition to evoking the Arthurian settings portrayed in part of *The Mabinogion,* the poem recalls the Welsh scenery in Tennyson's *Idylls of the King:* "For Arthur . . ./Held court at old Caerleon upon Usk." These echoes from the colorful and adventurous world of King Arthur seem to function as a contrast to the plainer and more difficult modern world; in Arthurian times the quest for the Holy Grail, purity, salvation was glorious and noble, while today man's search for spiritual fulfillment is lacking in glamor, requiring quiet determination and steady effort.

The poem is divided into two rather distinct parts. In the first six lines, the speaker, like the speaker of the lines from "Little Gidding" quoted above, makes clear that the seeking soul does not come to Usk to see its Roman walls or its medieval castle. Using the forceful imperative voice, he asserts that the soul can find salvation neither in magic spells nor in old superstitions:

> Do not suddenly break the branch, or
> Hope to find
> The white hart behind the white well.

The first line recalls Aeneas's use of the golden bough to enter into the underworld and can be linked to the decayed Roman walls of the real landscape of Usk. The allusion to the hart suggests an old belief of the Middle Ages that a vision of a white stag by a white well would bring salvation. Although these are traditional Christian symbols, the hart conveying "solitude and purity" and the well, "pilgrimage and . . . salvation,"[11] Eliot seems to be suggesting that the way of true redemption is not so easily come by, that it requires a determined and disciplined effort of the spirit. The speaker counsels the sincere soul not to rely on the "Old enchantments" symbolized by the (implicit, to be sure) ruined walls and crumbling castle of Usk:

> Glance aside, not for lance, do not spell
> Old enchantments. Let them sleep.
> "Gently dip, but not too deep" . . . .

Thoughts of the glorious, magical world of *The Mabinogion* and of Tennyson's *Idylls of the King*, evoked by the references to "lance" and "Old enchantments," must be put aside and the way of devotion embraced.

The second half of the poem concerns what the soul *is* to do to attain salvation, and it focuses on an obscure element of the landscape, the "hermit's chapel," which may refer either to the thirteenth-century church in Usk or to the chapel in the castle ruins. There is also an echo from one of Peredur's adventures in *The Mabinogion:* "And in the evening he entered a valley, and at the head of the valley he came to a hermit's cell, and the hermit welcomed him gladly, and there he spent the night."[12] Later in this episode Peredur uses his skill in fighting to convince a giant and his family to receive baptism at the court of Arthur. However, instead of looking back to the magic of the past, the pilgrim is admonished to *"Lift* your eyes/Where the roads dip and where the roads rise." The roads leading to the chapel are, as in "Little Gidding," "rough road[s]," and the place itself is undistinguished, not to be found in guidebooks, "turn behind the pig-sty to the dull façade/And the tombstone." However, this is the setting in which rebirth can occur through discipline and effort:

> Seek only there
> Where the grey light meets the green air
> The hermit's chapel, the pilgrim's prayer.

The grey light of the chapel's interior (and perhaps of a late fall afternoon), which is contrasted to the green air of day, suggests the quietness, the steadiness, the plainness of that unadorned effort.[13] There is neither trumpet nor fanfare nor magnificent cathedral, but simply a secluded chapel, symbolic of the humility and prayer necessary for redemption. Thus, the Roman walls, the medieval castle, and the obscure, unnamed chapel of this little known Welsh landscape function as highly complex symbols in this third poem of "Landscapes."

Poem IV, "Rannoch, by Glencoe," shifts to a landscape of death as the poet meditates on the destructive, violent quality of the soul devoid of spiritual significance. For his symbolic landscape Eliot has chosen a Scottish terrain well known both geographically and historically for its harsh and treacherous qualities. Indeed, its name by tradition means "Valley of Weeping" in Gaelic, and the traditional Judeo-Christian symbol of the Valley of the Shadow of Death underlies the poem. There are also affinities with "East Coker" and its archetypal symbol of earth, suggesting man's imprisonment in human history, destruction, and death:

> Earth feet, loam feet, lifted in country mirth
> Mirth of those long since under earth
> Nourishing the corn. . . .
> Feet rising and falling.
> Eating and drinking. Dung and death.

Glencoe is a long valley or glen in Argyll, in the western middle area of Scotland. It is a narrow, rocky corridor with steep walls and "glowering dark hills of andesite lava."[14] Heavy grey clouds often shroud the tops of the hills and even descend into the valley. The land is unarable, and there is virtually no human habitation in the desolate vale. Rannoch is the name of both a moor and a lake. The moor is a "melancholy expanse of peat bog and ancient forest ringed by sombre hills and broken by a chain of irregular lochs . . . ,"[15] one of which is also named Rannoch. As there is no mention of water in the poem, it seems evident that Eliot intends "Rannoch" to indicate the moor rather than the lake.

These geographical characteristics of the region give an added dimension to the symbolism of the first five lines of the poem:

> Here the crow starves, here the patient stag
> Breeds for the rifle. Between the soft moor
> And the soft sky, scarcely room
> To leap or soar. Substance crumbles, in the thin air
> Moon cold or moon hot.

This is surely one of Eliot's most desolate and sinister landscapes. The season appears to be early winter, as the land broods under a lowering sky heavy with clouds. The sharp, jarring rhythm immediately evokes a sense of violence. The land of Glencoe itself is so sterile that even the black crow, symbol of scavenging death, goes hungry. The destruction suggested by the crow is reinforced through the reference to the stag, existing only to be shot. In contrast to the previous poem where the male deer symbolized life, here the deer connotes a cruel and meaningless death. The wild moor, soft with peat bogs, conspires with the lowering sky to form a prison for both deer and bird; there is "scarcely room/To leap or soar." Decay is pervasive, as everything crumbles "in the thin air." This air, barely able to support life, is in direct contrast to the abundance suggested by the "green air" of the preceding poem. The description closes with a sinister allusion to the changeable moon, depicted as being completely indifferent to either human or animal existence. Thus in a few lines Eliot has created a cold and eerie landscape symbolic of death and violence. And, as is often the case with the middle and late poems, there are uncanny affinities with a Tennysonian landscape, as seen in the following scene from "The Palace of Art":

> And one a foreground black with stones and slags;
>   Beyond, a line of heights; and higher
> All barr'd with long white cloud the scornful crags;
>   And highest, snow and fire.

The second part of the poem focuses on the violent historical associations of Glencoe. When William III and Mary came to the throne of England after the Bloodless Revolution, many Scottish chieftains disliked the new regime, and two refused to take the Oath of Allegiance by the deadline of January 1, 1692. One of them was MacIan, head of the MacDonald clan of Glencoe. He relented, however, and did take the Oath later that month. Yet on February 13 he was punished for his disloyalty by Royalist forces who treacherously massacred forty of his clan in the rocky glen after living with them as guests for twelve days. The cold-blooded military orders are chilling; for example, Duncanson sent the following to Glenlyon: "You are hereby ordered to fall upon the rabelle, the MacDonalds of Glenco, and to putt all to the sword under seventy. You are to have a special care that the old fox and his sones doe not escape your hands. You are to secure all the avenues, that no man escape. . . ."[16] Today a Celtic cross recalls the violent tragedy to all who visit Glencoe. The region itself then is an historical emblem of the destructiveness and brutality of man's soul acting on its own and is a highly appropriate objective correlative for Eliot's meaning.

In the poem the road,[17] which twists in and out of the rocky cliffs and passes the commemorative cross as well as the site of the clansmen's homes, evokes the anguish in the havoc of massacre:

> The road winds in
> Listlessness of ancient war
> Languor of broken steel,
> Clamour of confused wrong. . . .

The irony is that these deaths, signifying the violence of the human soul, are wounds that will not be healed within the course of human history. The hatred continues, as the skeletal bones of the dead merge with the living bones of their descendants:

> Memory is strong
> Beyond the bone. Pride snapped,
> Shadow of pride is long. . . .

These lines seem to be a direct reference to the Celtic cross erected in 1883 by the last descendant of the clan, to urge remembrance of the brutal massacre:

> *Nec Tempore Nec Fato*
> This cross
> Is reverently erected
> In memory of
> McIan chief of the MacDonalds
> Of Glencoe
> Who fell with his people
> In the massacre of Glencoe
> Of 13 Feb: 1692
> By his direct descendant
> Ellen Burns MacDonald of Glencoe
> Aug. 1883
> Their Memory Liveth For Evermore.

Thus, in the long, desolate corridor of Glencoe, there is no unity: "in the long pass/No concurrence of bone." Once again in a minimum of lines Eliot has used an actual landscape to symbolize brilliantly a state of being, here specifically the state of the soul without God.

The last poem returns to an American landscape as Eliot presents the coastal region of Cape Ann, Massachusetts. It has affinities with "Burnt Norton" and "Little Gidding" because of its use of the garden symbol and with "The Dry Salvages" because of its specific New England locale associated with Eliot's youth. Through a depiction of the numerous birds that inhabit this area in the spring, he communicates the sense of joy and innocence with which the series began. However, there is an important difference; "New Hampshire" portrayed the joyous innocence of childhood, while "Cape Ann" seems to point toward a purity earned through effort, a purity restored after sin and thus doubly ecstatic. And the poem ends, like Section VI of "Ash Wednesday," with a willing renunciation of the beauties of earth in favor of the greater beauties of paradise.

The first ten lines of the poem are a call to celebrate the glories of the earth, symbolized by the birds of Cape Ann. Cape Ann itself is an idyllic place where Eliot spent his childhood summers. The Eliots' summer home faces the sea, which is at some distance from the house. In the front the setting has been left in its natural state: hilly terrain, large granite rocks, and numerous low trees. Birds fly singing through the luxuriant foliage, and other natural creatures such as small snakes are in evidence. In contrast to this untamed setting is the yard behind the house with its tall trees, lilacs, and grass. Concrete details of the landscape itself do not actually appear in the poem except for the reference to the bay-bush, an aromatic shrub with gray berries native to this northeastern region. The landscape functions only, and very generally, as the locale in which the birds are found.

In the poem the birds catch up the essence of delight, as the human being is urged to be quick to love its time on earth:

> O quick quick quick, quick hear the song-sparrow,
> Swamp-sparrow, fox-sparrow, vesper-sparrow
> At dawn and dusk. Follow the dance
> Of the goldfinch at noon. Leave to chance

The Blackburnian warbler, the shy one. Hail
With shrill whistle the note of the quail, the bob-white
Dodging by bay-bush. Follow the feet
Of the walker, the water-thrush. Follow the flight
Of the dancing arrow, the purple martin. Greet
In silence the bullbat. All are delectable. Sweet sweet sweet. . . .

In this catalogue of birds, Eliot has evoked sounds, colors, and movements to enrapture the senses: the songs of many varieties of sparrows, the trill of the warbler, the shrill note of the quail; the bright yellow body of the goldfinch, the white markings of the quail, the purple of the martin; and the dancing flights of the goldfinch and the martin. Even the bullbat, a nighthawk, is to be greeted, though in respectful silence. They are all symbolic of the sweetness of human existence as lived by the purified soul.

Yet this earthly existence must finally be renounced; it must be given back to the seagull, for the soul has another destination: "But resign this land at the end, resign it/To its true owner, the tough one, the sea-gull." Thus, having examined the soul in positive and negative spiritual conditions, the cycle ends: "The palaver is finished."

In the "Landscapes" Eliot has chosen five rather obscure rural settings to convey elusive spiritual conditions, both negative and positive. Through these settings he presents the soul in states of innocence and experience and continues his search for the meaning in human existence, relying entirely on landscapes as his symbols. The question of why he has selected these particular settings is intriguing. Of the three American locales used, two are from New England and carry positive meanings of original or regained innocence and purity. Two possible explanations exist. Since the locales are associated with Eliot's own childhood, they would, from a personal point of view, represent the innocence of the child. Second, New England has historically been the seat of the Puritan ethic of religious devotion and discipline. On the other hand, Virginia may have been chosen to symbolize stagnation of the soul because of its southern heritage. As a result of slavery, the

South (at least the Old South) has traditionally been seen as evil and corrupt. It may also be significant that Eliot first visited Virginia as an adult, after having been away from his native country for many years.

The other two settings are from the British Isles. The choice of Scotland's Glencoe as a symbol for the violence and destruction of the godless soul is easily understood because of its well known geographical and historical significance. By far the most difficult setting to explain is the Welsh town of Usk, symbol of the soul's striving to find fulfillment through prayer and meditation. One can, I think, only speculate as to why Eliot chose it, although several possibilities exist. The setting's historical association with Roman times and its literary association with the age of chivalry and quests for the Holy Grail perhaps suggested to Eliot earlier, easier, and more glorious methods of attaining salvation in contrast to the difficult struggle in modern times. Perhaps he himself entered the old church to pray or imagined entering the ruined castle chapel, so that a personal experience is the basis of his choice. Or perhaps simply the existence at Usk of the old church or the chapel where for centuries people had prayed for redemption lies behind its selection. All of these possibilities seem to be entirely plausible. At any rate, "Usk" is without doubt the most elusive of the poems, and this elusiveness seems closely related to the ambiguity surrounding its choice.

Because these poems clearly serve as experiments in preparation for *Four Quartets,* we must consider what Eliot retains and what he alters in writing the *Quartets.* Obviously, he continues to use landscapes as his major symbols for states of the soul and to use the names of the settings as titles. Further, while these landscapes are drawn from his personal experiences in the British Isles and the United States, they have their foundations in traditional symbols. However, he makes several refinements both in choice of locale and in specificity of detail. In the *Quartets* he employs settings even more particular and even more personal, and thus obscure, than those in "Landscapes." In the latter, he uses two states, New Hampshire and Virginia; two general areas or locales, Rannoch, by Glencoe and Cape

Ann; and one town, Usk; whereas in the *Quartets* he uses a particular manor house, Burnt Norton; a small, virtually unknown village, East Coker; a rock cluster off the coast of New England, the Dry Salvages; and a tiny, isolated country chapel, Little Gidding. Second, the details of the settings are more concrete and more numerous in the *Quartets* than in "Landscapes." If it were not for the titles of the poems in "Landscapes," one would have no idea of the *specific* locations of the settings. The apple orchard, for example, could be located anywhere. In the *Quartets,* on the other hand, the details are so many and so exact that one can recognize them immediately if one visits the sites. The actual garden of Burnt Norton, for example, does have drained pools, a gate, rose bushes, and an alley. This alteration gives an added sense of reality to the *Quartets.* Finally, in "Landscapes" Eliot departs from his established method of using urban landscapes to symbolize negative spiritual states, for two of the rural settings, "Virginia" and "Rannoch, by Glencoe," assume this function. However, in the *Quartets* he abandons this experiment and again employs city scenes as symbols of spiritual sterility, perhaps because he felt that contrasting settings (rural vs. urban) more effectively present the powerful contrast between positive and negative states.

The "Landscapes," both as works in their own right and as experiments anticipating *Four Quartets,* form a much more impressive part of Eliot's poetic creation than generally recognized. Their content is highly significant, portraying complex and elusive conditions of the human soul, and they exhibit brilliant technical mastery, especially in the use of landscapes as symbols of these conditions. Thus in theme, technique, and symbol these five "minor" poems are outstanding and serve as a fitting prelude to *Four Quartets.*

v · *Four Quartets*

In *Four Quartets* Eliot's quest for the meaning behind human experience comes to culmination. The pilgrimage began in the Inferno of the modern urban metropolis where dim rooms, dingy stairs, and sooty streets bespoke the emptiness of the human soul. It progressed through the Purgatorio of spiritual struggle, of putting off the world. Dark castle stairs and snow-clogged roads as well as bent goldenrod and white sails suggested the difficulty of that struggle, while misty gardens, fragrant pines, and apple orchards evoked the joy and ecstasy of union with God. With *Four Quartets* the pilgrimage reaches its destination, for here in Eliot's Paradiso is disclosed that which invests human life with enduring significance: the "intersection of the timeless/With time." Specifically, Eliot sees the Incarnation of Christ as the supreme union of the temporal and the eternal, of human and divine love. The Incarnation redeems man's soul from the formless chaos of "Gerontion" and *The Waste Land* and makes significant the spiritual struggle to ascend seen in "Ash Wednesday" and "Usk." Thus, these final poems bring together and reconcile all the previous poems. Yet, as Matthiessen points out, they are "scarcely poems of easy faith."[1] Throughout them, the world of the early poems, of the grasping body and the dirty, sterile soul, alternates with the world of the spirit, of the fulfilled soul and the dissolved body, for the union of human and divine love must be fought for relentlessly.

Artistically, too, *Four Quartets* marks the high point in Eliot's poetic style, and nowhere is his consummate technical mastery better illustrated than in his use of symbolic landscapes. As noted in Chapter IV, in the majority of his poetic works through "Marina" Eliot uses a persona, a central intelligence,

131

as his major symbol for elusive spiritual or emotional states. However, in the "Landscapes" and in *Four Quartets* landscape becomes the foremost symbol. It is the dominant element in the *Quartets'* code of symbols, providing the central symbol of each of the four separate poems. In addition to the four major settings denoted by the poems' titles, numerous minor landscapes are found throughout the *Quartets.* Together they reveal Eliot's system of symbolic landscapes at its most highly developed level.

In the *Quartets* the poet uses both rural and urban landscapes, whereas in previous poems he generally employs one or the other. The countryside, however, is unquestionably the dominant symbol, representing "the unseen world of inner unchanging pattern whose centre is 'the still point.'"[2] As in the middle poems and in three of the "Landscapes," the country is generally symbolic of the meaningful element in life. Eliot's treatment of natural landscapes in the work reflects in general method as well as in specific details Tennyson's influence as a landscape artist. Yet the city symbolism also plays an important though lesser role, suggesting the corruption and apathy which can render sterile the human soul. As pointed out at the end of Chapter IV, Eliot experiments in the "Landscapes" with rural landscape as a symbol of this negative condition, but in *Four Quartets* he restores this function to urban settings. The two opposing types of landscape symbols (urban vs. rural) reflect the conflict between the way of man alone and the way of God with man, between the body and the soul, essentially between Evil and Good. Yet the very predominance of rural landscapes in the late poems suggests the final dominance of the spiritual, as the preponderance of urban settings in the early poems so forcefully conveys the iron rule of the material.

Further, the landscapes, described in the *Quartets* by carefully chosen details, are strikingly realistic and more concrete than those in "Landscapes." They are drawn almost exclusively from Eliot's personal experience; Burnt Norton, East Coker, the Dry Salvages, and Little Gidding are all rather obscure places and have no traditional or well known literary associations. However, despite their personal origins, they possess universal meanings for they are basically linked with the archetypal symbols of the garden, earth, water, and the chapel. Again Eliot demonstrates, in this respect, his ability to merge poetic tradition and his individual talent. While retaining their particularity and originality, the settings go beyond mere reality and exactitude; Eliot transforms them into symbols conveying elusive states of the soul. As such, they transcend the personal to suggest universal human feelings and experiences often extremely difficult to capture in words. In "Burnt Norton" and "Little Gidding" particularly, the poet is dealing with spiritual and emotional states which are much more elusive than the degradation of the soul portrayed in the early poetry. In his essay on Dante, Eliot makes an especially relevant statement as he clearly points out this problem: "It is apparently easier to accept damnation as poetic material than purgation or beatitude; less is involved that is strange to the modern mind." However, despite its difficulty, Eliot succeeds in expressing the "inexpressible." In so doing, he accomplishes that feat which he so admired in Dante: "One can feel only awe at the power of the master [Dante] who could thus at every moment realize the inapprehensible in visual images."[3] In the *Quartets* Eliot's symbolic landscapes reach a high mark in poetic communication.

In "Burnt Norton,"[4] the first and most crucial of the *Quartets*, the poet uses an extremely complex symbolic landscape to present an experience central to the work as a whole. The well known mystical moment in the rose garden is introduced in Section I, and its meaning is developed and explored in the remaining four sections and in the three following poems. Its meaning has also been explored by all the major Eliot critics, most of whom limit it to one single concept. In reality, however, it has multiple levels that seem to be endless in their variety.

Burnt Norton is a spacious manor house and garden located near the town of Chipping Campden in Gloucestershire, England. It is called *Burnt* Norton because it stands on the site of a country mansion which was burned to the ground in the eighteenth century by its owner, Sir William Kyte.[5] At present the manor belongs to Lord Sandon, elder son of the Earl of Harrowby.[6] The house itself is large, partially covered with ivy. To one side of the house is a plot of roses beyond which lies the large formal garden, enclosed by a brick wall with an arched opening. One passes under the arch, goes down a walkway bordered by rose bushes, and arrives at another bed of roses. To the right one looks out over a low brick wall to an impressive view of the valley of Evesham; to the left are two drained pools, one rectangular and the other in the shape of a semicircle. A grassy knoll on the opposite side of the garden gives one a fine view down into the pools. Large trees shade the edges of the garden, and all is silent except for the sounds of birds.

Eliot visited Burnt Norton in the summer of 1934, at which time it was vacant, and in the poem the protagonist wanders first through the empty house, as Eliot himself no doubt did:

> Footfalls echo in the memory
> Down the passage which we did not take
> Towards the door we never opened
> Into the rose-garden.

While the house itself is not directly presented in the poem, it does function as a symbol since it provides both the locale and the title of the work. Like many of Tennyson's houses, it is vacant and deserted, conveying an état d'âme of spiritual desolation. Also the house, again like Tennyson's, suggests the transitory quality of human existence. This transience is expressed first by the emptiness of the house, indicating that its owners have departed or died, and second by the fact that the original mansion was destroyed by fire. As Northrop Frye indirectly points out, it suggests "the endless destruction of physical substance . . . [in contrast] to the eternity of spiritual substance."[7] From this standpoint "Burnt Norton" anticipates the crumbling houses of "East Coker." Finally, it seems to me that the vacancy of the house, with its overtones of burning, evokes the desolation of Eden after the exile of the fallen Adam and Eve. The gate, it will be remembered, was then guarded by cherubim and a flaming sword. Thus, in all its aspects, the house stands as a symbol in direct contrast to the meaning of the rose garden.

The rose garden of the manor house functions as the major landscape symbol in the poem. As always, Eliot grounds his symbols in reality. Through significant selected details the poet portrays a concrete view of the actual garden. It is enclosed, with a gate at its entrance, "the first gate." It is laid out in "a formal pattern" with walkways or alleys bordered by shrubbery. In its center is a circle of boxwood enclosing an empty pool or fountain:

> So we moved, and they, in a formal pattern,
> Along the empty alley, into the box circle,
> To look down into the drained pool.
> Dry the pool, dry concrete, brown edged. . . .

The garden is filled with rose bushes and birds, and falling autumn leaves litter the ground. Further, Helen Gardner, referring to Section IV, points out that there "are sunflowers in the borders and clematis hanging from the wall and clipped yews."[8]

The garden has been skillfully created, however, to stand for much more than itself. It is a symbolic landscape with multiple associations. Basically, its meanings fall into two broad categories: first, the meaning of the experience itself, which could take place anywhere; second, the meaning of the rose garden, which, being the locale of the experience, qualifies and intensifies its significance.

Let us look first at the visionary experience. In the center of the ordered garden, within the box circle,[9] the protagonist comes to the drained pool. Suddenly, unexpectedly, it is

> filled with water out of sunlight,
> And the lotos rose, quietly, quietly,
> The surface glittered out of heart of light. . . .

This mystic illumination is symbolic of the "intersection of the timeless/With time," the entrance of the supernatural into the natural, the manifestation of the invisible through the visible. It is a fleeting but ecstatic vision of the union of human and divine love. Eliot uses the ancient Oriental symbol of the lotos which "from remote times [has] symbolized the possibility of superhuman or divine life existing in the context of nature and yet unsullied by its context."[10] Significantly, he also employs the parallel symbol in Western culture, the rose, representing both mortal and immortal love. It is, I think, not by chance that the verb "rose" follows "lotos" in the description of the vision. Also the glittering water and the dazzling sunlight traditionally suggest abundant life. In his awareness of this insight the protagonist feels ecstasy, wholeness, and serenity. Yet the intensity of mystic experience is necessarily brief, and the vision passes as abruptly as it appeared:

> Then a cloud passed, and the pool was empty.
> Go, said the bird, for the leaves were full of children,
> Hidden excitedly, containing laughter.
> Go, go, go, said the bird: human kind
> Cannot bear very much reality.

Thus Eliot brilliantly evokes the elusive quality of mystic illumination. By itself it is not specifically Christian but a universal type of experience by which existence within time is rendered meaningful. Eliot speaks in general terms of the "kind of unexplainable experience which many of us have had, once or twice in our lives, and been unable to put into words."[11] And in his essay on Pascal he remarks on the universal and not necessarily Christian aspects of this phenomenon: "[W]hat can only be called mystical experience happens to many men who do not become mystics. . . . You may call it communion with the Divine, or you may call it a temporary crystallization of the mind."[12] These remarks clearly suggest the universal category into which Eliot places the rose garden experience. However, when considered in the context of Four Quartets as a whole, this ecstatic vision takes on more specifically Christian connotations. It is what I would term a "lesser" incarnation, one of the hints spoken of in "The Dry Salvages," pointing to the supreme "intersection of the timeless/With time" which is Christ's Incarnation. In every man's lifetime there are some fleeting moments—as in the rose garden—in which timelessness and time are merged; these, Eliot suggests, are bits of evidence attesting to the ultimate union of eternity and time, of immortality and mortality, of divine and human in and through Christ. The rose garden experience suggests the sense of innocence, joy, and serenity which are conditions of union with the timeless. Here then is the meaning of the experience itself: to present the reader with concrete evidence of this kind of union in man's timebound existence.

But the specific setting is integral to the vision and cannot be separated from it. The rose garden is a complex symbol releasing a multiplicity of richly meaningful associations, all of which deepen the significance of the revelation itself. It is a framework suggesting the spiritual condition necessary for union of the human with the Divine.

Critics have cited numerous works as sources for Eliot's garden: Carroll's *Alice in Wonderland*, D. H. Lawrence's short story "The Shadow in the Garden," Conrad's "The Shadow Line," Kipling's short story "They," and Walter de la Mare's "The Looking Glass," as well as the Bible and Dante's *Purgatorio* and *Paradiso*. In addition, I have noted many similarities in Frances Hodgson Burnett's popular children's book, *The Secret Garden*, and of much greater significance there are amazing correspondences with much of Tennyson's garden symbolism. Finally, it seems unquestionable that Eliot is also drawing on the archetypal symbol of the garden as a place of perfection. In his *Landscape Into Art* Sir Kenneth Clark calls this landscape symbol "one of humanity's most constant, widespread and consoling myths." He explains further that it has always been associated with paradise, adding that "paradise" is the Persian word for "a walled enclosure." He comments that the garden represents a place where "love, human and divine, could find fulfillment."[13] Eliot's garden does possess these archetypal qualities. And, despite this list of literary and archetypal influences, the rose garden is also a highly personal and original creation. Eliot's own experience in the actual rose garden of the rather obscure Burnt Norton manor forms the basis of the symbol in the poem.

The garden thus evokes numerous associations. In its astounding complexity the symbol contains at least six significant levels of meaning. They will be discussed in ascending order, progressing from a completely earthbound experience giving value to human existence to a completely spiritual experience that invests man's time with meaning. These six levels are the eighteenth century garden, the Tennysonian garden, the garden of childhood, the garden of Eden, the Dantean earthly paradise of Purgatory, and finally the Dantean Paradiso. The first four are places of natural innocence, while the last two connote spiritual illumination.

On the first level, the actual formal garden of Burnt Norton suggests a way of life, totally within man's time, which rendered human existence meaningful. The balanced design, the "formal pattern," of the garden itself evokes the sense of order and dignity of the eighteenth century way of life, while the "dignified, invisible" figures moving quietly along the paths indicate those who were a part of this ceremonial and serene civilization. Bodelsen speaks of this aspect of the garden in his book: "The atmosphere is peaceful and harmonious: it belongs to a past age, to which a contrast is later on provided by the time-bound hurry of present-day life, symbolized by the London tube."[14] Thus, on this first plane the garden symbolizes an earthly way by which life is made meaningful.

The second level is what I have called the Tennysonian garden. Throughout his poetry, Tennyson constantly uses the garden to symbolize the innocent bliss of fulfilled *human* love. His gardens are filled with rose bushes and apple trees, the former symbolizing human love and the latter innocence and purity. Further, they contain winding alleys, perhaps symbolic of the sense of wonder which accompanies the ecstasy of mortal union. Finally, they are usually secret or isolated, creating quiet refuges from the turmoil of the world.[15] Eliot's garden certainly possesses all these characteristics and can easily bear interpretation as a place where two human lovers experience the joy of passionate love, particularly in the light of Eliot's use of the garden in the early poems through *The Waste Land* and in *The Family Reunion*. Its roses especially evoke these associations, not only from Tennyson but also from the *Roman de la Rose*, Lawrence's short story, and Kipling's "They." The latter even suggests a further possible meaning, i.e., that children born of human love also add immeasurable value to human life. On the second level, then, the rose garden of "Burnt Norton" symbolizes the joy of mortal love, another earthly way by which human experience is given meaning.

On a higher plane, many aspects of the garden suggest the world of the pure and innocent child. Here the allusions to "our first world" refer to childhood, and "they" represent the protective parents. These evocations of children do not indicate that this extremely intense spiritual experience occurred to a child,[16] but rather children are meant to symbolize the innocence of the sin-free soul. The final reference to "the leaves . . . full of children,/Hidden excitedly, containing laughter" conveys the ecstatic joy and happiness of this child*like* state of purity.

From the natural innocence of the as yet untainted child, we move to the higher innocence of as yet unfallen man, for the setting also evokes the Biblical Garden of Eden. In his article "The Aesthetic Moment in Landscape Poetry," Marshall Mc-Luhan notes that "the practitioners of Zen Buddhism have long had a doctrine . . . concerning the momentary and unexpected transport from the realm of time to eternity, which has played an important role in the poetry of Mr. Eliot. A Zen moment is reputed to present us *in an instant of time with a landscape strange, yet familiar, showing us the original face of our being, as it were, in the landscape of our birthplace*" (italics mine.)[17] Although Eliot's vision is of the lotos in the shining water and not of the garden itself, the garden does certainly recall "the landscape of our birthplace." The repeated references to "the *first* gate" and "our *first* world" immediately suggest Eden, and the "dignified, invisible" figures which move along the pathways looking at the roses evoke both Adam and Eve, our first parents, and the Lord walking in the garden in the cool of the day.

While these first four planes convey types of natural innocence, the fifth symbolizes innocence and bliss attained through spiritual effort and struggle. Here Eliot's garden calls up associations with Dante's Earthly Paradise which rests atop the mount of Purgatory and is reached only through active striving and purgation of sin. As Dorothy Sayers points out, Dante's Earthly Paradise "represents the recovery of that original perfection of human nature which was impaired by the Fall."[18] Many details of the garden of Burnt Norton resemble aspects of the Earthly Paradise. Both are filled with sunlight; both contain bird song, red flowers, and shining water; both even have mysterious hidden music (*Purgatory*, XXVII, 133, and XXVIII, 13–18, 57, 61–2). And from this viewpoint Eliot's invisible figures are those souls who have attained the purity of Dante's Eden.

The final, and highest, level is that of Dante's Paradiso, of spiritual illumination, of the vision of the Godhead. Again, several aspects of the garden evoke Dante's climactic revelation. The boxwood circle surrounding the pool recalls the geometrical design of the vision, for Dante sees God as the center with the ranks of angels in concentric circles around him.[19] In addition, Dante describes the Trinity as three circles:

> That light supreme, within its fathomless
> Clear substance, showed to me three spheres, which bare
> Three hues distinct, and occupied one space. . .
> (*Paradise*, XXXIII, 115–117).

Traditionally, the circle symbolizes perfection, wholeness, and infinity, while the evergreen boxwood represents everlasting life. Second, the brilliant sunlight parallels the radiance of Dante's vision of the Empyrean:

> "We have won beyond the worlds, and move
> Within that heaven which is pure light alone:
>
> Pure intellectual light, fulfilled with love,
> Love of the true Good, filled with all delight,
> Transcending sweet delight, all sweets above"
> (*Paradise*, XXX, 38–42).

Third, the roses in the garden evoke the Dantean rose, symbol of divine love: "a rose/Of snow-white purity . . . ," "the Flower of the countless leaves" (*Paradise*, XXI, 1–2, 11). Eliot's garden on its highest level, then, symbolizes the ultimate spiritual illumination in which the human soul is united with the Divine.

Thus the garden as presented in Section I is indeed an astounding complex of meanings. In the poem the garden experience of the protagonist is a fleeting moment in which time and the timeless are united only temporarily in a particular earthly garden (i.e., the real garden of the country house named Burnt Norton). This experience *symbolizes* the permanent union of human and divine outside time (i.e., after death), and the garden of Burnt Norton *symbolizes* the paradisal garden in which this ultimate union takes place. The quality of this union is also suggested by the garden experience (ecstasy, joy, serenity, wholeness, fulfillment) as is the spiritual condition necessary for its attainment (purity, simplicity, the state of grace). Each time Eliot uses the garden symbol in *Four Quartets,* he implies one, several, or all of these meanings by the context in which it appears.

Having set up the multileveled symbolism of the rose garden in Section I, Eliot uses it in three of the remaining four sections of the poem. In Sections II and V he refers directly to the experience evoked in the opening passages, while in Section IV he plays a brilliant variation on it. In the third section he does not use the garden at all, but rather shifts to a contrasting urban setting. This virtuosity in dealing with the established symbolism of the rose garden further attests to Eliot's poetic genius.

In Section II Eliot is concerned to define, rather than to symbolize as in the previous section, the worlds of time and the timeless. He explores first the order of the natural world guided and regulated within a meaningful but limited pattern of creation, destruction, and re-creation:

> Ascend to summer in the tree
> We move above the moving tree
> In light upon the figured leaf
> And hear upon the sodden floor
> Below, the boarhound and the boar
> Pursue their pattern as before
> But reconciled among the stars.

This world of meaningful movement in time is contrasted with the stillness of eternity, as the second passage defines the ''still point" in negative and then in positive terms. It is first described as "Neither flesh nor fleshless;/Neither from nor towards." It has neither time nor place, not being of this world. Positively, it is delineated in terms that point back to the ecstatic vision in the rose garden:

> a grace of sense, a white light still and moving,
> *Erhebung* without motion, concentration
> Without elimination, both a new world
> And the old made explicit. . . .

The section closes with a direct evocation of the garden along with two other settings symbolic of the "intersection of the timeless/With time."

> To be conscious is not to be in time
> But only in time can the moment in the rose-garden,
> The moment in the arbour where the rain beat,
> The moment in the draughty church at smokefall
> Be remembered; involved with past and future.
> Only through time time is conquered.

Although eternity is outside time, it is through time that one attains fleeting glimpses of the timeless. These specific landscapes evoke "timeless" moments in Eliot's poetry from the present, the past, and the future: "the moment in the rose-garden" is the "now" of "Burnt Norton"; the "moment in the arbour where the rain beat" suggests two past experiences, the moment under "les saules trempés" of "Dans le Restaurant" and the moment in the hyacinth garden of *The Waste Land*; and the "moment in the draughty church at smokefall" indicates the future moment in "Little Gidding" when the "light fails/On a winter's afternoon, in a secluded chapel."

While the first two sections are concerned with aspects of eternity, Section III turns to the emptiness, monotony, and chaos of time-bound existence. Appropriately Eliot does not use the rose garden at all in this section but introduces a symbolic setting in direct contrast to it. He chooses an urban landscape to suggest the wretched condition of the human soul existing without the timeless. The specific locale is the London tube,[20] a dim underground world recalling Dante's Inferno and

Eliot's own twilight kingdom of "The Hollow Men." The section begins by locating the reader in this place which stands in complete contrast to the rose garden of Section I and the *"There we have been"* (italics mine) of eternity of Section II:

> *Here* is a place of disaffection
> Time before and time after
> In a dim light . . . (italics mine).

The dimness of the drab Underground is juxtaposed to the "heart of light" of the garden and the "white light" of eternity, for it connotes the half-life, the dullness, the disease of the time-bound soul. The latter aspect is reinforced by the adjectives "tumid," "unwholesome," "unhealthy," and "torpid." The picture of the "strained time-ridden faces" glimpsed through the window of a waiting train confirms this suggestion, for they are

> Distracted from distraction by distraction
> Filled with fancies and empty of meaning
> Tumid apathy with no concentration. . . .

As the passengers come up out of the station, a blast of cold wind whirls about them, stirring up the litter of used tickets and dirty paper on the floor: "Men and bits of paper, whirled by the cold wind. . . ." The wind, as always in Eliot's poetry, communicates a sense of emptiness and futility; however, the particular horror of this devastating image lies in the equation of men with bits of paper, suggesting the lack of control and direction in both. These lost souls are belched out of the Underground and emerge sluggishly into the "faded air" of a winter's day, a striking contrast to the "vibrant air" of the autumnal rose garden. The reference to the "gloomy hills of London" suggests that it is as dim outside as it is in the Underground; the emptiness haunts all of life. Finally, the naming of several suburban districts of London, all actually located on hills, has symbolic significance in two ways.[21] First, being tube stations in different parts of London, they reinforce the idea that the gloomy vacancy is everywhere. Second, the monotonous listing of these *seven* rather drab areas suggests the dull days of the week in which meaningless time imprisons man. On a realistic level, they portray the tube passengers returning home to the suburbs after work.

After a brief passage which presents the meaningful purgative darkness of St. John of the Cross, there is a final reference to the tube:

> the world moves
> In appetency, on its metalled ways
> Of time past and time future.

Elizabeth Drew remarks that "the 'metalled ways' on which the urban world now moves, suggest not only a picture of it as a vast network of roads and railways leading nowhere, but the whole quality of the mechanistic culture of today. . . ."[22] The sense of constant movement and cold impersonal materialism is particularly strong.

The dingy Underground setting of the time-bound subway is juxtaposed to the garden in concrete details as well as in symbolism. There is dimness rather than brilliant light, "faded air" rather than "vibrant air," imprisonment rather than freedom, movement rather than stillness, mechanical metal rails rather than natural objects such as birds, roses, and leaves. The urban setting is an effective symbol for the emptiness, dullness, and disease of the soul trapped in time. Thus, while the natural landscape of the garden symbolizes the timeless moment which invests human experience with significance, the landscape of London and its subway system conveys "the waste sad time/Stretching before and after."

In the lyric of Section IV we see an outstanding example of Eliot's virtuosity in using the complex symbol of the garden. In this section the poet portrays the protagonist-soul in a condition of doubt. After the devastating view of the world of time presented in Section III, the reality of the timeless vision experienced earlier in the rose garden is questioned. The soul asks, does the timeless truly exist and can it overcome the seemingly unconquerable hold of the time-bound world? Or will time and death gain the victory? The section ends, however, with an assertion of the reality of the Divine and the conquest of time.

With brilliant artistic insight, Eliot chooses the rose garden to symbolize this état d'âme of doubt. It is the same garden of Section I, but it is seen in a different light. Whereas previously it was entered in the bright sunlight of midday, now evening is falling, and suggestions of death, rather than life, abound. The first two lines evoke a funereal atmosphere: "Time and the bell have buried the day,/The black cloud carries the sun away." The light and warmth of the moment of vision have utterly disappeared, and the garden is cold and dark. The bell ringing out the vesper hours symbolizes the power of the endless movement of time, which has destroyed and buried the light of day. In league with the malign black cloud, symbolic of flux and change, time has hidden the sun, traditional symbol of Christ. In this setting, the earlier vision of the timeless seems only an illusion, and the protagonist-soul questions its validity through references to plants growing in the garden. He asks first if the Divine and its accompanying offer of rebirth really exist:

> Will the sunflower turn to us, will the clematis
> Stray down, bend to us; tendril and spray
> Clutch and cling?

The golden sunflower is an archetypal symbol for the life-force and a Christian symbol for Christ, while the white and blue clematis suggests the Virgin Mary.[23] Or, he wonders as the branches of a tall yew brush against him, is death the only reality?

> Chill
> Fingers of yew be curled
> Down on us?

While the evergreen yew is associated with everlasting life, it also symbolizes the finality of death, being often found in cemeteries. In this passage Eliot is certainly drawing on the latter with the words "chill" and "curled down" used for further emphasis. However, at this moment of agonizing doubt, when time, darkness, and death seem to hold the upper hand, a bird again points to the timeless as a kingfisher's wing reflects one of the last rays of the setting sun:

> After the kingfisher's wing
> Has answered light to light, and is silent, the light is still
> At the still point of the turning world.

The kingfisher himself is symbolic of immortality and is even a type of Christ.[24] Thus, this second moment of sudden, brief illumination, in which both the kingfisher and the light symbolize eternity, reaffirms not only the reality but also the significance of the rose garden's moment out of time.

With the existence of the eternal firmly established, the poet turns in Section V to a consideration of the difficulty of attaining it within time. The opening passage is concerned with this problem in artistic creation, and, except for the brief reference to Christ's temptation in the desert, landscape symbolism is not used. However, the closing passage returns again to the garden as a symbol of the manifestation of the timeless, here specifically divine love, within time. In its pure form outside time, divine love is

> unmoving,
> Only the cause and end of movement,
> Timeless, and undesiring. . . .

However, hints of it exist on earth, as Eliot reveals in the description of the children in the garden:

> Sudden in a shaft of sunlight
> Even while the dust moves
> There rises the hidden laughter
> Of children in the foliage
> Quick now, here, now, always—

The garden symbol again brings out the qualities of the union between human and divine: the sunlight conveys its beauty and its life-giving aspects; the children suggest its innocence and their laughter its ecstatic joy; and the foliage (possibly of an apple tree) evokes connotations of life, purity, and renewal.

Thus the rose garden in "Burnt Norton" is revealed to be perhaps Eliot's most complex landscape symbol. While it draws upon many associations, it is yet an original and particular symbol with a significance totally its own. On whatever level the reader chooses to take it, and on all the levels combined together, Eliot's garden symbolizes what gives meaning, purpose, and direction to human existence in time and beyond time. It functions not only as the major symbol of this important Eliotean theme in "Burnt Norton," but also in the remaining three *Quartets* where it appears continually and is indeed the symbolic landscape with which the work closes. The rose garden is, to my way of thinking, one of the most brilliantly comprehensive symbols in modern literature.

While the emphasis in "Burnt Norton" is on eternity, in "East Coker" it is on man's time. The poem's central symbolic landscape is another rural English setting, the village of East Coker. Located in southeast Somerset not far from the sea, it is, as Eliot explained in a letter to H. W. Hausermann, the place where his ancestors lived for two hundred years[25] and from which they emigrated to Massachusetts in 1667. It is, as Helen Gardner remarks, "a landscape full of human history"[26] and thus an appropriate symbol for man's life within time.

The actual village is quite small and completely charming. Set in the midst of the lush English countryside of Somerset, it is approached down a narrow country road bordered by tall trees which form a canopy of leaves in summer. The village has one main street that winds among twenty or so thatch-roofed cottages with colorful flower gardens. On a hill overlooking the village is St. Michael's Church, where Eliot's ashes are buried. One reaches the church by walking up a pathway bordered on the right by a tall hedge and passing through an iron gate with a cross on it. To the left and right are worn tombstones "that cannot be deciphered," and straight ahead is the small grey stone church with its modest clock tower. The oval memorial plaque to Eliot is to the right as one enters the door. It is inscribed with the first and last lines of "East Coker," "In my beginning is my end. In my end is my beginning," and the following words:

Of your charity
Pray for the repose
Of the soul of
Thomas Stearns Eliot
Poet
26th September 1888—4th January 1965

Eliot apparently visited East Coker several times; according to Grover Smith he was there in August of 1937,[27] and Sir Rupert Hart-Davis noted in his speech at Eliot's memorial service (St. Michael's Church, September 26, 1965) that the poet's last visit was in the late summer of 1939, at which time he took photographs of the village and the church.[28] He may have begun the poem soon after this final visit, for it was completed by February of 1940 and was published the next month.

The poem opens with a statement of its theme of man's imprisonment in time and mortality, "In my beginning is my end," followed by an illustration of that statement through what Raymond Preston describes as "a rapid sketch of the changing face of the village in the course of several centuries. . . ."[29]

In succession
Houses rise and fall, crumble, are extended,
Are removed, destroyed, restored, or in their place
Is an open field, or a factory, or a by-pass.
Old stone to new building, old timber to new fires,
Old fires to ashes, and ashes to the earth. . . .

The village is pictured as its old stone and timbers give way to the signs of modern "progress"; a vacant lot, a sooty factory, a traffic-crammed by-pass, symbols from urban landscape suggesting the encroaching menace of mechanistic existence. In addition, these lines, which echo Baudelaire's "Paris change! . . . palais neufs, échafaudages, blocs,/Vieux faubourgs," convey the sense of the inevitable decomposition and death of time-bound objects, including man. There is a swift and relentless movement to the earth which "is already flesh, fur and faeces,/Bone of man and beast, cornstalk and leaf." The completeness of death's power is communicated by the details from human, animal, and vegetable life. The passage ends with a bleak setting:

> [There is] a time for the wind to break the loosened pane
> And to shake the wainscot where the field-mouse trots
> And to shake the tattered arras woven with a silent motto.

The broken window, the moldering wainscot, the gnawing field-mouse, and the ragged tapestry describe a deserted, dilapidated house through which the wind sweeps, a symbol often used in Eliot's poetry to suggest decay and desolation. These meanings are reinforced by the echoes from Tennyson's "Mariana," in which a desolate landscape symbolizes the desolation of the soul. As Bradbrook points out, Eliot uses the borrowed symbols of the mouse and the crumbling house creatively: "The mouse may come from Tennyson's 'Mariana,' which also describes a decaying house: 'The mouse/Behind the mouldering wainscot shrieked.' It is characteristic that in Eliot's poem the mouse has become a field-mouse, thus adding a new touch to the scene of desolation; the house is being invaded by the creatures of the field."[30]

In the second passage the poet presents a setting at the outskirts of the present village just beyond the path which leads up to St. Michael's Church. There is a sharp curve in the narrow rural road leading into East Coker where the bordering trees block out the summer sun almost completely, leaving the curve in dark shadow. On one side is a high wall while on the other is a steep bank, so that the pedestrian does indeed feel imprisoned in a "deep lane"; and the narrowness of the road forces him to lean against the bank if a truck passes. In the passage Eliot portrays his protagonist in this lane, and he uses the setting, a rural landscape menaced by hints of the urban, to symbolize the paralysis of the modern soul. Every detail of the scene suggests hypnotized apathy:

> In my beginning is my end. Now the light falls
> Across the open field, leaving the deep lane
> Shuttered with branches, dark in the afternoon,

> Where you lean against a bank while a van passes,
> And the deep lane insists on the direction
> Into the village, in the electric heat
> Hypnotised. In a warm haze the sultry light
> Is absorbed, not refracted, by grey stone.
> The dahlias sleep in the empty silence.
> Wait for the early owl.

The "electric heat," "warm haze," and "sultry light" of the late summer afternoon evoke a sense of heavy inertia, similar to that of "Virginia." This état d'âme is reinforced by the "empty silence" in which the dahlias sleep. The fact that the lane is "deep," echoing the "ways deep" of "Journey of the Magi," and "shuttered with branches" conveys a feeling of imprisonment. Finally, the word "electric" indicates the mechanization of modern civilization, while the truck which passes by represents its continual movement toward commercial gain and recalls "the world mov[ing]/In appetency on its metalled ways." Thus the rural landscape with its urban overtones is an effective symbol for the listless indifference of the modern human soul.

In the third passage the protagonist returns at night to the open field which was described at mid-afternoon in the previous passage. The landscape of the present fades into the landscape of the past as the protagonist has a vision of the field in the time of Eliot's ancestors:

> In that open field
> If you do not come too close, if you do not come too close,
> On a Summer midnight, you can hear the music
> Of the weak pipe and the little drum
> And see them dancing around the bonfire . . .
> Round and round the fire
> Leaping through the flames, or joined in circles,
> Rustically solemn or in rustic laughter
> Lifting heavy feet in clumsy shoes,
> Earth feet, loam feet, lifted in country mirth. . . .

This exuberant scene displays an ordered, meaningful existence within time much like the eighteenth century way of life suggested in Section I of "Burnt Norton." However, despite the fullness of their existence, it is limited by decay and inevitably by death as indicated by the reference to "Earth feet, loam feet" and the final lines, "Feet rising and falling./Eating and drinking. Dung and death." Arthur Mizener sums up the implication of these lines when he remarks that "the modulation at the end of this passage from 'East Coker' does not deny the reality of this life or its goodness; it only suggests the insufficiency of such a life."[31] Only the timeless can conquer decay and death and thus invest life with eternal significance, as Eliot will suggest more directly later in the *Quartets*.

Having described East Coker in the afternoon (the present) and at night (the past), the protagonist ends Section I with a meditation on dawn (the future). It is a dawn without hope of rebirth, a dawn within time, promising only the same soul-paralyzing heat and silence of yesterday: "Dawn points, and another day/Prepares for heat and silence." The next line, evoking a dawn wind which wrinkles the surface of a vast and desolate sea, recalls the emptiness of a similar seascape in *The Waste Land*, I: "*Oed' und leer das Meer.*" Both suggest the sterility of human experience bound by the temporal, and the protagonist's final words on the vagueness and rootlessness of his own personal experience serve to reinforce this idea:

> Out at sea the dawn wind
> Wrinkles and slides. I am here
> Or there, or elsewhere. In my beginning.

In the opening passage of Section II, Eliot stresses further the limitations of life within time. Here, however, he turns from the ordered life of his sixteenth century ancestors to the disorder and chaos of a "wasteland" existence, symbolized first by a garden setting and then by outer space. The garden is described in a state of upheaval with the normal patterns of nature totally confused:

> What is the late November doing
> With the disturbance of the spring
> And creatures of the summer heat,
> And snowdrops writhing under feet

> And hollyhocks that aim too high
> Red into grey and tumble down
> Late roses filled with early snow?

Although it is November, the flowers of summer are still blooming in the falling snow. The word "writhing" emphasizes the anguish of this tortured disturbance of nature. Not only upon earth does discord reign, but also among the planets and stars of outer space, where brutal warfare suggests a more comprehensive chaos:

> Scorpion fights against the Sun
> Until the Sun and Moon go down
> Comets weep and Leonids fly
> Hunt the heavens and the plains
> Whirled in a vortex that shall bring
> The world to that destructive fire
> Which burns before the ice-cap reigns.

In this vision of cosmic destruction, the universal strife culminates in the total annihilation of man's world, the earth itself being, to quote Helen Gardner, "burnt out to an icy cinder."[32] Thus these two settings, one terrestrial and the other extraterrestrial, skillfully convey the disorder and ultimate destruction of human existence confined totally within the boundaries of time.

   In the second passage, the poet rejects the preceding poetic style as inadequate and repeats the same idea in straightforward proselike verse, discounting the idea that earthly knowledge is all-sufficient:

> There is, it seems to us,
> At best, only a limited value
> In the knowledge derived from experience.

Even here in this "unpoetic" section, however, he uses three similar landscapes to symbolize the perplexity and insecurity of the soul's journey through life:

> In the middle, not only in the middle of the way
> But all the way, in a dark wood, in a bramble,
> On the edge of a grimpen, where is no secure foothold. . . .

The dark wood, of course, is borrowed from Canto I of Dante's *Inferno*, where it very clearly indicates the darkness, desolation, and danger of human existence. The bramble perhaps has its origins in Eliot's own childhood experience on the New England coast, where berrypickers are often ensnared and scratched by the prickly shrubs. The grimpen, highly symbolic of danger and death, is a bog or mire probably taken from A. Conan Doyle's *The Hound of the Baskervilles*. There, Dr. Watson remarks, "Life has become like that great Grimpen Mire, with little green patches everywhere into which one may sink and with no guide to point the track."[33] Eliot concludes that the wisdom necessary to guide the soul through these treacherous, trackless landscapes of life is "the wisdom of humility." Section II closes with two empty landscapes which comment literally on the decay and dissolution of East Coker's sixteenth century houses and inhabitants but apply symbolically to the ultimate plight of all mankind: "The houses are all gone under the sea./The dancers are all gone under the hill." Finite man, his works, and his meaningless history dissolve into the elements of sea and earth; in the prison of time death is inescapable.

Section III opens with a powerful description of the black void of death which awaits all men who have led meaningless lives, and particularly the inhabitants of a materialistic civilization. Eliot uses both Miltonic echoes and the setting of outer space to suggest the horror and emptiness of this grim end:

> O dark dark dark. They all go into the dark,
> The vacant interstellar spaces, the vacant into the vacant,
> The captains, merchant bankers, eminent men of letters,
> The generous patrons of art, the statesmen and the rulers,
> Distinguished civil servants, chairmen of many committees,
> Industrial lords and petty contractors, all go into the dark. . . .

John Bradbury remarks that this empty darkness is "the symbol of the damned state into which the worldly physical life must hurl its victims, 'the captains, merchant bankers,' and the rest." He then points out that "in contrast to this infernal darkness . . . Eliot immediately invokes the already established purgatorial dark, the 'darkness of God.' "[34] The empty but fertile quality of this darkness, interestingly enough, is symbolized by three urban settings. The first is a theatre, darkened so that the scenery on stage can be changed:

> The lights are extinguished, for the scene to be changed
> With a hollow rumble of wings, with a movement of darkness on
> darkness,
> And we know that the hills and the trees, the distant panorama
> And the bold imposing façade are all being rolled away—

The expectant waiting, the vacant blackness, and the removal of earthly trappings are all properties of the way down of St. John of the Cross. The second setting is in a train stopped at an Underground station:

> [W]hen an underground train, in the tube, stops too long
> between stations
> . . . the conversation rises and slowly fades into silence
> And you see behind every face the mental emptiness deepen
> Leaving only the growing terror of nothing to think about. . . .

Using this ordinary and daily phenomenon, Eliot suggests the waiting and the silence associated with the dark night of the soul. But even more important he communicates through this image the quality of "mental emptiness"; i.e., the mind must completely void itself of any personal thought and wait to be filled with the thought of God. Thus Eliot uses a mundane experience with negative connotations to suggest the positive qualities of self-denial, humility, and patient waiting associated with spiritual purgation. The final scene in the operating room of a hospital again stresses the condition of mental emptiness. Under the anesthetic, the mind is numbed but not extinguished, and thus it is "conscious but conscious of nothing."

Having evoked the qualities of purgatorial darkness through city settings, Eliot points to the qualities of moments of illumination through natural settings:

> Whisper of running streams, and winter lightning.
> The wild thyme unseen and the wild strawberry,
> The laughter in the garden, echoed ecstasy
> Not lost, but requiring, pointing to the agony
> Of death and birth.

These garden and woodland settings are concrete images, evoking sensations that are auditory ("Whisper of running streams"), visual ("winter lightning"), and olfactory ("The wild thyme unseen and the wild strawberry"). Further, they are specific symbols of ecstatic timeless moments and suggest freshness, vitality, beauty, and joy. All of them appear elsewhere in the poetry with the same connotations. The "running streams" recall "a running stream" in the temperate valley of "Journey of the Magi," and they anticipate the waterfall of "The Dry Salvages" and "Little Gidding." The brilliant intensity of winter lightning is found again in "The Dry Salvages," and of course a flash of lightning heralds the commands of the thunder in *The Waste Land,* V. While the "wild thyme unseen" reappears only in "The Dry Salvages," the joyous children's laughter in the garden is used in various forms in a number of poems: "Marina," "New Hampshire," "Burnt Norton," and "Little Gidding." These rural settings are, as Preston suggests, "moments of illumination in the flux of time which are assurances of a reality that conquers the flux."[35] Because they assure the soul of the ecstasy of the timeless, they require it to undergo the agony of purgation; they ascertain the validity of the two purgative passages which frame them.

In Section IV Eliot elaborates on the necessity of purgatorial suffering, using the setting of an operating room in a hospital as his central symbol. The willing, regenerative pain of purgation is suggested by the sharp scalpel of the surgeon (Christ) which cuts out the diseased matter (sin) of the patient (mankind):

> The wounded surgeon plies the steel
> That questions the distempered part;
> Beneath the bleeding hands we feel
> The sharp compassion of the healer's art
> Resolving the enigma of the fever chart.

The second stanza develops the idea further with the dying nurse (perhaps the church) whose duty is not to comfort the patient but to remind him constantly of his state of sin ("our, and Adam's curse") and of his need for purgation. In the third stanza the poet reveals that "The whole earth is our hospital," endowed by Adam with sin. The remainder of the passage has two possible meanings. First, if man does well in a material sense, he will die in sin. The "absolute paternal care" in this case would refer to Adam, the father of mankind, whose heritage of sin will not leave man and thus prevents his entering paradise. Second, if man does well in a spiritual sense (i.e., if the sick patient is cured of his illness of sin), he will die in a state of purity. The "absolute paternal care" would refer to God and to his grace which remains with man to prevent his continuing in the state of sin. The second interpretation seems to me more valid, considering the metaphors of the hospital and the sick patient, although both interpretations could be valid.

In the brilliant fourth stanza Eliot evokes the suffering of the patient (the human soul) as it is cured of the disease of sin by the refining fires:

> The chill ascends from feet to knees,
> The fever sings in mental wires.
> If to be warmed, then I must freeze
> And quake in frigid purgatorial fires
> Of which the flame is roses, and the smoke is briars.

The concrete details of physical pain render the passage agonizingly realistic: the chill of death rising toward the heart, the burning fever in the brain, the uncontrollable shaking of the body, and the sharp piercing sensation implied by the reference to briars. The symbolic overtones are no less striking in that Eliot has made very specific the quality of the cleansing fires. They are cold rather than hot fires and cause the soul to freeze and quake. (This concrete detail seems to be original with Eliot; for example, Dante's purgatorial fires of the seventh ledge do not have this characteristic.) Their flame of roses suggests the love of God as well as the consuming of human love by divine love; the last lines of "Little Gidding," which employ the same symbols, echo and reinforce these concepts:

> All manner of thing shall be well
> When the tongues of flame are in-folded
> Into the crowned knot of fire
> And the fire and the rose are one.

The smoke of briars suggests the pain of suffering demanded by God. The final stanza focuses on the Eucharist and Good Friday as symbols of man's redemption through Christ's love from Adam's endowment of sin: "The dripping blood our only drink,/The bloody flesh our only food. . . ." Man's pride and perversity, however, lead him to think that he is "sound, substantial flesh and blood," that he is healthy and strong enough to stand alone, that he is not sick with sin and in need of salvation. Yet, in spite of that foolish belief, the day of Christ's sacrifice for man is still called *good* Friday. Thus the complex symbolic cluster of hospital, diseased patient, surgeon, and nurse works to suggest that purgation is the only cure for man's state of sin.

Finally, in Section V the poet emphasizes the necessity of the *effort* to attain perfection. The first passage considers this theme in the realm of art and has no landscape symbolism. On the other hand, the second passage, which considers the theme in the realm of ordinary human experience, employs four different symbolic settings. But a discussion of their meanings requires elucidation of the significance of the passage itself. Eliot seems to be saying that one cannot live solely in the ecstatic moment of illumination:

> Not the intense moment
> Isolated, with no before and after,

> But a lifetime burning in every moment
> And not the lifetime of one man only
> But of old stones that cannot be deciphered.

Since man is of the earth, he must live meaningfully within its boundaries of time and place: "Home is where one starts from." Using the insight gained from the timeless moments, he must endow the ordinary moments and human history as a whole with significance. The reference to the "old stones that cannot be deciphered" evokes the churchyard of St. Michael's Church in East Coker where many of Eliot's ancestors are buried. As a symbol, the churchyard suggests all of mankind that has lived on earth. The idea Eliot proposes is that the timeless can give meaning and validity, not just to individual human beings, but to mankind and human history as a whole. When human life is lived within the framework of the timeless, the simple human pleasures, suggested by the two following settings, become part of a meaningful whole:

> There is a time for the evening under starlight,
> A time for the evening under lamplight
> (The evening with the photograph album).

The first setting echoes Tennyson's Canto XCV of *In Memoriam*:

> By night we linger'd on the lawn,
>   For underfoot the herb was dry;
>   And genial warmth; and o'er the sky
> The silvery haze of summer drawn. . . .

Both Tennyson's and Eliot's settings communicate serenity and human warmth, as does the living room scene with its lamps and photograph album. The Eliotean settings have further symbolic overtones in connection with time: the first suggests youth and the present; the second, age and the past. Eliot seems to be saying that, although there is a time for simple pleasures, youth and age, present and past, memory and desire, there is also a time for spiritual effort, for the future of the soul. Old men particularly should not be content to reminisce about the past, but should consider their future and the state of their souls:

> Old men ought to be explorers
> Here and there does not matter
> We must be still and still moving
> Into another intensity
> For a further union, a deeper communion. . . .

Again the lines echo Tennyson; his poem "Ulysses" expresses the idea of the old man continuing his travels, and its seascape may have suggested the setting that Eliot uses in the final lines:

> I cannot rest from travel; I will drink
> Life to the lees. . . .
>   There lies the port; the vessel puffs her sail;
> There gloom the dark, broad seas. My mariners,
> Souls that have toil'd, and wrought, and thought with me—
>   . . . you and I are old;
> Old age hath yet his honor and his toil.
> Death closes all; but something ere the end,
> Some work of noble note, may yet be done. . . .
> 'Tis not too late to seek a newer world.

The description of the wintry night-time seascape with which the poem closes catches up the anguish and difficulty of the struggle for spiritual purity:

> Through the dark cold and the empty desolation,
> The wave cry, the wind cry, the vast waters
> Of the petrel and the porpoise.

Yet despite the "dark cold" and the "empty desolation," the effort has its rewards as suggested by the petrel and the porpoise. While in *The Waste Land* the bird and the fish carried negative connotations, here they function as symbols of fertility and renewed life; although the sea still appears to be "*Oed' und leer*," the bird no longer says "Jug jug to dirty ears" and the dolphin is no longer "carvèd" and immobile. Being alive and free, they suggest the possibility of rebirth: "In my end is my beginning." The word "end" implies both death and goal. Thus the final setting of "East Coker" is a complex one, communicating both the horror and the glory of the battle for spiritual fulfillment.

In "The Dry Salvages" Eliot considers the problems of time, change, and death in human experience, suggesting in the fifth section that the Incarnation of Christ overcomes them and thus renders human life meaningful. In expressing this theme, Eliot uses as his major symbols two complex landscapes from his childhood. The dominant setting, anticipated in the closing lines of "East Coker" and confirmed by the title of the third Quartet, is the sea and the coastal region of Cape Ann, Massachusetts where Eliot spent his summers as a child and as a young man. The other setting is that of the Mississippi River at St. Louis, the city in which he was born and lived until he went off to Milton Academy at the age of sixteen.

A valid analysis of the symbolism of these two settings requires mention of certain facts. In the poem Eliot uses five different aspects of the coastal area around Cape Ann: the Eliot house, the sea, the Dry Salvages, the town of Gloucester, and Our Lady of Good Voyage Church.[36] The Eliot house was built by Eliot's father on Edgemoor Road at Eastern Point, East Gloucester, and the family spent the summers there, arriving in June and departing in October. Eliot himself stayed there for nineteen summers, from 1893 through 1911, a period covering his childhood and young manhood. The house is set on a hill, and in Eliot's boyhood it overlooked the sea and had a panoramic view of the surrounding area. (At present, trees and houses partially block such a view.) It is a large, two-story house with a spacious porch along the side and the front where one could sit and gaze out at the sea and boats in the harbor, as evidenced by several photographs taken by Henry Ware Eliot, Jr. in the early 1900s. In front of the house large granite rocks and numerous trees filled with birds create a terrain which surely delighted the Eliot children. In the yard behind the house are lilac bushes, and in the neighborhood in spring goldenrod and climbing wild roses are rampant. This idyllic setting provides Eliot with the basis for much of the landscape symbolism in the poem.

A second aspect of the region is the sea itself. Eliot saw the sea in varied conditions, both from land and on the water. He had wandered its beaches, climbed among the granite rocks, discovered its inhabitants, "the starfish, the hermit crab," "the more delicate algae and the sea anemone." The latter he mentions in *The Use of Poetry and the Use of Criticism* with what are surely autobiographical overtones: "the experience of a child of ten, a small boy peering through sea-water in a rock-pool, and finding a sea-anemone for the first time."[37] However, on the same beaches he had also found evidence of the sea's violence: bits of broken oar or a torn fishing net or fragments of a lobsterpot. In addition to this landsman's knowledge of the sea's variety he had much experience on the sea itself. An accomplished sailor, Eliot cruised up and down the coast with his companions (often Harold Peters or his brother Henry Ware Eliot, Jr.), and he knew the sea well. He was familiar with the different sounds of the sea and used them in the poem: the noise of the ropes in the sails, the splashing of a wave on the water, the crashing of the surf against the granite rocks, the groaning sound of a whistling buoy as it heaves in the water, the cry of the seagulls, the tolling of a bell buoy. All of these sea sounds are authentic, as S. E. Morison points out in his article, "The Dry Salvages and the Thacher Shipwreck":

> Take, for instance, "the menace and caress of wave that breaks on water," which Eliot could have observed at Flat Ground or Milk Island Bar. When a moderate wave from the ocean strikes a shoal, it suddenly lifts—a warning to an approaching mariner—and then breaks, with a susurration that may be rendered as a hissing menace or a wooing caress. Notice also "the distant rote." *Rote* or *Rut* is an old English word now seldom heard outside New England. It means a distant, continuous roar made by waves dashing on a long rocky coast. Often have I heard a Maine man say, "Sea's making up. Hear that rote!" . . . T. S. Eliot doubtless listened to the rote from his parents' house, during the windless calm after a storm, or on a "weather-breeder" day when swells from the eastward begin crashing on the "granite teeth" of Cape Ann before a storm breaks.

Further, Morison notes that there is a diaphone (a fog signal which gives a blast of two tones, "the wailing warning from the approaching headland") on Thacher Island and a groaner in the waters east of the island.[38] However, John Boyd in his article, "The Dry Salvages: Topography as Symbol," suggests that the "wailing warning" is a reference to the Eastern Point Lighthouse, quoting a description from Copeland and Rogers' *The Saga of Cape Ann:* " 'For the seafarers of Cape Ann, Eastern Point has always been an outstanding landmark. Located at a sharp angle on a rocky shore, it indicates dangerous rocks and reefs to be shunned and marks the entrance to Gloucester Harbor from the east, a point to be rounded to reach a haven of safety in foul weather.' "[39] Eliot also recreates authentic visual images of the sea from his own experience, such as drifting débris in the water and the "silent fog" (the latter combining both the visual and the auditory). Finally, he depicts the beauty and the destruction of the sea through references to weather conditions: on a halcyon day the sea is calm and smooth, while on a stormy day it becomes a "sudden fury."

A third element of the regional setting, the Dry Salvages, provides the title of the poem and, although it appears only once within the poem, is a central symbol. The death and destruction it represents pervade the entire work. Eliot identifies the obscure rock cluster in the headnote of the poem, for, as John Hayward explains in a letter to Frank Morley, "Tom was worried that the title might appear too remote and, particularly, that it might not occur to his readers (as it did'nt [sic] to me) that it was a proper name."[40] The headnote reads: "The Dry Salvages—presumably *les trois sauvages*—is a small group of rocks, with a beacon, off the N.E. coast of Cape Ann, Massachusetts." Specifically, the rock formation is located about a mile from Rockport's Straitsmouth Island and, as Morison informs us, has two neighboring ledges, the Little Salvages and Flat Ground. While the Dry Salvages are visible even at high tide (hence the adjective "dry"), the Little Salvages are visible only at low tide; and Flat Ground lies below the water's surface at all times. Thus, these three, and the Dry Salvages in particular, pose a great danger for ships and have caused many a shipwreck, even as recently as the 1950s. Morison notes, "When an easterly gale is raging the entire group—Dry Salvages, Little Salvages and Flat Ground—becomes a seething mass of foam, as heavy swells from the Atlantic break and roar over it; and at all times it is a menace to navigators attempting to round Cape Ann."[41] And John Boyd quotes the following description from *The Saga of Cape Ann:* " 'The hazards of navigation in the neighborhood of Thachers and Straightsmouth are rendered substantially more serious by the Salvages—the 'savage rocks'—which lie outside Straightsmouth. The Little Salvages are about a mile offshore and the Big Salvages [the Dry], a half-mile farther out. On a clear day the Big Salvages glisten in the sun, whitened by the droppings of myriads of gulls, but in stormy weather those ledges have brought disaster to many a ship' "[42]

Thus, quite literally the Dry Salvages is an instrument of death and destruction. Eliot, of course, knew the rock cluster well from his sailing experiences, as Morison points out: "Cruising in college days with his friend Harold Peters, the Dry Salvages was the last seamark they passed outward bound, and the first they picked up homeward bound. . . . They doubtless learned to allow an extra quarter point for set of current when sailing from the Maine coast to Cape Ann, as insurance against running on the Salvages."[43] As to the derivation of the name, Eliot said he owed it to his brother but added that perhaps he owed "more to my own imagination than to any explanation that I heard."[44] The adjective "dry" in the anglicized title indicates, as previously mentioned, that the rocky formation is never completely covered by water. *Les trois sauvages* literally means *the three savages* and perhaps refers to all three ledges. Whatever the case, the Dry Salvages and its neighbors are without doubt savages in their ability to destroy.

Another part of Cape Ann used in the poem is the town of Gloucester, famous for over three hundred years as a flourishing fishing port and maritime center. Built on a hill, the town looks out over Gloucester Harbor, called by Eliot "the most beautiful harbor for small ships on the whole of that coast."[45] Along its picturesque waterfront are docked numerous fishing boats, and drying nets line the shore. Just west of the water-front is the bronze fishermen's memorial, *The Man at the Wheel*, which honors over eight thousand Gloucester fishermen lost at sea. Its inscription from Psalms 106:23, "They that go down to the sea in ships," is echoed in the poem. Although the statue was not in existence during Eliot's childhood summers on the Cape (it was not erected until 1923), he perhaps saw it on a visit as an adult. While the town is not mentioned specifically in the poem,[46] it is the home of the fishermen and their families who are portrayed in various ways in the work. Eliot must often have visited the harbor and seen the fishing fleets departing on or returning from long journeys. Surely he saw the fishermen upon their return receiving their wages and drying their sails and nets along the waterfront, "drawing their money, drying sails at dockage." Morison tells us that he and his brother "talked with James B. Conolly [sic], author of *Out of Gloucester*, and with numerous fishermen and sailors."[47] Eliot himself, in his preface to another of Connolly's works, *Fishermen of the Banks*, speaks of fish drying on racks behind the wharves and sailors telling their stories while they lounged at the corner of Main Street and Duncan Street.[48] Perhaps some had told him of the work at sea, "bailing,/Setting and hauling," or of the terrors of an approaching storm or a thick fog. No doubt he heard accounts of those who had lost their lives at sea,

> those who were in ships, and
> Ended their voyage on the sand, in the sea's lips
> Or in the dark throat which will not reject them. . . .

The wives of the fishermen are also portrayed in the poem in attitudes of anxiety or sorrow. In Section I they appear as

> anxious worried women
> Lying awake, calculating the future,
> Trying to unweave, unwind, unravel
> And piece together the past and the future,
> Between midnight and dawn . . .

and in Section IV as "Women who have seen their sons or husbands/Setting forth, and not returning." As John Boyd notes, Gloucester contains more than one house with a " 'widow's walk,' a mute reminder of the terror of the sea. It is a porch high atop a house where an anxious wife would pace while awaiting the uncertain return of her husband at sea."[49] Thus, the town of Gloucester is the fourth aspect of the region used in the poem.

Finally, Our Lady of Good Voyage Church in Gloucester is the actual setting referred to in Section IV of the poem. The section begins with an address to the "Lady, whose shrine stands on the promontory." The church is located on Prospect Street, high on the hill (promontory) overlooking the harbor, and a small sign proclaims it "Our Lady of Good Voyage Church: Shrine of the Fishermen." As the name of the church indicates, the Virgin Mary is the patroness of the fishermen, guarding and protecting them on their long and dangerous sea voyages. The theme of Mary as the protectress of fishermen is carried out in many ways in the church's décor. The façade is white with blue doors and two towers capped in blue, the color associated with the Virgin. Between the towers and facing the harbor is a large statue of Mary, her left arm holding a fishing vessel and her right arm raised in a gesture of blessing or peace. Inside the church the dominant color is blue, and numerous replicas or models of various types of ships line the sides and the back wall. Also on the back wall are fishing nets and a life preserver. Over the altar at the front of the church is another statue of Mary with the Christ Child in her left arm and a fishing boat in her right hand. She is wearing a golden crown, a white dress, and a blue cape, and her facial expression seems sad and sombre. Finally, to the left of the sanctuary is a fishing boat in gold with its mast in the shape of a cross. Thus, it seems unquestionable that it is the Virgin of Gloucester's Our Lady of Good Voyage Church whom the speaker asks to pray for fishermen, for their wives and mothers, and for those destroyed at sea.

This New England coastal region, then, serves as the main geographical background of the poem, furnishing Eliot with concrete images which fill the lines with beauty. It is in this imagistic use of the setting that John Hayward sees the poem's greatness. In a letter to Frank Morley, he writes, ''I attribute its excellence to the beauty of the marine images, which provides a haunting background to the recurrent 'Time Past—Time Present' theme. And you know, probably better than I do, with what nostalgic longing the sea affects Tom's sensibility. (Some of the great passages in his poetry—the end of 'Gerontion,' the Phoenician sailor, 'Marina' & c. are evocations of the coast of New England and of white sails flying).''[50] However, perhaps even more important is the pervasive and many-leveled symbolism which, as we shall see later, is based on the coastal setting.

Eliot's use of the Cape Ann area is complex, and the region dominates the poem; however, the second important landscape, while also deriving from his childhood, neither has such a varied background nor plays so important a role in the work. (It appears only twice, in the opening passage and at the end of Section II.) The setting is the Mississippi River at St. Louis. St. Louis, a busy industrial port, extends approximately nineteen miles along the west bank of the river. In this location the Mississippi is extremely muddy as the waters of the Missouri River flow into it just north of the city. It is approximately fifteen hundred feet wide and nine feet deep. During floods it can be extremely treacherous with high waters and swift, raging currents. Two bridges spanned the river in Eliot's time, the older of which (Eads Bridge, built in 1874) served as a vantage point where the young boy watched the swollen waters in flood time. The waters, of course, rise every spring; in addition, five floods were recorded in St. Louis during Eliot's childhood (in 1892, 1893, 1897, 1903, and 1904), and he surely would also have observed these.

St. Louis was Eliot's birthplace and his home until he was sixteen and as such influenced him strongly, as he has said numerous times. In an early draft of an address delivered in 1953 at Washington University in St. Louis, he remarks on the value to him of his birthplace. After noting that it was hard for him to prepare the speech because ''so much of my past life—of the early formative years—so many memories were aroused . . . ," he says, "in my opinion St. Louis was a good place to have been born in: at any rate, a good place for a poet to have been born in; and I think that I personally was fortunate to have been born here, rather than in Boston, or New York, or London."[51] In a letter published in 1930 in the *St. Louis Post-Dispatch*, Eliot reveals even more clearly his feelings about his childhood home and particularly about the Mississippi:

> As I spent the first 16 years of my life in St. Louis, with the exception of summer holidays in Maine and Massachusetts, . . . it is self-evident that St. Louis affected me more deeply than any other environment has done. These 16 years were spent in a house at 2635 Locust street, since demolished. . . . The river also made a deep impression on me; and it was a great treat to be taken down to the Eads Bridge in flood time.
> . . . And I feel that there is something in having passed one's childhood beside the big river, which is incommunicable to those who have not. Of course my people were Northerners and New Englanders, and of course I have spent many years out of America altogether; but Missouri and the Mississippi have made a deeper impression on me than any other part of the world.[52]

Eliot mentions the Mississippi again and again in other remarks on St. Louis. In his preface to Mowrer's *This American World*, he speaks of the landscape with "the long dark river, the ailanthus trees, the flaming cardinal birds, the high limestone bluffs where we searched for fossil shell-fish . . . ,"[53] and in an address entitled "The Influence of Landscape upon the Poet" he describes the impact of the river even more directly: "[M]y scenery was almost exclusively urban. . . . It was also, however, the Mississippi, as it passes between St. Louis and East St. Louis in Illinois: the Mississippi was the most powerful feature of Nature in that environment."[54]

The data concerning the two settings of Cape Ann and St. Louis provide a solid basis for an interpretation of their symbolism in the poem. Appropriately, Section I presents both landscapes, beginning, as Eliot has said, "where I began, with the Mississippi,"[55] and then shifting to the ocean off the Massachusetts coast. The river is described in some detail. It is a "strong brown god," powerful and muddy as is the Mississippi at St. Louis, and it has served several functions, listed chronologically in the poem. First, it was "recognised as a frontier." In 1783 when the United States received its independence from England, the Mississippi River was the western boundary of the nation and thus in the late 1700s and early 1800s served as the frontier for westward expansion. St. Louis itself, founded in 1764 as a fur trading post, was a crossroads for traders and settlers moving west. And Eliot tells us that even in his childhood (the 1890s) the city limits of St. Louis seemed to him "on the verge of the Wild West."[56] Second, the Mississippi was (and is) "a conveyor of commerce." In the days before the development of the steamboat, rafts and barges carried products and people downstream to New Orleans and the Atlantic Ocean. After the advent of the steamboat in 1811, the river became one of the busiest commercial waterways in the world, with St. Louis as a major port. Finally, the Mississippi was "only a problem confronting the builder of bridges." Eliot here may be referring to the building of the Eads Bridge. Completed in 1874, it was the first bridge to span the Mississippi at St. Louis and was considered an engineering wonder. The river thus has been "patient to some degree," "useful," and finally "almost forgotten/By the dwellers in cities." However, it is always capable of unleashing its fury, as in a storm or flood, when it becomes a raging destructive agent. The Mississippi is especially well known for its disastrous floods, the most catastrophic of which occurred in modern times (1927).[57] Numerous descriptive words suggesting a malign aspect of the river dominate the passage: "sullen, untamed and intractable," "untrustworthy," "ever . . . implacable,/Keeping his seasons and rages, destroyer, reminder/Of what men choose to forget," "unpropitiated," "waiting, watching and waiting."

This emphasis on its ominous destructive qualities would suggest that the river symbolizes death and man's inevitable mortality: "destroyer, reminder/Of what men choose to forget." It represents man's life within time, a constant flow moving relentlessly toward death:

> His rhythm was present in the nursery bedroom,
> In the rank ailanthus of the April dooryard,
> In the smell of grapes on the autumn table,
> And the evening circle in the winter gaslight.

In these lines Eliot uses sensory images from the setting of his childhood home on Locust Street in St. Louis, combining references to childhood, seasons of the year, and times of day to create an impression of human life flowing inexorably toward death. The rhythm of the river, representing the tick of clock-time, is present in all phases of man's life, each of which is symbolized by one of the four settings. The nursery bedroom clearly symbolizes infancy, while the flowering yard in April suggests youth. (The ailanthus, or Tree of Heaven, has large pinlike leaves and clusters of small greenish flowers that give off an unpleasant odor.) The kitchen setting with its mellow autumnal grapes is maturity, and the wintertime living room with its evening gaslight recalling the "evening under lamp-light" of "East Coker" conveys old age. Eliot's mastery in choosing concise but highly evocative details is illustrated especially well in this passage.

Eliot's varied symbolic uses of rivers throughout his poetry follow a general pattern. In *The Waste Land* the Thames for the most part symbolizes commercialism, sterility, and death, although the possibility of fertility is implied in the references to fishing and fishermen. One other river, the Ganges, is mentioned in the poem; it is described as being "sunken," waiting for rain, and hence stagnant and sterile. In "The Hollow Men" the barren spirits gather by an unnamed "tumid river" (intended, I think, to evoke the Acheron) which suggests the corruption and sterility of a meaningless death. "Journey of the Magi" includes a reference to a "running stream and a water-mill beating the darkness," the first use of a river to convey a positive meaning; it symbolizes the life, freshness, and vitality associated with the birth of Christ. However, the minor poem "The Wind Sprang up at Four O'Clock" returns to the river as a negative symbol, here of suffering, pain, and bitterness:

Is it a dream or something else
When the surface of the blackened river
Is a face that sweats with tears?
I saw across the blackened river
The camp fire shake with alien spears.

The Rivanna river at Charlottesville, Virginia appears in "Virginia" as a symbol of paralysis and hence sterility of the spirit. It is portrayed as muddy, slowly moving, stagnant: "Red river, red river,/Slow flow heat is silence. . . ." A river is mentioned twice in "Choruses from 'The Rock' " as a symbol of time's passage, "The river flows, the seasons turn," and "the running streams" in Section III of "East Coker" evoke again connotations of renewed spiritual life. Of course, in Section I of "The Dry Salvages" the Mississippi River represents the inexorable movement of time toward death, and in Section II it suggests sin and evil. The flood waters (presumably of the Mississippi) described in Section II of "Little Gidding" clearly are destructive, death-dealing agents. However, at the end of this final Quartet the river appears as a symbol of purity, life, and renewal. This summary shows, then, that the river is used predominantly as a negative symbol but that it has a great variety of meanings. And approximately half the references are to specific rivers, while the other half are to river generally.

To return to "The Dry Salvages," the second passage moves from the river to the sea: "The river is within us, the sea is all about us. . . ." The detailed description of the sea depicts its great variety, and its symbolism is correspondingly complex: "The sea has many voices,/Many gods and many voices." The sea represents all of time; as Bergsten puts it, "the sea is not only the time of a past infinitely removed, but it also implies an endless future. It is, that is to say, all time. It is temporal existence seen in the widest possible perspective; so wide, in fact, as to appear similar to eternity. . . . But the sea does not stand for eternity in the sense of timelessness."[58] Though it includes man's time, it stretches before and after, having begun before the creation of the earth and extending infinitely into the future. Eliot suggests its tremendous range by picturing man's history as simply a tiny portion of it:

Footfalls echo in the memory
Down the passage which we did not take
Towards the door we never opened
Into the rose-garden.
"BURNT NORTON," 11. 11-14.

Hopkins.

Burnt Norton Manor, Chipping Campden, Gloucestershire.

Through the first gate,
Into our first world, shall we follow
The deception of the thrush? Into our first world.
"BURNT NORTON," 11. 20-2.

M. J. Hopkins.

The gate at Burnt Norton, Chipping Campden, Gloucestershire.

The drained pools in the garden of Burnt Norton,
Chipping Campden, Gloucestershire.

So we moved, and they, in a formal pattern,
Along the empty alley, into the box circle,
To look down into the drained pool.
Dry the pool, dry concrete, brown edged. . . .
"BURNT NORTON," ll. 31-4.

> *Now the light falls*
> *Across the open field, leaving the deep lane*
> *Shuttered with branches, dark in the afternoon, . . .*
> *And the deep lane insists on the direction*
> *Into the village . . . .*
> "EAST COKER," 11. 14-16, 18-19.

The country lane leading to the village of East Coker, Somersetshire.

In a warm haze the sultry light
Is absorbed, not refracted, by grey stone.
The dahlias sleep in the empty silence.
"EAST COKER," 11. 20-2.

The village of East Coker, Somersetshire.

St. Michael's Church, East Coker, Somersetshire.

W. H. Rendell.

And not the lifetime of one man only
But of old stones that cannot be deciphered.
"EAST COKER," 11. 195-6.

W. H. Rendell.

The gravestones at St. Michael's Church, East Coker, Somersetshire.

In my beginning is my end.
In my end is my beginning.
"EAST COKER," ll. 1, 209.

The memorial plaque to T. S. Eliot, St. Michael's Church,
East Coker, Somersetshire.

In that open field
If you do not come too close, if you do not come too close,
On a summer midnight, you can hear the music
Of the weak pipe and the little drum. . . .
"EAST COKER," ll.23-6.

An open field, East Coker, Somersetshire.

I do not know much about gods; but I think that the river
Is a strong brown god—sullen, untamed and intractable. . . .
"THE DRY SALVAGES," 11. 1-2.

The Mississippi River and the Eads Bridge, St. Louis, Missouri.

His rhythm was present in the nursery bedroom,
In the rank ailanthus of the April dooryard,
In the smell of grapes on the autumn table,
And the evening circle in the winter gaslight.
"THE DRY SALVAGES," 11. 11-14.

Front view of the Eliot house at 2635 Locust Street,
St. Louis, Missouri, about 1905.

The inner hall of the Locust Street house , about 1905.

The sea is the land's edge also, the granite
Into which it reaches, the beaches where it tosses
Its hints of earlier and other creation. . . .
"THE DRY SALVAGES," 11. 16-18.

The Eliot house at Cape Ann, Massachusetts. The photo was taken
by Henry Ware Eliot, Jr. about 1909. A note on the back reads:
"Outer harbor and piazza. Morning."

Where is the end of them, the fishermen sailing
Into the wind's tail, where the fog cowers?
"THE DRY SALVAGES," 11. 68-9.

A fishing schooner, Gloucester, Massachusetts. The photo was
taken by Henry Ware Eliot, Jr. about 1900.

And the ragged rock in the restless waters,
Waves wash over it, fogs conceal it;
On a halcyon day it is merely a monument,
In navigable weather it is always a seamark
To lay a course by: but in the sombre season
Or the sudden fury, is what it always was.
"THE DRY SALVAGES," 11. 119-24.

Samuel Eliot Morison.

The Dry Salvages, near Rockport, Massachusetts.

Jerry Klinov

Lady, whose shrine stands on the promontory,
Pray for all those who are in ships, those
Whose business has to do with fish. . . .
"THE DRY SALVAGES," 11. 176-8.

Jerry Klinow.

John N. Cole.

The Virgin, Our Lady
of Good Voyage Church,
Gloucester, Massachusetts.

Our Lady of Good Voyage Church,
Gloucester, Massachusetts.

So, while the light fails
On a winter's afternoon, in a secluded chapel
History is now and England.
"LITTLE GIDDING," 11. 236-8.

The chapel at Little Gidding, Huntingdonshire.

Photo Precision Ltd.

The interior of the chapel at Little Gidding, Huntingdonshire.

After the dark dove with the flickering tongue
  Had passed below the horizon of his homing
  While the dead leaves still rattled on like tin
Over the asphalt where no other sound was
  Between three districts whence the smoke arose. . . .
"LITTLE GIDDING," ll. 82-6.

A London street after a World War II bombing raid.

> The sea is the land's edge also, the granite
> Into which it reaches, the beaches where it tosses
> Its hints of earlier and other creation:
> The starfish, the hermit crab, the whale's backbone;
> The pools where it offers to our curiosity
> The more delicate algae and the sea anemone.

These lines move us back to the very dawn of earth's existence. In addition to conveying the great scope of universal time, the sea symbolizes its all-inclusiveness. The lines quoted above portray the beauty and creativity of the sea and hence of all time, while lines 22–24 (below) express the terrors and mystery of its death-dealing powers:

> It tosses up our losses, the torn seine,
> The shattered lobsterpot, the broken oar
> And the gear of foreign dead men.

Like the sea, universal time includes both birth (the creation of living beings) and death (the future destruction of the world as well as the constant destruction of its individual inhabitants).

Between the second and third passages of Section I are two lines describing literal scenic details of the coastal region: "The salt is on the briar rose,/The fog is in the fir trees." Howarth notes, "In East Gloucester in July the wild roses climb on fence and low seawall and wherever they can find a hold; the salt moisture clings to them and creeps through the trees."[59] The fir trees are specifically recalled by Eliot as he reminisces about New England in his preface to *This American World,* and he must often have seen fog from the sea drifting among them. The images are beautiful in their own right, but they also carry symbolic overtones; Eliot modulates the symbolism of the sea from all time to eternity, leading into the third passage. The uniting of sea and land in the images thus suggests the "intersection of the timeless/With time," the salt and the fog of the sea representing the timeless and the rose and the fir trees representing time. Both the rose and the mist among the firs are used elsewhere in Eliot's poetry (for example, "Burnt Norton" and "Marina") to evoke the beauty and ecstasy of the moment in and out of time.

The third passage juxtaposes the anguish, danger, and inevitable death of human time to the serenity and stability of
eternity through the further use of the sea as symbol. In the
first nine lines life is symbolized as a sea voyage with potential
dangers of shipwreck and death on every hand. "The menace
and caress of wave that breaks on water" could indicate, as
Morison has noted, an underwater shoal or rocky ledge. The
"wailing warning" and "the heaving groaner" are auditory
signals indicating perilous waters, while the oppressive fog
traps man in a silent, isolated blindness that increases the
possibility of wrecking. Finally, the reference to the noise of the
surf is particularly sinister, "The distant rote in the granite
teeth." Bodelsen explains the realistic aspect of this symbol:
" 'Rote' is the sound of the surf pounding on the beach, with a
hint, I think, of the grinding noise of the pebbles which it drags
to and fro. The granite teeth are, of course, the rocks of the
beach."[60] Further, Morison remarks that this sound may indicate the approach of a storm.[61] Symbolically, this coastal setting is the devouring mouth of death ready to swallow up
human victims. Two landscapes in Tennyson's poetry are strikingly similar to this angry seascape. In "The Palace of Art," the
protagonist describes one picture in the following terms:

> One show'd an iron coast and angry waves.
> You seem'd to hear them climb and fall
> And roar rock-thwarted under bellowing caves,
> Beneath the windy wall.

And an even closer echo is found in *Maud,* where the young
man speaks of walking in his dark garden and "listening now
to the tide in its broad-flung shipwrecking roar,/Now to the
scream of a madden'd beach dragg'd down by the wave." With
the added force of Tennyson's seascapes behind it, Eliot's sea
powerfully symbolizes the constant, terrifying presence of
death in human existence.

Contrasted to these dangers is the stability and timelessness
of eternity, symbolized by the ocean's ground swell which
rings the bell buoy. The ground swell is a broad, deep, and
constant undulation portrayed as being older than man's time:

>The tolling bell
>Measures time not our time, rung by the unhurried
>Ground swell, a time
>Older than the time of chronometers. . . .

The everlasting time measured by the tolling bell buoy is juxtaposed to human time filled with anxiety and suffering; human time is symbolized by the fishermen's wives who, during their husbands' absences at sea, lie awake in the depths of night trying to make a coherent whole out of time:

>time counted by anxious worried women
>Lying awake, calculating the future,
>Trying to unweave, unwind, unravel
>And piece together the past and the future,
>Between midnight and dawn, when the past is all deception,
>The future futureless, before the morning watch
>When time stops and time is never ending. . . .

The imagery of weaving recalls the futility of the empty shuttles in "Gerontion" and suggests the anguish of the women, trapped in a dark, lonely "no-time" with neither past nor future. In those hours before dawn, time seems to have stopped; yet it drags on endlessly. In the last three lines of the passage, Eliot again uses juxtaposition, setting over against this tortured vision of human time the serenity and permanence of eternity, symbolized by the ground swell and the bell buoy:

>And the ground swell, that is and was from the beginning,
>Clangs
>The bell.

Yet beneath this primary meaning runs a secondary connotation of the constant presence of death; the ocean waters are always instruments of death, and the clanging bell buoy, in addition to warning quite literally of underwater danger and thus of potential death, calls up associations of a tolling funeral bell.

In the first passage of Section II, composed in the difficult sestina form, Eliot uses the sea as a symbol of human life and the Gloucester fishermen as a symbol of mankind voyaging through life. The vision presented is indeed bleak; humanity's voyage on the sea of life is made up of suffering, decay, destruction, and death, and, being without a goal, it is meaningless and monotonous. The first stanza presents all these themes in the form of a question: "Where is there an end of the agony in human existence?" The various kinds of agony are symbolized through four images, two of which are seascapes. The first image, "the soundless wailing," recalls the lonely, anxious fishermen's wives pictured in Section I and suggests further, it seems to me, the anguish of those who lose loved ones at sea. The second image, "The silent withering of autumn flowers," is a conventional symbol for decay. The third and fourth images, views of desolate beaches and of silent, débris-strewn ocean waters, also evoke devastating aspects of human life. The "drifting wreckage" of shattered ships suggests lack of control or direction, the fragmented quality of human existence, and the destruction of ideals, hopes, or even life itself. The beaches, deserted except for the bleached bones of fishermen drowned at sea, strikingly convey the sterility and terror of death.

In the second stanza the speaker answers his own question. There is no end to man's anguish; rather there is more anguish. Echoing the image of the drifting wreckage, he asserts his disillusioned concept of life: "the emotionless/Years of living among the breakage/Of what was believed in as the most reliable. . . ." The third stanza moves to old age and its bitter impotence, using another image drawn from the New England coast:

> In a drifting boat with a slow leakage,
> The silent listening to the undeniable
> Clamour of the bell of the last annunciation.

One can hardly imagine a more terrifying symbol of old age: man is alone in a boat over which he has no control, the boat is slowly sinking into the waters of death, and all the while the clanging funeral bell (literally a bell buoy) warns of death's imminence. The juxtaposition of the vast silence with the onomatopoeic "clamour" of the bell makes that death knell even more horrifying.

In the fourth and fifth stanzas Eliot focuses on the Gloucester fishermen, using them to represent all men on the dangerous voyage through life: "Where is the end of them, the fishermen sailing/Into the wind's tail, where the fog cowers?" The poet then says that we cannot think of a time in human history when life was not difficult and "littered with wastage"; further, we fear that the future, like the past, has no meaningful goal. Thus, to avoid the terror of this reality, we think of the fishermen in more positive terms; stanza five portrays them in their ordinary, daily occupations:

> We have to think of them as forever bailing,
> Setting and hauling, while the North East lowers
> Over shallow banks unchanging and erosionless
> Or drawing their money, drying sails at dockage;
> Not as making a trip that will be unpayable
> For a haul that will not bear examination.

The first lines refer to their work at sea, bailing out water to keep from sinking, setting out their lines or nets and then hauling in their catch; all the while a Northeaster (a nautical term for a storm or high wind from the northeast) threatens darkly in the distance, symbolizing the ever-present threat of disaster and death in the human journey. The third line describes the fishermen back in port (the Gloucester harbor) receiving their salaries and drying their sails and nets along the docks. The last two lines, however, rip away the illusion of productivity and progress to reveal a possibility we are loathe to look at—the possibility that the fishing voyage (human life) is a failure, the catch so meager it is not worth either inspection or payment. Once again Eliot has taken a traditionally positive symbol and reversed its meaning; in this case, the lack of fish and the unsuccessful fishing trip are reversed symbols of fertility, or what we might call "double negatives" of sterility.

The final stanza of the sestina comes full circle, returning to the opening stanza's rhymes and images of wailing, withering flowers, and desolate seascapes. However, whereas in the first stanza the speaker *asks* where suffering, decay, and death end, in this stanza he asserts with grim finality, "There is no end of it." Yet in the two closing lines the barest whisper of hope is heard: "Only the hardly, barely prayable/Prayer of the one Annunciation." The only possible salvation from the dismal human life presented in the sestina is in the surrender of man's will to that of God; Mary's prayer at "the one Annunciation" was "Be it unto me according to thy Word." Thus at the end of the passage Eliot makes a brilliant reversal of the meaning of the word "annunciation." In the final lines of the first and third stanzas "annunciation" means the announcement of death, but here in capitalized form it has been transformed to mean the announcement of the Incarnation, the joining of human and divine, and thus salvation from sterile death.

In the second passage of Section II Eliot uses prose-like rhythms and plain language in contrast to the elaborate and difficult sestina form of the first passage. Yet his theme remains basically the same as he meditates on the permanence of agony and death in man's life. Overall he considers what is permanent in the flux of time and presents three constant elements: moments of happiness, moments of agony, and death. In the first twelve lines the speaker states rather straightforwardly that the "moments of happiness" and "the sudden illumination[s]" that occur in human life give ecstatic significance to it:

> We had the experience but missed the meaning,
> And approach to the meaning restores the experience
> In a different form, beyond any meaning
> We can assign to happiness.

However, the remaining twenty-seven lines of the passage deal with the permanence of the negative elements, suffering, sin, and death. The "backward half-look/Over the shoulder, towards the primitive terror" I take to refer to the terror of death, always stalking man. ("But at my back I always hear/ Time's wingèd chariot hurrying near.") This is a permanent fear, and "the moments of agony" of daily living

> are likewise permanent
> With such permanence as time has. . . .
> People change, and smile: but the agony abides.

Eliot then returns to the settings of the Mississippi River and the Dry Salvages to symbolize the constancy of death in the human experience. The Mississippi River is pictured during a destructive flood, when it bears evidence of its destruction:

> Time the destroyer is time the preserver,
> Like the river with its cargo of dead Negroes, cows and chicken
>   coops,
> The bitter apple and the bite in the apple.

The word "cargo" is used ironically here; at most times the Mississippi bears cargo in the sense of the merchandise or goods transported on her by boat, but during a flood the river carries its own merchandise of drowned human and animal bodies and fragments of destroyed property. "The bitter apple and the bite in the apple" allude, of course, to Adam's cursing man with the bitterness of death by eating of the forbidden fruit in the Garden of Eden. Simultaneously, the river symbol works on another level, for, it seems to me, it also represents the sin or evil that is permanent in man. Like the collective history of mankind as well as the personal histories of individual men, the river destroys (sins) and then preserves the evidence of that evil. The allusion to the apple on this level suggests original sin from which humanity cannot escape, while the "cargo of dead Negroes, cows and chicken coops" indicates the daily, individual sins of individual men.[62]

The passage closes with the description of the treacherous "ragged rock in the restless waters" of life. It is highly significant, though rarely pointed out, that this is the rocky shelf of the poem's title, a fact necessary for valid interpretation of its symbolism. While this rock has been interpreted by several critics to be symbolic of "good," eternal stability, even Christ, a knowledge of its actual geographic location and history (as described earlier) as well as a close reading of the lines themselves reveals its sinister and negative symbolism. The fact that it is "ragged," meaning jagged, sharp, and dangerous, suggests its malign nature. Further, it is deceptive, seeming to be totally harmless, as on a clear "halcyon day" or "in navigable weather" when it is "a seamark/To lay a course by." Even more treacherous, it can be hidden: "Waves wash over it, fogs conceal it. . . ." However, despite its benign appearance or "disappearance," the ragged rock is violently destructive, death itself: "but in the sombre season/Or the sudden fury, is what it always was." In reality, this New England rock cluster, significantly called "les trois *sauvages*" (italics mine) in the epigraph, caused many a shipwreck; symbolically, it is the death agony which wrecks and destroys every man's existence. It does represent permanance, but it is the negative permanence of death. Thus the two landscapes of the Mississippi River and the rocky Dry Salvages are used to symbolize the permanent agony of sin and death in man's time.

Section III is based on the sacred Indian poem *The Bhagavad-Gita,* in which Krishna tells Arjuna that the way to salvation is through action in the *present,* completely free of selfish, personal motives. Among other symbols, Eliot uses the settings of a train and an ocean liner to suggest human time conceived of as wholly present, with neither past nor future:

> Fare forward, travellers! not escaping from the past
> Into different lives, or into any future;
> You are not the same people who left that station
> Or who will arrive at any terminus,
> While the narrowing rails slide together behind you;
> And on the deck of the drumming liner
> Watching the furrow that widens behind you,
> You shall not think "the past is finshed"
> Or "the future is before us."

The concrete images of the railroad tracks and the ship's wake receding into the distance, while still being parts of train and ship, become symbols of the past connected to the present, while the traveller of course represents man voyaging through life. The points of departure and the destinations (whether train stations or harbors) indicate past and future with the voyager forced to exist solely in the present. To make clock time meaningful, man must live totally in the present moment, conducting himself as if it were the only moment:

> "You can receive this: 'on whatever sphere of being
> The mind of a man may be intent
> At the time of death'—that is the one action
> (And the time of death is every moment)
> That shall fructify in the lives of others:
> And do not think of the fruit of action."

The section ends with an address to all men symbolized as Gloucester fishermen, both those who safely return to the harbor after a fishing trip and those who meet death at sea. The speaker admonishes us through the words of Krishna that our "real destination" is to live unselfishly in the present:

> "O voyagers, O seamen,
> You who come to port, and you whose bodies
> Will suffer the trial and judgement of the sea,
> Or whatever event, this is your real destination."
> So Krishna, as when he admonished Arjuna
> On the field of battle.
> > Not fare well,
> But fare forward, voyagers.

Section IV is a lyrical prayer to the Virgin. It is a prayer not only for fishermen and their families but for all men, for all sojourners in time. Again the themes of the danger, suffering, and death in the human experience are sounded. There are two uses of landscape here, one indirect and the other direct. The literal setting is indirectly evoked in the first line, "Lady, whose shrine stands on the promontory," and it is significant in establishing the complex symbolism of the Virgin in the passage. While Eliot is calling upon several traditional associations, the Virgin as a symbol of the timeless taking the temporal unto itself ("Figlia del tuo figlio"), as Mater Dolorosa, as the "Queen of heaven," he is also setting up a more specific association linked to the Cape Ann environment. As pointed out earlier, the shrine on the promontory is Our Lady of Good Voyage Church high on a hill overlooking Gloucester Harbor. The Virgin of this church is the patroness of the Gloucester fishermen, their protectress and guardian. (It should be remembered that these fishermen function in the poem as symbols for all mankind.) Thus she has a special concern for all those associated with fishing, and it is appropriate that the speaker make his prayer for the men and their families to her. He asks first of all for protection:

> Pray for all those who are in ships, those
> Whose business has to do with fish, and
> Those concerned with every lawful traffic
> And those who conduct them.

Then he asks for consolation for grieving widows and mothers:

> Repeat a prayer also on behalf of
> Women who have seen their sons or husbands
> Setting forth, and not returning. . . .

Finally, he petitions for peace and comfort for those killed at sea. In this stanza three brief and generalized seascapes serve as places of death, recalling similar settings in Sections I and II:

> Also pray for those who were in ships, and
> Ended their voyage on the sand, in the sea's lips
> Or in the dark throat which will not reject them
> Or wherever cannot reach them the sound of the sea bell's
> Perpetual angelus.

The metaphor of the sea as a devouring mouth is echoed from Section I, "The distant rote in the granite teeth," while the allusion to the sand reminds us of Section II's desolate "bone on the beach." The final words of the prayer evoke the ringing of the bell buoy: "the sound of the sea bell's/Perpetual angelus." Earlier in the poem Eliot uses the clanging bell as a symbol of death, a funeral bell. Here, however, it functions as a symbol of the Incarnation, being associated with the Roman Catholic Angelus, the bell rung at morning, noon, and night to announce the devotional prayer commemorating the Annunciation. The bell buoy thus suggests the possibility of redemption from the suffering and death inherent in human life.

In Section V Eliot makes no use of the symbolism of the New England coast which has dominated the poem, and there is only an oblique reference to the river. These have been for the most part representative of man's suffering and mortality; since in this section Eliot emphasizes man's redemption from his sorrows, he perhaps felt that a corresponding shift to settings symbolic of joy and fulfillment was necessary. This section embraces at its core the mystery of the Incarnation, the point toward which the poetry as a whole has been moving. Yet the passage begins, significantly, in the wasteland world of time where men rely on magic, superstition, and psychology rather than religion to solve the enigma of time and life. The catalogue of varied methods used to pry into the past and the future, thus avoiding the present altogether, includes science fiction, seances, fantasy, astrology, horoscopes, analysis of handwriting, fortune-telling by reading palms, tea leaves, or playing cards (the Tarot pack), drugs, and Freudian psychology. Each is represented by a concrete image (palm reading, for example, is "[to] evoke/Biography from the wrinkles of the palm/And tragedy from fingers"), and all are summed up by the lines, "To explore the womb, or tomb, or dreams; all these are usual/ Pastimes and drugs, and features of the press." To suggest the universality in both time and space of these secular devices, Eliot utilizes two settings. The general "shores of Asia" with overtones of ancient times evoke the Eastern cultures. In contrast, the specific reference to London's Edgeware Road indicates modern European civilization. Bodelsen suggests that Eliot chose this particular street because "it appears to him to epitomise some of the features of modern commercial civilization: a heavily trafficked street with ugly architecture and cheap shops and restaurants."[63] While on the surface these two cultures are diametrically opposed, Eliot reveals that underneath they employ the same useless methods to find significance in life: "Men's curiosity searches past and future/And clings to that dimension."

Eliot now turns to what *will* render human existence meaningful, "The point of intersection of the timeless/With time." While the saint may attain the ultimate vision of God, ordinary men have only sudden moments of illumination which point to, which hint at, the Ultimate Illumination. In "Burnt Norton" Eliot employed the rose garden experience to symbolize a lesser incarnation pointing to the Incarnation; here he uses several elements of an unidentified natural landscape and a musical concert as symbols of these revelatory moments, which are symbols themselves of the Incarnation:

> For most of us, there is only the unattended
> Moment, the moment in and out of time,
> The distraction fit, lost in a shaft of sunlight,
> The wild thyme unseen, or the winter lightning
> Or the waterfall, or music heard so deeply
> That it is not heard at all, but you are the music
> While the music lasts.

This setting, which recalls scenes from the other Quartets, catches up in physical terms the qualities of ecstatic spiritual experience: the warmth and dazzling light of the sunshine ("And the pool was filled with water out of sunlight," "Sudden in a shaft of sunlight," "Burnt Norton," I and V, "The brief sun flames the ice," "Little Gidding," I); the freshness and fragrance of wild thyme ("The wild thyme unseen," "East Coker," III); the sudden brilliance of winter lightning ("and winter lightning," "East Coker," III); and the clear beauty, the coolness, and the musical sound of the waterfall ("Whisper of running streams," "East Coker," III, "At the source of the longest river/The voice of the hidden waterfall," "Little Gidding," V). The music of the concert room, evocative of timelessness and harmony, also recalls the "unheard music hidden in the shrubbery" in the rose garden of Burnt Norton. Eliot has taken archetypal symbols of fertility and life—light, water, green plants, music—and has made them particular and concrete. Thus they carry their universal connotations, but they gain added impact and increased powers of communication through their realism, fresh originality, and vitality. These symbols have all the weight and authority of traditional meaning as well as the vigor and freshness of newly created significance. They are hints, or emblems, of Christ's Incarnation:

> These are only hints and guesses,
> Hints followed by guesses; and the rest
> Is prayer, observance, discipline, thought and action.
> The hint half guessed, the gift half understood, is Incarnation.

The brief moments of ecstatic illumination provide man with evidence of the Incarnation; the rest of his time is then devoted to the less spectacular, more difficult daily pursuit of spiritual fulfillment through "prayer, observance, discipline, thought and action."

For those who attain this goal, "the past and future/Are conquered, and reconciled" and their lives are lived in a meaningful present. Always a realist, the poet admits that this goal is almost impossible for ordinary men to reach; yet he asserts that the very effort to attain union with the timeless is valuable in itself:

> For most of us, this is the aim
> Never here to be realised;
> Who are only undefeated
> Because we have gone on trying;
> We, content at the last
> If our temporal reversion nourish
> (Not too far from the yew-tree)
> The life of significant soil.

The last lines contain two implicit landscape symbols. One is the yew tree of a churchyard cemetery. Here, in opposition to "Burnt Norton," IV, the evergreen tree suggests spiritual rebirth at the close of a fruitful life. The other landscape is found in the reference to "significant soil," which evokes the fertile, abundant land of a fulfilled soul. It is in direct contrast to the barren, unproductive wasteland of the empty, defiled soul which has been seen so often in Eliot's poetry and which will appear a final time in the allusion to the "parched, eviscerate soil" in "Little Gidding."

Thus Eliot's brilliant symbolic use of river, sea, and rock to suggest the agony of decay and death in the first four sections of the poem gives way in the fifth section to a masterful blending of urban and natural settings which point to the Incarnation as the ultimate significance for human life.

"Little Gidding," a poem of gathering together, of reconciliation, of transformation, is the culmination of Eliot's quest for meaning. Like most of the masterpieces of literature, Eliot's poetry as a whole and *Four Quartets* particularly offer us a significant way of living on earth. This final poem of the *Quartets* is especially concerned to show that one must combine the ecstatic joy of the transitory moment out of time with the spiritual effort of the countless moments in time. For this reason, Eliot's choice of the landscape of Little Gidding is an especially happy one, for the place symbolizes both the ecstasy and the disciplined work of the meaningful spiritual life. The latter quality is inherent in Little Gidding's historical past. This remote Huntingdonshire village is the site of a religious community founded by Nicholas Ferrar in 1625. Ferrar's ideal was to lead an ordered life of devotion and good works similar to the life in a Catholic monastery or nunnery. With discipline and prayer as the focus of daily routine, the chapel was the center of the community. In Shorthouse's novel, *John Inglesant*, there are several passages which admirably set forth the quality of life at Little Gidding:

> This was Mr. Nicholas Ferrar, who had founded a religious house at Little Gidding, in Huntingdonshire, or, as it was called in the world, the "Protestant Nunnery," in which he lived with his mother and several nephews and nieces, in the practice of good works and the worship of God.
>
> . . . For his own part, he said he had adopted that manner of life through having long seen enough of the manners and vanities of the world; and holding them in low esteem, was resolved to spend the best of his life in mortifications and devotion, in charity, and in constant preparation for death.
>
> . . . [Little Gidding] was a solitary, wooded place, with a large manor house, and a little Church close by. It had been for some time depopulated, and there were no cottages nor houses near. The manor house and Church had been restored to perfect order by Mr. Ferrar, and Inglesant reached it through a grove of trees planted in walks, with latticed paths and gardens on both sides. A brook crossed the road at the foot of the gentle ascent on which the house was built.

. . . The family proceeded to Church in procession, Mr. Ferrar and Inglesant walking first. The Church was kept in great order, the altar being placed upon a raised platform at the east end, and covered with tapestry stretching over the floor all round it, and adorned with plate and tapers. . . . The Church was very sweet, being decked with flowers and herbs; and the soft autumn light rested over it. . . . The whole scene, strange and romantic as it appeared to him, the devout and serious manner of the worshippers—very different from much that was common in churches at that day—and the abstracted and devout look upon the faces of the girls struck his fancy.[64]

Thus, as Bradbrook suggests, Little Gidding is "perhaps the most perfect example of that exquisite blend of piety, learning, decency, and comeliness of life which distinguished the religious life of the 17th century at its best."[65]

Additional historical events connected with the place deepen its significance even further. It was visited by the meditative poet, George Herbert; more important, King Charles, who had come to Little Gidding in 1633 and 1642, took refuge there after his defeat at Naseby in 1646. Quoting his last sentence from Carter's *Life of Nicholas Ferrar,* Preston describes Charles's last visit: "He had been to [Little Gidding's] religious house before . . . , and in his desolation he remembered the peaceful hours he had spent there. 'Very privately, in the darkness of night, he came once more to Gidding.' "[66] As a place of sanctuary, it stands for serenity and peace. Finally, the community and the chapel itself were destroyed by Cromwell's troops in 1647. Thus, while being a place of religious effort and of union with the timeless, it is at the same time firmly enmeshed in the turbulence of man's historical time.

On another level Little Gidding is symbolic of the moment of ecstasy, and this quality seems to come mainly from Eliot's personal experience. On May 25, 1936 in the company of Dr. H. F. Stewart, Eliot visited the chapel, which had been restored in 1714 and again in 1853,[67] and it is plausible to suppose that the mystical experience described by the protagonist in Section I had its roots in that visit. Eliot's description of the site is certainly quite accurate:

> It would be the same, when you leave the rough road
> And turn behind the pig-sty to the dull façade
> And the tombstone.

Little Gidding was at the time of Eliot's visit (and still is today) a tiny village made up of a farmhouse, a few cottages, and the chapel in the countryside of Huntingdonshire. It is remote and isolated, the closest villages (Great Gidding, Alconbury, Hamerton, and Sawtry) also being small communities. A narrow, rough country lane leads to the farmhouse and the adjoining chapel, and one must go through the farmyard ("turn behind the pig-sty") and across a field to reach the chapel which is in a clearing in a grove of tall shade trees. It is quite small (approximately sixty feet long by seventeen feet wide), and its exterior is plain and unimpressive. The sides and back are of red brick, while the façade is of dull gray stone. To the right are numerous tombstones, and a little pond is at the bottom of the hill. Before the door is the raised, gray stone tomb of Nicholas Ferrar (1592–1637), referred to in the poem as "the tombstone." An inscription over the door reads, "This is none other but the house of God and the gate of heaven." The interior of the chapel is warm and intimate, the pews, walls, and the barrel-vaulted ceiling being of richly colored wood and the font, eagle lectern, chandelier, and candle holders being of gleaming brass. Much of the décor, including the font and the lectern, dates from 1625.

Thus the symbol is complex both in its sources and in its meanings, for it combines the personal and the general, the present and the past, the discipline of devotion and the ecstasy of revelation.

Section I begins with a passage describing a moment out of time on the road leading to the restored chapel of Little Gidding. The experience is complex and is composed of three elements: the actual landscape, the symbolism of that landscape, and the emotional/spiritual response of the protagonist as he perceives both aspects of the setting. Beginning with the first element, the details reveal that it is a rural setting in winter; the ground is "sodden" and muddy, "pond and ditches" are covered with ice or frost, leafless bushes are white with snow, and a freezing atmosphere of "windless cold" penetrates all. It seems to be a sterile, desolate, frozen waste land: "There is no earth smell/Or smell of living thing." Yet it is transformed by the piercing rays of the early afternoon sun into an intensely brilliant vision of light and spring:

> When the short day is brightest, with frost and fire,
> The brief sun flames the ice, on pond and ditches,
> In windless cold that is the heart's heat,
> Reflecting in a watery mirror
> A glare that is blindness. . . .
> Now the hedgerow
> Is blanched for an hour with transitory blossom
> Of snow. . . .

The exterior landscape is highly symbolic. It represents the divine intersection of the timeless with time and the transforming power which the supernatural has on the natural. The sunlight symbolizes the love of God which brings rebirth (spring) to the deadened soul (the winter landscape). The outer landscape suggests the inner landscape of the sterile soul being reborn into significant spiritual existence: "glow more intense than blaze of branch, or brazier/Stirs the dumb spirit. . . ." The qualities of this ecstatic timeless moment, which is like that in the rose garden of Burnt Norton, are conveyed through a complex of symbolic details and paradoxes. It is a brief moment in time, "in the early afternoon" in winter on the road to Little Gidding, but also out of time, "Suspended in time," "not in time's covenant." Numerous words suggest the paradox of the unity of time and the timeless. Those indicating the former are "sundown," "short day," "brief sun," "an hour," and "transitory," while those evoking the latter are "Sempiternal," "Suspended in time," "not in time's covenant." Contrasting seasonal images reinforce this paradoxical unification. Literally, the season is winter as evidenced by "Midwinter," "short day," "frost," "ice," "windless cold," "dark time of the year," "freezing," "snow." Symbolically, the soul is in midwinter, sterile, passive, dead. However, as the sun brings light and life to the barren geographical surroundings, so God's love brings a spiritual spring or rebirth to the barren soul. The seasonal images of spring include "spring," "melting," "sap," "spring time," "blossom," "bloom." In addition to the contrasting symbols of time vs. the timeless and winter vs. spring, there are those of heat vs. cold and light vs. dark. The light/heat images symbolize God's love, divine illumination, the timeless, and/or the Holy Spirit, all of which can transform a lifeless soul into a fulfilled one as the sun transforms the bleak winter setting into a brilliant one. These images occur no less than twelve times: "tropic," "brightest," "fire," "sun," "flames," "heat," "glare," "glow," "blaze," "brazier," "fire," and "summer." The reference to "pentecostal fire" recalls the Holy Spirit's descent on the apostles, symbolized as tongues of flame and as a dove: "And there appeared unto them cloven tongues like as of fire" (Acts 2:3). The symbol of fire will appear throughout the poem with varied meanings. The dark/cold imagery is more complex in its symbolism, being negative or positive depending upon the context. The negative images, associated with sterility or mortality, are "frost," "ice," "dark," and "snow." However, these are transformed by the sunlight into things of beauty. The two dark/cold images which seem to have more positive meanings are the "glare that is blindness" and the "windless cold that is the heart's heat." Concerning the latter, since the wind throughout Eliot's poetry has been associated with futility, the absence of wind could be interpreted as a positive sign.

Finally, there is the element of the protagonist's emotional and spiritual involvement in the setting and its symbolism. In opposition to the souls which peopled the early poetry and particularly *The Waste Land,* his soul responds eagerly to the stimulus of the spiritual spring. Indeed, his response echoes that of Chaucer's Canterbury pilgrims: "(So priketh him Nature in hir corages);/Than longen folk to goon on pilgrymages."[68] The flame of divine love kindles his human love: "The brief sun flames the ice . . ./In windless cold that is the *heart's heat* . . ." (italics mine). In addition, two images of the vitality of spring are used to suggest his positive response. The stirrings of new life in the soil provide the image in the line, "And glow more intense than blaze of branch, or brazier,/*Stirs the dumb spirit*" (italics mine). The same image is used in the opening lines of *The Waste Land* ("April is the cruellest month . . . stirring/Dull roots with spring rain"), but there the inhabitants fear and reject it. The first flowing of a tree's sap in springtime serves as the second image of spiritual reawakening: "Between melting and freezing/The soul's sap quivers." The word "quivers" is particularly effective because it suggests the first, tentative trembling movements of life. The use of "sap" is appropriate not only because of its associations with spring but also because it is quite literally the life-bearing element, responsible for health and vigor.

The protagonist's intense experience is, to quote Raymond Preston, "a moment, a condition which seems timeless. It is not 'spring' in time; it is not the awakening of the life of nature. It is a spiritual awakening, an earnest of eternity. . . ."[69] Like the rose garden experience, it is a symbol of the supreme union of time and the timeless. It is, to use Eliot's own metaphor, a spring which points to "the unimaginable/Zero summer" of Christ's Incarnation and the purified soul's individual union with divine love after death.

In the second and third passages, the speaker universalizes his own personal experience, indicating that the chapel holds the same significance for all men in all situations. No matter where one comes from, whether by night or by day, whether in spring or in winter, whether commoner or king, "It would be the same." The broken king who came at night alludes to King Charles who sought sanctuary at Little Gidding after his defeat at Naseby in 1646, and Eliot's own visit to the chapel in May, 1936 is indicated in the lines, "If you came this way in may time, you would find the hedges/White again, in May, with voluptuary sweetness."

These passages involve the reader personally, for the protagonist, addressing him as "you," takes him along the actual road and into the chapel. He describes the unimpressive surroundings quite literally. The "rough road" is lined with hedges, white with snow in winter and with fragrant blossoms in spring. However, to reach the chapel one must leave this road and "turn behind the pig-sty to the dull façade/And the tombstone." The "dull façade" refers to the plain gray stone front of the chapel, and the tombstone is that of Nicholas Ferrar before the front door. The little chapel with its cemetery is firmly mired in the dullness and dirt (the mud suggested by the pig-sty) of everyday living. Yet it holds within itself an access to the timeless:

> And what you thought you came for
> Is only a shell, a husk of meaning
> From which the purpose breaks only when it is fulfilled
> If at all. Either you had no purpose
> Or the purpose is beyond the end you figured
> And is altered in fulfillment.

There are other places like Little Gidding where the world of time touches the infinity of the timeless:

> There are other places
> Which also are the world's end, some at the sea jaws,
> Or over a dark lake, in a desert or a city. . . .

All these places are connected with saints, as Eliot revealed in a letter to his brother.[70] The sea jaws refer to the islands of Iona and Lindisfarne, associated with St. Colomba and St. Cuthbert respectively; the dark lake is Ireland's Glendalough where St. Kevin established a hermitage; the desert alludes to St. Anthony's temptations; and the city is the Padua of the other St. Anthony. The speaker has chosen Little Gidding, associated with the "saint" Nicholas Ferrar, because it is "the nearest, in place and time,/Now and in England."

In the third passage we seem to be inside the chapel, kneeling in one of the pews. After explaining what the visitant does *not* come to do,

> You are not here to verify,
> Instruct yourself, or inform curiosity
> Or carry report,

the poet asserts that he comes to establish communication with the timeless through the spiritual effort of prayer:

> You are here to kneel
> Where prayer has been valid. And prayer is more
> Than an order of words, the conscious occupation
> Of the praying mind, or the sound of the voice praying.
> And what the dead had no speech for, when living,
> They can tell you, being dead: the communication
> Of the dead is tongued with fire beyond the language of the living.
> Here, the *intersection of the timeless moment*
> Is England and nowhere. Never and always (italics mine).

Once again the revelation of eternity is symbolized by fire: "the communication/Of the dead is *tongued with fire*. . ." (italics mine). Thus Little Gidding serves as a brilliant symbol of religious devotion, of spiritual fulfillment, of the union of time and the timeless here on man's earth in very ordinary surroundings.

Section II returns to the decay, disintegration, and death inherent in earthly time. The first passage, composed of three eight-line stanzas with rhyming couplets, describes the final destruction of all man's constructions, of the four elements, of the world itself, in a vision echoing "Gerontion" and "East Coker," II. It is highly significant that these desolate settings recall those of earlier poems. The first is a Tennysonian house, abandoned or destroyed, whose air is choked with dust and ashes:

> Ash on an old man's sleeve
> Is all the ash the burnt roses leave.
> Dust in the air suspended
> Marks the place where a story ended.
> Dust inbreathed was a house—
> The wall, the wainscot and the mouse.

The first four lines may evoke Sir William Kyte, the eighteenth century owner of the country mansion which stood on the site of Burnt Norton. Having ruined his life through licentiousness and alcoholism, he set fire to the house and was himself destroyed in the blaze. An account of the story in *The Gentleman's Magazine* contains the following description: "When [the servants] had broken open [the] door, the flames burst out upon them with such fury, that they were all glad to make their escape out of the house, the principal part of which sumptuous pile was, in a few hours, burnt to the ground, and no other remains of Sir William were found the next morning than the hip-bone and the vertebrae, [the] bones of the back, with two or three keys, and a gold watch, which he had in his pocket."[71] The lines also recall Gerontion and his crumbling rented house as well as the present deserted house of Burnt Norton with "the dust on a bowl of rose leaves." The last two lines allude to the rotting edifice of "East Coker," I:

> Houses live and die: there is a time . . .
> . . . for the wind to break the loosened pane
> And to shake the wainscot where the field-mouse trots
> And to shake the tattered arras woven with a silent motto.

Reinforced by the traditional images of mortality, dust and ashes, all these houses are combined here into one house to symbolize brilliantly the decay of man and of his efforts within time.

The second stanza blends river, sea, and wasteland settings to suggest the destructive capacities of water and earth:

> There are flood and drouth
> Over the eyes and in the mouth,
> Dead water and dead sand
> Contending for the upper hand.
> The parched eviscerate soil
> Gapes at the vanity of toil,
> Laughs without mirth.
> This is the death of earth.

A complex of visual images is created by these lines: images of rotting bodies half buried under desert sands and of drowned bodies floating underwater or washed up on shore. They recall various images of death and dead bodies from earlier poems. Mme. Sosostris's warning to the protagonist in *The Waste Land*, "Fear death by water," culminates in Section IV with the sinister description of the body decomposing beneath the sea. In "The Dry Salvages" both ocean and river waters are death-dealing agents. The ocean itself is "littered with wastage," and the bones of drowned fishermen lie on desolate sandy beaches, "the bone on the beach"; and the flooding Mississippi River carries "its cargo of dead Negroes, cows and chicken coops." The dead sand operates on two levels; it is associated with the beaches of ocean or river, but it also is the sand of the desert. Thus, the "dead sand" and the "parched eviscerate soil" evoke the barren desert of *The Waste Land* and the no-man's land of "The Hollow Men," "This is the dead land/This is cactus land." Both water and earth in these lines from "Little Gidding" and in the earlier poems connote meaningless death and spiritual sterility.

Stanza three begins with a generalized landscape of decay and then focuses on the specific setting of the chapel at Little Gidding. Fire is used here as a negative symbol of destruction and death in opposition to Section I where it represents divine love and spiritual illumination. In the first two lines water and fire overcome the "town, the pasture and the weed." The town suggests, as it has throughout Eliot's poetry, the sterility and corruption of the soul as do the pasture and weed, which recall the urban vacant lots ("Preludes"), rural pastures ("Gerontion"), and open fields ("East Coker") used earlier. The next five lines evoke the chapel after its destruction by Cromwell's soldiers in 1647, although there are also overtones of the city churches damaged by fire and water during the bombing raids on London in World War II:

> Water and fire deride
> The sacrifice that we denied.
> Water and fire shall rot
> The marred foundations we forgot,
> Of sanctuary and choir.

The desecrated chapel functions here as a symbol for humanity's desecration and rejection of religion in general and of Christianity and the Christian church in particular. It suggests the destructive end of man's choosing to live wholly on his own without spiritual values or guidance. As Drew explains it, " 'History' is human experience lived without the framework of a Logos. . . . It is man relying on his own desires and 'whispers,' believing that he can control his own fate. . . ."[72]

The second half of Section II centers on a "disfigured street" in the Kensington district of London[73] just after a World War II bombing raid:

> In the uncertain hour before the morning
>> Near the ending of interminable night
>> At the recurrent end of the unending
> After the dark dove with the flickering tongue
>> Had passed below the horizon of his homing
>> While the dead leaves still rattled on like tin
> Over the asphalt where no other sound was
>> Between three districts whence the smoke arose
>> I met one walking, loitering and hurried. . . .

In the eerie half-light of dawn with smoke arising from the rubble of wartime destruction, the street resembles scenes in Dante's *Inferno*. The metallic sound of dead leaves emphasizes the sudden silence that has fallen with the departure of the last bomber, whose "flickering tongue" of flame (machine-gun fire) continues the image of fire as a destructive element. This sinister setting functions as a symbol of man's destructive capabilities, serving like the *Inferno* as a warning to turn from this way of life. The street also forms the background against which the protagonist, like Dante, meets the "familiar compound ghost" who reveals to him the results of man's living for self alone, without God. This meeting is based primarily on the episode in Canto XV of the *Inferno* where Dante talks with Ser Brunetto Latino, a scholar and writer whose works (the prose *Livre dou Tresor* and the poetic *Tesoretta*) had greatly influenced Dante. In addressing him with gratitude and affection, Dante reveals his admiration of Brunetto as a man and a literary figure:

[Y]ou were a radiance among men,

for that sweet image, gentle and paternal,
  you were to me in the world when hour by hour
  you taught me how man makes himself eternal,

lives in my mind, and now strikes to my heart;
  and while I live, the gratitude I owe it
  will speak to men out of my life and art (*Inferno*, XV, 81–87).

That Eliot had this episode in mind is evident from an early handwritten draft of the passage in which line ninety-nine reads, "And heard my voice: 'Are you here, Ser Brunetto?' "[74] Further, in his essay on Dante in *To Criticize the Critic* Eliot says: "Twenty years after writing *The Waste Land*, I wrote, in *Little Gidding*, a passage which is intended to be the nearest equivalent to a canto of the Inferno or the Purgatorio, in style as well as content, that I could achieve. The intention, of course, was the same as with my allusions to Dante in *The Waste Land*: to present to the mind of the reader a parallel, by means of contrast, between the Inferno and the Purgatorio, which Dante visited and a hallucinated scene after an air-raid."[75] In addition, the reference to "the brown baked features" echoes Dante's description of Ser Brunetto as having "baked features" (XV, 26) and a "burnt crust" (XV, 28).[76] Finally, the protagonist indicates a feeling of awe and admiration similar to Dante's in saying that the ghost had "the sudden look of some dead master." Hence it is clear that the ghost primarily symbolizes all those poets who influenced Eliot in the way that Ser Brunetto influenced Dante; this, then, is Eliot's tribute to Dante himself, Yeats, Shakespeare, Pope, Mallarmé, Swift (all of whom are echoed in this passage), Virgil, Milton, Donne, Tennyson, Baudelaire, and many others.

On a secondary level the episode seems partially based on Spencer Brydon's meeting of the ghost of his other self in James's "The Jolly Corner": "He saw, in its great grey glimmering margin, the central vagueness diminish, and he felt it to be taking the very form toward which, for so many days, the passion of his curiosity had yearned. It gloomed, it loomed, it was something, it was somebody, the prodigy of a personal presence. Rigid and conscious, spectral yet human, a man of his own substance and stature waited there to measure himself with his power to dismay. . . . As it came upon him nearer now—the face was the face of a stranger."[77] Thus the ghost seems to be a kind of alter-ego, a double, of the protagonist, or perhaps the protagonist himself as a spirit come back from the dead: " 'In streets I never thought I should revisit/When I left my body on a distant shore.' " Like Brydon's apparition, it is both "intimate and unidentifiable," a part of the speaker and yet separate:

> So I assumed a double part, and cried
> And heard another's voice cry: 'What! Are *you* here?'
> Although we were not. I was still the same,
> Knowing myself yet being someone other—
> And he a face still forming; yet the words sufficed
> To compel the recognition they preceded.

Therefore, the complex ghost seems to be poet in general, Eliot as poet, and all those poets from whom he learned, and man in general, Eliot as man (both as he is and as he may be), and all those men from whom he learned. The core of his message lies in "the gifts reserved for age," the fruits of selfish action; these are the horror of physical dissolution ("the cold friction of expiring sense"), the knowledge of man's endless folly ("the conscious impotence of rage/At human folly"), and the remorse of irrevocable deeds done in the past ("the rending pain of re-enactment/Of all that you have done, and been"). The only means by which to avoid this sterile and bitter ending of life is that of purgatorial cleansing. In Yeatsian phraseology (echoing and contrasting the Yeatsian "impotence of rage" of line 136) the ghost admonishes the protagonist to submit to the refining fire:

> From wrong to wrong the exasperated spirit
> Proceeds, unless restored by that refining fire
> Where you must move in measure, like a dancer.

Here fire is used in a positive sense as a purifying agent, a reversal of its symbolism in the preceding parts of Section II. It specifically recalls the purgatorial flames of Yeat's "Byzantium" as well as those of Canto XXVI of Dante's *Purgatorio* where Arnaut Daniel leaps willingly back into the fires which purge his sins. The vision ends as the ghost fades away at the sound of the all-clear siren, recalling the ghost of Old Hamlet ("It faded on the crowing of the cock") who also exhorted his listener to positive action. The protagonist finds himself alone in the débris-strewn street with day breaking, a sunrise perhaps symbolic of renewed hope.

An earlier, and remarkably different, draft of the ghost's speech reveals a much more extensive use of landscape as well as a less negative content. Beginning at line 121, the ghost exhorts the protagonist to "remember rather the essential moments,"[78] both good and bad. Following are several settings, or details of settings, which evoke some particular, personal moments. Most seem to be ecstatic:

> The dark night in the solitary bedroom . . .
> The wild strawberries eaten in the garden
> Remember Poitiers and the Anjou wine.
> The fresh new season's rope, the smell of varnish
> On the clear oar, the drying of the sails. . . .

The first creates a scene of agony and isolation, while the second suggests the joy and sweetness associated with most of Eliot's garden experiences and specifically recalls these lines from "East Coker":

> Whisper of running streams, and winter lightning,
> The wild thyme unseen and *the wild strawberry*,
> The laughter in the garden, echoed ecstasy . . . (italics mine).

While the third is somewhat obscure, evoking only the pleasurable taste of Anjou wine, the fourth recreates the sense of freedom and exhilaration through images from Eliot's own youthful sailing experiences on the New England coast. The last of the speech contains the heart of the message in rather straightforward terms. The ghost says that human life has one constant goal, the eternal love of God; all else is transitory:

> Remember, as you go this dreary round,
> So shall time pass from you. . . .
>
> This is the final gift on earth accorded,
> One soil, one past, one future, in one place
>
> Nor shall the eternal thereby be remoter
> But nearer: seek or seek not, it is here.
> This is the last love on earth. The rest is grace.

Section III, which asserts the power of God's love to overcome sin, evil, and death, employs very little landscape. However, with a minimum of selected details—the "hedgerow," "this place," "a king at nightfall"—Eliot establishes the reader again in the setting of the chapel at Little Gidding. Here in this chapel built by men of dedication, the protagonist has an insight into the unifying love of God and the larger pattern of eternity:

> See, now they vanish,
> The faces and places, with the self which, as it could, loved them,
> To become renewed, transfigured, in another pattern.

The second passage evokes spirits of men of the past who were divided in life, chiefly by war, but are reconciled by God in death, "folded in a single party." They symbolize the imperfect "perfected in death" through the infinite love of God. Both those men dead in past wars and those men dying in the present one ("Why should we celebrate/These dead men more than the dying?") are purged of their sins by the power of God's love:

> And all shall be well and
> All manner of thing shall be well
> By the purification of the motive
> In the ground of our beseeching.

The lyric of Section IV clearly sets forth man's two choices of eternal life or eternal death. Fire is again the major symbol, suggesting on the one hand the positive flames of God's love and of purgation and on the other hand the negative flames of self-love, lust, and ultimately hell itself. The constructive fires are brilliantly juxtaposed to the destructive fires at the close of each stanza. Eliot relies on Christian and Classical symbols associated with fire, neither of which involves setting directly. However, the "dove descending" recalls London during the blitzkreig, and the funeral pyres and fires suggest the landscapes of Dante's Inferno and Purgatory.

In the first stanza Eliot uses a Christian symbol to suggest the terrifying power and intensity of divine love. The German bomber, the "dark dove with the flickering tongue," which in Section II symbolized man's capacities for hatred and destruction, has been transformed by God's love into the pentecostal dove of the Holy Spirit:

> The dove descending breaks the air
> With flame of incandescent terror
> Of which the tongues declare
> The one discharge from sin and error.

As he has done throughout "Little Gidding," Eliot uses words associated with light and heat to convey the qualities of spiritual illumination; "flame" and "incandescent" suggest a glowing, brilliant, white-hot intensity. In addition, "breaks" and "terror" indicate the powerful, even violent, aspects of that intensity, as does the description of the Holy Spirit as a dive-bomber. Finally, the word "tongues," which has also appeared earlier in the poem (ll. 52 and 82), reinforces the concept of spiritual communication, revelation, insight. "The one discharge from sin and error" is the refining fire of purgation:

> The only hope, or else despair
> Lies in the choice of pyre or pyre—
> To be redeemed from fire by fire.

Man's two choices are symbolized by the two kinds of fire, the negative burning of lust and self-love which leads to the sterile finality of a funeral pyre (an allusion to the Heracles myth in stanza two) or the positive burning of purgatorial fire which leads to union with God. Man's only hope is to be redeemed from the fires of self-love by the fires of God's love, a reiteration of the ghost's closing message in Section II.

The second stanza employs the classical symbol of the burning Nessus shirt but transforms it into a Christian symbol of God's love. (Eliot seems to be using Dante's technique of reworking classical characters, places, or symbols into Christian ones.) In the myth the Nessus shirt represents the destructive burning of human passions. Since Heracles could not escape this unbearable torture, he destroyed himself on a funeral pyre. As Eliot describes the terror and intensity of the Holy Spirit in terms of a German dive-bomber in the first stanza, so here he describes the inescapable power of divine love and the pain of purgatorial cleansing in terms of the Nessus shirt:

> Who then devised the torment? Love.
> Love is the unfamiliar Name
> Behind the hands that wove
> The intolerable shirt of flame
> Which human power cannot remove.

The stanza closes with two lines repeating the paradox of man's alternatives, the fire of purgation and eternal life in paradise or the fire of self and eternal death in hell: "We only live, only suspire/Consumed by either fire or fire." Man himself must choose to love God or to love self, to achieve intense union with the timeless or to sigh ("suspire") with the damned souls of the Inferno.

In the fifth movement, *Four Quartets* comes full circle, arriving at the beginning (the Garden of Eden) which is the end of meaningful human existence, the end toward which the aspiring soul struggles. It is also the end of Eliot's quest for the meaning behind experience, a quest which has involved the whole of his poetry. Significantly he uses two major landscape symbols to convey the qualities of this spiritual end, the chapel with its connotations of devotion and discipline and the garden with its associations of love, purity, and ecstasy.

The section opens with a meditation on beginnings and endings, exploring this theme first in the realm of art and then in terms of human life and death. Every success in artistic creation ("every phrase/And sentence that is right") is both an end and a beginning. Similarly, every action in man's life is a movement toward death, which is both an end and a beginning. Characteristically, Eliot suggests man's inevitable death through four details, two of which are landscapes:

> And any action
> Is a step to the block, to the fire, down the sea's throat
> Or to an illegible stone: and that is where we start.

Each detail evokes death in a specific Quartet: "the block" ("scaffold" in an earlier draft)[79] returns us to Section III of "Little Gidding"; "the fire," in addition to being a means of death in Sections II and IV of "Little Gidding," also recalls the burning of the original house at Burnt Norton; "down the sea's throat" suggests not only all of "The Dry Salvages" but the specific lines in Section IV which allude to drowned fishermen, "pray for those . . . in the sea's lips/Or in the dark throat which will not reject them"; and "an illegible stone" refers to the "old stones that cannot be deciphered" in the graveyard of St. Michael's Church in East Coker. Although these deaths seem to be sterile and sinister endings, they are transformed into beginnings by the love of God:

> We die with the dying:
> See, they depart, and we go with them.
> We are born with the dead:
> See, they return, and bring us with them.

Eliot echoes here the earlier lines in Section III,

> See, now they vanish,
> The faces and places, with the self . . .
> To become renewed, transfigured, in another pattern.

The poet now re-locates the protagonist inside the chapel of Little Gidding on the winter afternoon of his visit for a moment of ecstatic insight:

> The moment of the rose and the moment of the yew-tree
> Are of equal duration. A people without history
> Is not redeemed from time, for history is a pattern
> Of timeless moments. So, while the light fails
> On a winter's afternoon, in a secluded chapel
> History is now and England.

The first sentence is somewhat ambiguous and has been interpreted in several ways. If we take the rose to represent human life or time (literally the rose lasts for only a short period of time) and the yew to represent eternal life or the timeless (literally the yew endures for hundreds of years), then the protagonist is equating life and afterlife. This interpretation is weak and unconvincing; however, a more satisfactory explication follows. Throughout Eliot's poetry, and particularly in the *Quartets,* the rose has been associated with the ecstatic experience of timelessness within time, and in several poems (for example, "Ash Wednesday" and "East Coker") the yew has been associated with eternal life or the experience of timelessness in the timeless. What the protagonist seems to be saying is that the timeless has the same value whether experienced briefly in time or in its absolute, ultimate form. It is not a part of sequential time and cannot be judged in conventional terms of "duration." It is what gives significance to the human experience of life and death:

> A people without history
> Is not redeemed from time, for history is a pattern
> Of timeless moments.

With this definition of history, Eliot replaces Emerson's inadequate definition which was refuted in "Sweeney Erect":

> (The lengthened shadow of a man
> Is history, said Emerson
> Who had not seen the silhouette
> Of Sweeney straddled in the sun.)

If man himself were the sum total of human history, it would be meaningless. Thus the protagonist's discovery here at the end of "Little Gidding" culminates Eliot's poetic search for what can give value to mankind's existence. Amid the rushing tumult of time, suggested by the dying light of late afternoon, by the dead season of the year, and by the secluded chapel once desecrated and abandoned, comes the significant timeless moment manifesting God's love: "With the drawing of this Love and the voice of this Calling. . . ."[80]

The second passage presents a garden setting, symbolic of the state of innocence and joy which the soul attains through the agony of effort and the suffering of purgation:

> We shall not cease from exploration
> And the end of all our exploring
> Will be to arrive where we started
> And know the place for the first time.
> Through the unknown, remembered gate
> When the last of earth left to discover
> Is that which was the beginning;
> At the source of the longest river
> The voice of the hidden waterfall
> And the children in the apple-tree. . . .

The place "where we started" is meant to suggest several gardens: the rose garden of Burnt Norton with which we started the *Quartets*, the Garden of Eden where mankind in general started, and the garden of childhood innocence where each individual human being begins. Most important, however, for the protagonist as a sinner seeking redemption is the garden evoked by the phrase, "the *end* of all our exploring": the Garden of Eden at the top of Dante's Mount of Purgatory, symbolic of spiritual purity regained through purgatorial suffering. Each detail of the setting reveals an element of spiritual bliss. The "unknown, remembered gate" suggests the privacy and security of this walled enclosure as well as the idea of beginning or entering. That the gate is familiar, "remembered," implies the innocence of Adam and of the child ("that which was the beginning"); that it is "unknown" reflects man's present fallen condition (he has not been in the garden for a long time). It also recalls the gate of the rose garden in "Burnt Norton," "Through the first gate,/Into our first world," and thereby the ecstasy of the timeless moment. Finally, it may perhaps allude to the inscription over the front door of the actual chapel: 'This is none other but the house of God and the *gate of heaven*" (italics mine). The "longest river" seems to have two functions. First, as a symbol of human history or individual human lives, it locates the garden in time. The garden is "at the source of the longest river," and therefore at the beginning of human history in general and of each human life in particular. Second, in conjunction with the "hidden waterfall" it carries connotations of freshness, rebirth, and fertility.[81] The children in the apple tree are symbolic of the joy and innocence of this condition of the soul, having carried these meanings in "Marina" ("Whispers and small laughter between leaves"), in "New Hampshire" ("Children's voices in the orchard/Between the blossom- and the fruit-time"), and in "Burnt Norton" ("The leaves were full of children,/Hidden excitedly, containing laughter," and "There rises the hidden laughter/Of children in the foliage"). Visions of this garden are given to man in brief moments of timelessness: "heard, half-heard, in the stillness/Between two waves of the sea." The garden with its gate, its river and waterfall, its children, and its apple trees is one of Eliot's most significant symbols, being the means by which he expresses the qualities of spiritual fulfillment. And that spiritual fulfillment, which gives meaning, purpose, and direction to human life and death, is without question the climactic point toward which the poetry as a whole has been moving.

Eliot closes the poem and the *Four Quartets* with a brilliant and ecstatic vision:

> All manner of thing shall be well
> When the tongues of flame are in-folded
> Into the crowned knot of fire
> And the fire and the rose are one.

The details of the vision are symbolic of majesty ("crowned"), of intense love ("tongues of flame," "fire"), and of unity ("in-folded," "knot," "one"). Concerning the latter, George Williamson notes that the "crowned knot" is a nautical term for a knot whose strands are interwoven so that they cannot become untwisted.[82] The symbolism of the fire and the rose is complex and inclusive. On one level, it recalls Dante's vision of the Godhead as a golden light at the center of a white rose:

> the gold of the eternal rose,
> Whose gradual leaves, unfolding, fragrantly
> Extol that Sun which spring for aye bestows. . .
> (*Paradise,* XXX, 124–6).

The rose in medieval literature was the symbol of mortal love, but Dante transformed it into the symbol of divine love. Its whiteness, of course, conveyed purity. The brilliant light represented the glory and power of God as well as absolute Good: "Light I beheld which as a river flowed,/Fulgid with splendor" (*Paradise,* XXX, 61–2). In "Little Gidding," then, the fire and the rose reflect the very essence of God—his intensity or power and his love or goodness. On another level, they symbolize the union of human love (the rose) and divine love (the fire), suggesting the union after death of individual human souls with the Divine as well as the fusion of both human and divine in the Godhead itself. Concerning the latter, Sayers points out in her notes on Dante's vision in Canto XXXIII that he perceives the dual nature of God: "By a flash of insight, or by an instantaneous participation of the bliss of souls in Heaven, Dante understands how the human and the divine are joined in God. To the souls who see Him in His essence, this union is self-evident as axiomatic truth."[83] On a third and final level, the rose has served in *Four Quartets* as a symbol of the ecstatic revelation of timelessness within time and the fire as a symbol of the timeless itself. The closing line would then also indicate the ultimate blending of time and the timeless in two ways. First, Christ himself is the supreme manifestation of the timeless entering into and merging with time. Second, as the culmination of the brief experiences of timelessness on earth, man at his death is taken into and becomes a part of eternity.

Thus, the poem closes with an assurance that "all shall be well" followed by a climactic vision revealing the union of human love and divine love, mortality and immortality, time and the timeless. "Little Gidding" is, as John Hayward said in a letter to Frank Morley, "a fine confirmation of the old tag—*finis coronat opus.*"[84] It is significant that Eliot wrote no more serious poetry after "Little Gidding," for with its completion he ended his quest successfully.

Four Quartets stands as the climax of Eliot's poetic creation both thematically and technically. Certainly, this work marks the high point in his use of landscape symbolism. With consummate artistry, he has taken four little-known settings from his own experience and forged them into extremely effective symbols which convey highly complex and highly elusive ideas and emotions. These brilliant landscape symbols are one of the means by which he attains that poetic accomplishment which he felt to be the ultimate goal of the poet. As he himself expresses it, "the poet . . . [has] the obligation to explore, to find words for the inarticulate, to capture those feelings which people can hardly even feel. . . . The task of the poet [is] making people comprehend the incomprehensible. . . ."[85]

Conclusion

This study has shown the importance and the complexity of landscape in Eliot's poetry. While time has long been recognized, and analyzed, as a significant element, place has been largely overlooked. Yet I contend not only that Eliot's settings give great reality to his works but also that they provide the central symbol of his poetry as a whole, that they lie at the very center of his poetic craft. In his use of settings Eliot merges the traditions of landscape poetry with his individual talent so that while he is a landscape poet he is unusually original, provocative, and exciting. Indeed, he has given a new meaning to the term "landscape poetry" and has opened new and unexplored uses of landscape.

He has employed, as I have shown, settings of every kind, urban as well as rural, interior as well as exterior, imaginary as well as actual, personal as well as traditional, obscure as well as familiar. In his early poetry the urban scene is of greatest importance. His sources are largely American and British cities from his own experience—St. Louis, Boston, and London. He portrays not only their exteriors—their streets, slums, industrial districts—but also their interiors—elegant drawing rooms, sordid flats, the bare rooms of brothels or low class hotels. London is described in the greatest detail. In *The Waste Land* the actual City area and its landmarks, King William Street, the Cannon Street Hotel, the churches of St. Mary Woolnoth and St. Magnus Martyr, London Bridge, Moorgate, are evoked as the central setting; but there are also scenes of the Thames, Richmond and Kew Gardens, an ordinary pub, Greenwich Reach, and the Isle of Dogs. In addition, he has used other great cosmopolitan cities in the early works. Paris is the scene of "Rhapsody on a Windy Night," it furnishes portions of the settings in "Preludes," and it is evoked by the references to Baudelaire in *The Waste Land;* Munich, Vienna, Athens, Jerusalem, Alexandria, Antwerp, Brussels, and Venice appear in several poems.

In the middle and later poetry Eliot shifts to settings predominantly rural and exterior. Rarely are we inside a room or building as we often are in the early poetry. With the exception of the vague reference to "the shores of Asia" in "The Dry Salvages," all these middle and later settings are drawn from his experiences in America and the British Isles. The American landscapes are largely those of his childhood and thus center on New England and St. Louis. From New England he chooses a variety of scenes—Maine's Casco Bay, New Hampshire, the coastal areas of Gloucester and Cape Ann—and a variety of concrete details—grey rock, goldenrod, mist in pine trees, sandy beaches. The muddy and treacherous Mississippi at St. Louis provides him with another major setting. The British landscapes reveal an even greater scope as he ranges from the lush countryside of Somersetshire and Gloucestershire to the plainer region of Huntingdonshire to the rocky crags of Scotland's Glencoe.

Eliot also uses literary or imagined landscapes, often in juxtaposition to the actual ones. The technique can be found in many poems: in "Prufrock" the literal setting of the elegant house is contrasted to an imagined setting beside and in the sea; in *The Waste Land,* landmarks of London abruptly dissolve into the literary setting of the arid desert; and in "Ash Wednesday" the imagined/literary garden and desert are strikingly juxtaposed to the New England coastal scene of Section VI. The whole of "The Hollow Men" takes place in a barren nightmare landscape drawn largely from Dante, and the scenes of "Journey of the Magi" are Biblical. In "Landscapes" and in *Four Quartets* these literary or imagined settings are not used at all, although there are literary echoes and undertones.

Eliot's landscapes also reveal a brilliant balance between the personal and the traditional, the obscure and the familiar. The early poems deal almost exclusively with great cities which are world-famous, while the later poems are based on locations which are small and virtually unknown to the majority of readers. Yet Eliot seems to have chosen the latter carefully in that each is associated with a traditional and thus familiar setting. Burnt Norton, for example, is linked to the garden and the Dry Salvages to the sea. In this way Eliot assures that the settings will possess both the freshness of the unknown and the security of the familiar.

The variety in Eliot's treatment of landscape can be seen in yet another way. In the early poetry and again in the middle and late poetry, there is a development, a movement, from the general and vague to the particular and concrete. In the poems written prior to *The Waste Land,* the city is unspecified; that is, although the details are concrete and exact, it is difficult or impossible to say definitely that a certain city is being described. Sometimes we may have a feeling that a particular city or cities are being evoked, as in "Prufrock" which contains aspects of both Boston and St. Louis or in "Rhapsody on a Windy Night" whose street lamps, "sunless dry geraniums," and "smells of chestnuts in the streets" suggest Paris. However, it is not until *The Waste Land* that Eliot grounds us in the clearly identifiable metropolis of London by references to specific landmarks such as St. Mary Woolnoth and the Cannon Street Hotel. Again in the middle and late poems we find the same kind of development. The former contain for the most part generalized settings so that exact locations cannot be determined with assurance, although occasionally details do suggest specific places. "The Hollow Men" is set in a nightmarish "cactus land"; the landscapes of "Ash Wednesday" are a garden, a desert, a tower stairway, a springtime meadow; and "Journey of the Magi" describes a Biblical temperate valley full of green, growing vegetation. However, in Section VI of "Ash Wednesday" and in "Marina" are striking details of the New England coast. In "Landscapes" Eliot becomes more specific, using the names of particular American, Welsh, and Scottish settings as titles and describing these settings in some detail. Finally, in *Four Quartets* he has moved to highly personal, definite, and obscure locations, again using them as titles and including numerous concrete details in the poems. We are not just in an American state or Welsh town, as in "Landscapes," but at a precise manor house outside the town of Chipping Campden in Gloucestershire or in a tiny chapel in the lonely countryside of Huntingdonshire. Concerning the numerous exact details of the landscapes in these poems, Helen Gardner has commented, "[T]he moment I entered the garden of *Burnt Norton* I recognized it. I felt that if I had been blindfolded and dropped there by helicopter, and the bandage taken off had been asked to say where I was, I should have replied at once that I was in the garden of Eliot's poem. And similarly, as I walked through the streets of Gloucester every detail of *The Dry Salvages* came to life before my eyes."[1]

Even more significant than the varied kinds of landscapes and the varied ways in which Eliot presents them are the functions that they serve. In the past, landscape had been used simply as description or decoration, it had provided a locale for the action or characters, it had consoled the speaker, or it had evoked a mood or atmosphere. The Victorian poets, notably Tennyson, and the French symbolists, notably Baudelaire, had begun to use it as a symbol for human emotions, generally negative ones. Eliot combines some of the traditional functions with some wholly new ones, so that he can again be seen as merging tradition and the individual talent. His landscapes certainly provide precise and realistic locations in which his characters move and speak. This concreteness lends a shocking sense of reality to his poems which involves the reader intimately in them. As noted in the chapter on *The Waste Land*, for example, seeing an actual, familiar place such as the City district of London dissolve abruptly into a sterile desert has a more shattering impact on the reader than if the setting were vague and unspecified. Further, the landscapes evoke moods or atmospheres, as in "Preludes" where the grimy city slums create a feeling of gloom and depression or in "Marina" where the fresh beauty of the New England coast sets a mood of joy and hope. These traditional uses of landscape appear throughout Eliot's poetry.

However, inspired largely by Tennyson's and Baudelaire's innovative uses of landscape, Eliot employs setting as a highly complex symbol for emotional, moral, and spiritual states that are difficult to portray. The physical landscapes become the inner landscapes of mind, heart, and spirit. Thus he is able to communicate the "inapprehensible," the "incomprehensible," with ever-increasing skill and precision as his poetry moves from depictions of man's spiritual and emotional sterility to those of his spiritual and emotional fulfillment, what Eliot himself calls "a satisfaction of the whole being."[2] In his essay on Dante, Eliot points out that "[i]t is apparently easier to accept damnation as poetic material than purgation or beatitude; less is involved that is strange to the modern mind."[3] As he shifts from portrayals of damnation in the early poems to those of purgation in the middle poems and beatitude in the later poems, he relies more and more heavily on landscapes to symbolize these elusive conditions. Urban settings are the dominant symbols for the emptiness of the human experience in the works from "Prufrock" to *The Waste Land*. The dirty streets and dingy buildings of the city slums as well as the elegantly furnished apartments of the well-to-do brilliantly suggest the degraded and futile quality of the modern human soul. The middle poems, however, mark a positive movement toward rebirth and renewal. Corresponding to this thematic shift in emphasis is a change in the landscape symbolism. Rural rather than urban settings are used, as gardens, meadows, streams, and flowers embody the soul's progress toward spiritual revitalization. The series of poems called "Landscapes," an anticipation in miniature of *Four Quartets*, employs country landscapes to symbolize both the purity and the corruption of the soul as it moves through life. The New Hampshire apple orchard, the Welsh countryside, and the Massachusetts sea coast evoke spiritual purity, while the red river of Virginia and the rocky crags of Scotland's Glencoe represent spiritual corruption. Finally, in *Four Quartets* Eliot fuses urban and natural settings to suggest the unending tension between the world of flesh and the world of spirit. Yet the very predominance of the rural and natural (the rose garden, the remote village, the sea coast, the country chapel) indicates the final triumph of the spiritual, and indeed the closing poem is a celebration of that triumph. It is in "Little Gidding" and in "Burnt Norton" that we find Eliot's most brilliant use of landscape to evoke states of intense spiritual illumination which are extremely difficult to communicate. In "Burnt Norton" the rose garden symbolizes the experience of timelessness merging with time, while in "Little Gidding" the wintry, sun-touched landscape surrounding the chapel becomes the landscape of the human soul undergoing an ecstatic spiritual rebirth. It seems to me that in literature only Dante has been as successful as Eliot in presenting these kinds of experiences. And Eliot's success is due in large part to his use of symbolic landscape.

It seems clear that landscape occupies a central position in Eliot's poetry and that any attempt to read his work must come to grips with this important element. In the past many fine critiques, essays, and analyses have barely mentioned or entirely overlooked it, perhaps because so much emphasis was placed on the new and original in his work. Scholars have focused on the literary and historical allusions, on the disjunctive form, on rhythm and diction, those aspects which were most startling, new, and difficult. Landscape, on the other hand, is one of the oldest and most traditional of poetic devices. Yet we have seen that Eliot's genius revitalizes this conventional element by using many new kinds of settings (the modern city and obscure rural areas, for example) and by enlarging its function as a symbol. Thus landscape provides both the sense of the traditional and familiar in his work and the excitement of the original and innovative. It may well be this combination of old and new in his use of landscape that accounts in part for his singular eminence among modernist poets. Landscape grounds the poems firmly in the actual by the use of a particular place and in the traditional, as it is a time-honored device of poetry. Yet in being used freshly and innovatively as a major symbol for intangible states of mind, it is integral to the fundamental meanings, concepts, and philosophy of the works.

The latter point has not often been recognized in Eliot criticism, for landscape has usually been seen simply as a locale for the action based on interesting, but basically irrelevant, outside sources. Thus, perhaps another reason the importance of land-scape has been overlooked is the too strict application of for-malist criticism. This school of thought with its emphasis on the organic elements of a work of art requires that one not look outside the poem in making critical evaluations. Since Eliot's use of landscape involves knowledge of the original geographi-cal sources, a formalist critic would therefore not be likely to concern himself with setting. Other critics would feel obliged to apologize or defend themselves for dealing with it.

Helen Gardner has written an excellent article entitled "The Landscapes of Eliot's Poetry," in which she suggests the impor-tance of place in his work and notes that it is interesting to the reader to know about the actual scenes from which he draws his poetic landscapes. She defends the validity of this kind of interest for the reader, but not for the critic. In fact she agrees that it has nothing to do with critical evaluation and keeps her discussion of the actual locations on a personal, rather than a critical, note: "[T]he sense of place is fundamental to these poems, as fundamental as the sense of time. It is their pro-foundly felt basis. This sense of the actual moves me very deeply in Eliot's poems. It can so easily be lost if we concentrate on his philosophical and religious thought, and his literary sources. At times scholarship seems in danger of turning him into a theorist on the nature of time, or a walking card-index of quotations. It may be simple and naive and retrograde to want to visit the places he lived in, and to indulge in this kind of rambling biographical and geographical annotation. *It has only slight relevance to critical evaluation.* It has, I think, great rele-vance to understanding. *If we think of a poem as a work of art, like a beautiful pot, a structure of meanings and symbols, self-consistent, to be judged for what it is, I would agree that discussion of sources, whether literary or actual, is irrelevant"* (italics mine).[4]

On the contrary, it seems to me that this kind of knowledge has much to do with valid critical interpretation of landscape in Eliot's work. Because landscape functions as a major symbol, lack of knowledge about the actual sources, as well as insuffi-cient or incorrect knowledge, can distort or even reverse its symbolic import. A case in point is the positive interpretations of the ragged rock in "The Dry Salvages" as a symbol of good and virtue. Many of these interpretations arise from lack of knowledge concerning the true nature of the literal rocky shelf called the Dry Salvages located off the coast near Rockport, Massachusetts. Knowledge of the real locations enriches and deepens our understanding of the poems as a whole.

However, even from the point of view of formalist criticism, a case can be made for close analysis of landscape in Eliot's poetry. As a dominant and complex symbol, it is an integral part of the organic whole, of the "structure of meanings and symbols" which is each individual poem as well as the entire body of Eliot's poetry. Indeed, landscape can be seen as *the* major symbolic expression of Eliot's total poetic subject and therefore deserves recognition from any viewpoint as a brilliant and highly complex achievement which lies at the very center of his poetry.

Notes

NOTES TO PREFACE

1. T. S. Eliot, *Selected Essays* (New York: Harcourt, Brace and World, Inc., 1950), pp. 360, 368.
2. Genesius Jones, *Approach to the Purpose: A Study of the Poetry of T. S. Eliot* (New York: Barnes and Noble, 1964), pp. 20–1.
3. Helen Gardner, "The Landscapes of Eliot's Poetry," *Critical Quarterly*, 10 (Winter, 1968), 330.

NOTES TO CHAPTER I

1. Wyndham Lewis, *Blasting and Bombardiering* (Berkeley: University of California Press, 1967), p. 282.
2. Stephen Spender, "Remembering Eliot," *T. S. Eliot: The Man and His Work*, ed. by Allen Tate (New York: Delacorte Press, 1966), pp. 38, 47.
3. W. H. Auden, as quoted by Nevill Coghill, "Sweeney Agonistes," *T. S. Eliot*, ed. by Tambimuttu and Richard March (London: Frank and Cass Co., Ltd., 1965), p. 82.
4. Lewis, *Men Without Art* (New York: Russell and Russell, Inc., 1964), p. 65.
5. Hugh Ross Williamson, *The Poetry of T. S. Eliot* (London: Hodder and Stoughton, 1932), p. 14.
6. See Eliot, "A Prediction in Regard to Three English Authors," *Vanity Fair*, 21 (February, 1924), 29, 98.
7. F. O. Matthiessen, *The Achievement of T. S. Eliot* (New York: Oxford University Press, 1959), p. 82.
8. F. R. Leavis, *New Bearings in English Poetry* (London: Chatto and Windus, Ltd., 1932), p. 25.
9. Structural innovation is an element seen in all fields of modernist art—in Stravinsky's music, Picasso's paintings, and Joyce's novels.
10. Eliot, *Collected Poems: 1909–1962* (New York: Harcourt, Brace and World, Inc., 1963), p. 144. All quotations from the poetry of T. S. Eliot are from this edition unless otherwise indicated.
11. Matthiessen, p. 83; Eliot, "The Three Provincialities," *The Tyro*, No. 2 (Spring, 1922), 13.
12. Matthiessen, p. 88.
13. Eliot, *To Criticize the Critic* (New York: Farrar, Straus and Giroux, 1965), p. 185.
14. Edmund Wilson, *Axel's Castle* (New York: Charles Scribner's Sons, 1931), p. 114.
15. Leavis, pp. 25–6.
16. Eliot, *To Criticize the Critic*, p. 19.
17. Eliot, *On Poetry and Poets* (New York: Farrar, Straus and Cudahy, 1957), p. 295.

18. Eliot, *To Criticize the Critic,* p. 58.
19. Ibid., p. 126.
20. Eliot did, of course, find *some* inspiration for technique and tone in the mainstream of the English tradition. He has often acknowledged the influence of Donne and the metaphysical poets as well as that of the Jacobean dramatists.
21. These three essays are "The Aesthetic Moment in Landscape Poetry," *English Institute Essays,* ed. by Alan Downer (New York: Columbia University Press, 1952), "Tennyson and Picturesque Poetry," *Essays in Criticism,* 1 (July, 1951), 262–82, and "Introduction," *Tennyson: Selected Poetry* (New York: Holt, Rinehart, and Winston, 1956), pp. xiv-xxiv.
22. Frank Kermode, *Romantic Image* (London: Routledge and Kegan Paul, 1957), p. 154.
23. Arthur Symons, as quoted by Kermode, p. 110.
24. Philip Wheelwright, *The Burning Fountain* (Bloomington: Indiana University Press, 1954), p. 19.
25. Eliot, *Selected Essays,* p. 377.
26. Ibid., pp. 124–5.
27. Eliot, as quoted by Matthiessen, p. 56.
28. Eliot, *The Use of Poetry and the Use of Criticism* (Cambridge, Mass.: Harvard University Press, 1933), p. 78.
29. Ibid., p. 148.
30. Eliot, *To Criticize the Critic,* p. 126.
31. Eliot, "A Brief Introduction to the Method of Paul Valéry," Paul Valéry's *Le Serpent* (London: The Criterion, 1924), pp. 12, 14.
32. Eliot, *On Poetry and Poets,* p. 299.
33. Robert Langbaum, *The Poetry of Experience* (New York: W.W. Norton and Co., Inc., 1957), pp. 65–6. Despite extensive searching, I have been unable to find any direct statement by Eliot on the multiple meanings of symbols. But he makes numerous indirect comments as in the essay "The Metaphysical Poets."
34. Elizabeth Drew, *T. S. Eliot: The Design of His Poetry* (New York: Charles Scribner's Sons, 1949), p. 98.
35. Herbert Howarth, *Notes on Some Figures Behind T. S. Eliot* (Boston: Houghton Mifflin Co., 1964), p. 202.
36. Georges Cattaui, *T. S. Eliot,* trans. by Claire Pace and Jean Stewart (New York: Funk and Wagnalls, 1966), p. x. Certainly many other paintings suggested symbolic landscapes to Eliot, but this is a facet of his work yet to be explored.
37. Eliot, "The Influence of Landscape upon the Poet," *Daedalus,* 89 (Spring, 1960), 421–22.
38. Eliot, "Preface," in Edgar A. Mowrer, *This American World* (London: Faber and Gwyer, 1928), p. xiv.
39. Eliot, "The Influence of Landscape upon the Poet," p. 422.
40. Eliot, "Preface," p. xiv.
41. Eliot, "The Influence of Landscape upon the Poet," p. 422.
42. Jay Martin, "T. S. Eliot's *The Waste Land,*" *A Collection of Critical Essays on The Waste Land,* ed. by Jay Martin (Englewood Cliffs, N.J.: Prentice-Hall, Inc., 1967), p. 13.
43. Eliot, *To Criticize the Critic,* pp. 54, 56.
44. Auden, as quoted by McLuhan, "Introduction," p. xiii.
45. Eliot, *Selected Essays,* pp. 288, 291.
46. Harold Nicolson, *Tennyson: Aspects of His Life, Character, and Poetry* (Boston: Houghton Mifflin Co., 1923), p. 237.
47. Alfred Lord Tennyson *The Complete Poetical Works,* ed. by W. J. Rolfe (Cambridge, Mass.: The Riverside Press, 1898), p. 12. All quotations from the poetry of Tennyson are from this edition.
48. Tennyson, as quoted by Joanna Richardson, *The Pre-Eminent Victorian* (London: Jonathan Cape, 1962), p. 34.
49. McLuhan, "Introduction," pp. xv–xvi.

50. McLuhan, "Tennyson and Picturesque Poetry," p. 279.
51. Elizabeth H. Waterston, "Symbolism in Tennyson's Minor Poems," *Critical Essays on the Poetry of Tennyson,* ed. by John Killham (London: Routledge and Kegan Paul, 1960), p. 114.
52. Ibid., p. 116.
53. Valerie Pitt, *Tennyson Laureate* (Toronto: University of Toronto Press, 1963), pp. 41-2.
54. Basil Willey, "Tennyson," *More Nineteenth Century Studies* (New York: Harper and Row, 1956), p. 80.
55. Ibid., p. 94.
56. Jerome Hamilton Buckley, *Tennyson: The Growth of a Poet* (Cambridge, Mass.: Harvard University Press, 1960), p. 173. I owe a general debt to Buckley in my discussion of the *Idylls.*.
57. Robert G. Stange, "Tennyson's Mythology: A Study of Demeter and Persephone," *Critical Essays on the Poetry of Tennyson,* pp. 146–7.
58. Eliot, *Selected Essays,* p. 249.
59. Ibid., p. 377.
60. Martin Turnell, *Baudelaire: A Study of His Poetry* (Norfolk, Connecticut: New Directions, n.d.), p. 162.
61. Tennyson deals almost exclusively with rural landscapes, although in a few instances he uses urban settings as symbols.
62. McLuhan, "Tennyson and Picturesque Poetry," pp. 280, 271.
63. Ibid., p. 281.
64. Turnell, p. 35.
65. McLuhan, "Tennyson and Picturesque Poetry," pp. 281–2.
66. Eliot, *To Criticize the Critic,* pp. 126–7.
67. Eliot, *Selected Essays,* p. 377.
68. Turnell, pp. 89–90.
69. Charles Baudelaire, *Oeuvres Complètes* (Paris: Bibliothèque de la Pléiade, 1961), p. 85. All quotations from the poetry of Baudelaire are from this edition.
70. See "Prufrock," "Preludes," "Mr. Apollinax," and "Sweeney Erect."
71. Sister M. Cecilia Carey, "Baudelaire's Influence in *The Waste Land,*" *Renascence,* 14 (Summer, 1962), 191.
72. Ibid., p. 186.
73. McLuhan, "Tennyson and Picturesque Poetry," p. 271.
74. Denis Donoghue, *The Ordinary Universe* (New York: The Macmillan Company, 1968), p. 103.

NOTES TO CHAPTER II

1. Hugh Kenner, "The Urban Apocalypse," *Eliot in His Time,* ed. by A. Walton Litz (Princeton: Princeton University Press, 1973), p. 27.
2. Drew, p. 33.
3. Grover Smith, *T. S. Eliot's Poetry and Plays: A Study in Sources and Meaning* (Chicago: The University of Chicago Press, 1956), p. 20.
4. Ibid., p. 24.
5. Cleanth Brooks, "T. S. Eliot: Thinker and Artist," *T. S. Eliot: The Man and His Work,* p. 320.
6. Kristian Smidt, *Poetry and Belief in the Work of T. S. Eliot* (Oslo: I Kommisjon Hos Jacob Dybwad, 1949), p. 112.
7. Conrad Aiken, "King Bolo and Others," *T. S. Eliot,* ed. by Tambimuttu and March, pp. 21–2.
8. Leonard Unger, *T. S. Eliot: Moments and Patterns* (Minneapolis: University of Minnesota Press, 1956), p. 20.
9. Kenner, "The Urban Apocalypse," p. 27.

10. Drew, p. 33.
11. While some critics, such as Langbaum, *The Poetry of Experience,* p. 189, see the overwhelming question as merely a sexual one, I feel that this interpretation is too limited and distorts the more devastating meaning which Eliot intended the poem to express. The sexual question is an objective correlative for the larger emotional and spiritual question about the sterility of Prufrock's life as a whole.
12. Eliot remarked in a speech given at the University of Minnesota in 1956 that he had been surprised to learn from a critic that the fog had somehow gotten *into* the drawing room. It is, of course, a part of the exterior urban landscape seen through the windows.
13. Drew, p. 33.
14. Helen Gardner, *The Art of T. S. Eliot* (New York: E. P. Dutton and Co., Inc., 1959), p. 82.
15. Philip Headings, *T. S. Eliot* (New York: Twayne Publishers, Inc., 1964), p. 45.
16. Eliot, *Selected Essays,* p. 342.
17. Eliot's Gerontion seems to be an ironic contrast, both in his personality and in his vision of life's end, to Newman's Gerontius.
18. John Crowe Ransom, "Gerontion," *T. S. Eliot: The Man and His Work,* p. 142.
19. Kenner, *The Invisible Poet: T. S. Eliot* (New York: MacDowell, Obolensky, Inc., 1959), p. 130.
20. Ibid., p. 132.
21. B. Rajan, "The Overwhelming Question," *T. S. Eliot: The Man and His Work,* p. 372.
22. Ibid., p. 373. Although the most common definition of "gulf" is "a large area of sea partially enclosed by land," either of two other definitions seems more appropriate to the violence of the context: "a deep, wide chasm; abyss" or "a whirlpool; an eddy." *The American Heritage Dictionary of the English Language,* 1969.
23. Brooks, "*The Waste Land:* An Analysis," *T. S. Eliot: A Study of His Writings by Several Hands,* ed. by B. Rajan (New York: Haskell House, 1964), p. 34.
24. Kenner, "The Urban Apocalypse," p. 27.
25. In the original manuscript Eliot had written "Königsee" rather than "Starnbergersee." The Königsee" is a small lake just south of Berchtesgaden in the extreme southeast tip of Germany. Perhaps he made the change because the Starnbergersee is quite close to Munich whereas the Königsee is at some distance.
26. Gardner, p. 90.
27. See Eleanor M. Sickels, "Eliot's *The Waste Land,* I, 24–30, and *Ash Wednesday,* IV–VI," *The Explicator,* 9, No. 1 (October, 1950), Item 4.
28. Wheelwright, p. 345.
29. Eliot, "The Death of Saint Narcissus," *Poems Written in Early Youth* (New York: Farrar, Straus and Giroux, 1967), p. 34.
30. Robert A. Day, "The 'City Man' in *The Waste Land:* The Geography of Reminiscence," *PMLA,* 80 (1965), 287.
31. The latter symbolism appears also in "Prufrock" as a yellow fog, in "Portrait of a Lady" as a grey and yellow smoke, in "Preludes" as the "burnt-out ends of smoky days," in "Morning at the Window" as "brown waves of fog," in "Burbank with a Baedeker" as "The smoky candle end of time," and in "Burnt Norton," III, as the "faded air."
32. Northrop Frye, *T. S. Eliot* (New York: Barnes and Noble, 1966), p. 64.
33. Eliot's copy of Baedeker's *London and Its Environs* (1908) is in the collection belonging to King's College, Cambridge. It is signed "Thomas S. Eliot" and is dated October 14, 1910. Many places are marked in pencil, including St. Magnus Martyr, St. Mary Woolnoth, and other City churches.
34. Eliot, *Poèmes: 1910–1930,* trans. by Pierre Leyris, notes by John Hayward (Paris: Editions du Seuil, 1947), note for 11. 63–8. Hayward's notes have been extremely helpful to me and would be, I think, for any nonBritish reader. A draft of these notes is located in the Eliot collection of King's College, Cambridge.

35. Day, p. 287.
36. See Dante's *Inferno,* III, 55–7, and IV, 25–7.
37. Brooks, "T. S. Eliot: Thinker and Artist," p. 325.
38. See E. C. Cook, *London and Environs* (Llangollen: Darlington and Co., n.d.), p. 263.
39. In his notes on *The Waste Land,* Eliot remarks that this dead sound on the stroke of nine is "A phenomenon which I have often noticed," p. 71.
40. Day, p. 289.
41. Ibid., p. 291.
42. In the myth, King Tereus raped his wife's sister Philomela and then cut out her tongue so that she could not reveal his crime. Philomela wove a tapestry depicting her story and sent it to her sister, whereupon the two gained revenge on Tereus and then were transformed into birds.
43. Matthiessen, p. 58.
44. Hayward's notes reveal that "the Thames, above London, from Richmond to Maidenhead and Henley, is a favorite resort for the kind of trippers described in ll. 179–80. . . . Spenser's bridal party has become a 'petting party.' "
45. George Williamson, *A Reader's Guide to T.S. Eliot* (New York: The Noonday Press, 1953), p. 140. In his "London Letter" to *The Dial,* Eliot described "Le Sacre du Printemps" in terms which apply equally well to this section of *The Waste Land;* its music transformed "the rhythm of the steppes into the scream of the motor horn, the rattle of machinery, the grind of wheels, the beating of iron and steel, the roar of the underground railway, and the other barbaric cries of modern life." *The Dial,* 71 (October, 1921), 453.
46. The hotel was destroyed during the bombing raids on London in World War II.
47. Hayward, note for 1. 213.
48. Other indications are his unshaven face (suggesting that he does not need to shave) and the currants (symbolic of shrivelled-up fertility).
49. Hayward, note for 1. 214.
50. Drew, p. 80, and Allen Tate, as quoted by Brooks, *"The Waste Land:* An Analysis," p. 21.
51. Frye, p. 52.
52. The sonnet is set into a long passage, but its form is readily detected. Beginning at line 235 ("The time is now propitious, as he guesses . . .") and ending at line 248 ("And gropes his way, finding the stairs unlit . . ."), it contains three quatrains and a couplet and has a rhyme scheme of abab, cdcd, efef, gg.
53. Sir John Betjeman, *The City of London Churches* (London: Pitkin Pictorials, Ltd., 1972), pp. 20–2.
54. Eliot, "Notes on *The Waste Land,"* p. 73. Eliot's strong feeling for the City churches can be seen in the following excerpt where he argues for their preservation: "To one who, like the present writer, passes his days in this City of London . . . the loss of these towers, to meet the eye down a grimy lane, and of these empty naves, to receive the solitary visitor at noon from the dust and tumult of Lombard Street, will be irreparable. . . ." "London Letter," *The Dial,* 70 (June, 1921), 691.
55. Day, pp. 290–1.
56. Cook, p. 453.
57. Eliot stayed at the Albemarle Hotel, 47 East Esplanade, Cliftonville, Margate.
58. The quotation is Augustine's complete sentence taken from his *Confessions.* The burning motif recalls the title of Section III, "The Fire Sermon." Eliot's note directs the reader to Warren's *Buddhism in Translation:* "All things, O priests, are on fire. . . . And with what are these on fire? With the fire of passion, say I, with the fire of hatred, with the fire of infatuation. . . ."
59. Spender, p. 43; Brooks, *"The Waste Land:* An Analysis," p. 24; Gardner, p. 95; Day, p. 289; Langbaum, "New Modes of Characterization in *The Waste Land," Eliot in His Time,* p. 115; and A. F. Beringause, "Journey through *The Waste Land," South Atlantic Quarterly,* 56 (1957), 87. The sea in Eliot's poetry is a complex symbol,

representing death as well as life, destruction as well as creation, sterility as well as fertility.
60. Gardner, p. 95.
61. Warren French, *The Twenties: Poetry, Fiction, Drama* (Deland, Fla.: Everett–Edwards, 1976), pp. 112–13.
62. *Encyclopedia Britannica*, 1975, I, 479–82, II; 262–69; X, 138–44; and XIX, 115–20.
63. Here is an echo of the destruction of Sodom and Gomorrah.
64. For an opposing view, see Leavis, p. 103.
65. Hugh Ross Williamson, p. 149.
66. Gardner, p. 98.

NOTES TO CHAPTER III

1. Drew, p. 98.
2. See "Portrait of a Lady," "Mr. Apollinax," "Dans le Restaurant," "Mr. Eliot's Sunday Morning Service," and Sections I and V of *The Waste Land*. In addition, the setting of "La Figlia che Piange" could be a garden.
3. Drew, p. 98.
4. A suggestion of coastal New England appears in Section V of *The Waste Land:*

> *Damyata:* The boat responded
> Gaily, to the hand expert with sail and oar
> The sea was calm, your heart would have responded
> Gaily, when invited, beating obedient
> To controlling hands. . . .

Although the setting is not directly identified, it clearly anticipates Eliot's use of the New England shore in his middle and late poetry.
5. Gardner, p. 100.
6. Warren French has suggested that some of the details of the landscape in Sections III–V may come from the American/Mexican Southwest, a locale that does not appear in any of Eliot's other poems. Cactus, particularly the prickly pear native to both North and South America, and tumid rivers are peculiar to this region of the world, and stone images especially suggest Mexico. While Eliot may only be recalling the desert stereotype familiar to him from his American childhood, he is usually quite specific in choosing concrete details from actual landscapes; he possibly visited the Southwest, for he had been to California by 1935 (See note 13, Chapter IV).
7. Dante, *Inferno*, trans. by John Ciardi (New York: The New American Library, 1954), III, 22–23, 29–39. All quotations from Dante's *Inferno* are from this edition.
8. Gardner, p. 111.
9. Joseph Conrad, "Heart of Darkness," *Conrad*, ed. by Morton Dauwen Zabel (New York: The Viking Press, 1947), pp. 497, 536–7.
10. Additional literary overtones are indicated in Eliot's handwritten note at the bottom of a typescript of the poem; the note reads, "Cf. 'The Hollow Land' by Wm. Morris [and] 'The Broken Men' by R. Kipling." This typescript is located in the Eliot Collection of King's College, Cambridge.
11. Although the meaning of death's other kingdom is ambiguous and has been variously interpreted, it seems to function in the poem as a direct contrast to death's dream kingdom. Eliot intended it to signify heaven, the "eyes" being those of God and the heavenly host.
12. *Inferno*, III, 23, 31, 72, 127.
13. For a different interpretation, see M. C. Bradbrook, "T. S. Eliot," *British Writers and Their Work*, ed. by Bonamy Dobree (Lincoln, Neb.: University of Nebraska Press, 1965), p. 21, and E. M. Stephenson, *T. S. Eliot and the Lay Reader* (London: The

Fortune Press, 1944), p. 46. Both critics feel that the reference is to Dante's *Purgatorio.*

14. Bradbrook, p. 21.
15. The figures of the early poems were self-centered and concerned only with self. See Prufrock, Sweeney, Gerontion, the young man in "Portrait of a Lady," and the inhabitants of *The Waste Land.*
16. Headings, p. 73. The original title of the poem, found on the first handwritten draft which now belongs to the Eliot Collection of King's College, Cambridge, was "All aboard for Natchez, Cairo, and St. Louis," indicating a trip on the Mississippi River. This secular title was replaced by the present religious one.
17. Hugh Kenner in *The Invisible Poet* says the source of Eliot's garden may be Tennyson's lines from "The Holy Grail," "But even while I drank the brook, and ate/The goodly apples, all these things at once/Fell into dust . . ." (p. 269). This Tennysonian garden, however, symbolizes the sensual in general, while Eliot's seems more specifically to suggest passionate human love. Thus a better Tennysonian source might be Maud's garden, a refuge and a place of mortal love.
18. For a similar idea, see Chaucer's "Troilus and Criseyde" as well as the "Retraction" of *The Canterbury Tales.*
19. "Hence the soul cannot be possessed of the divine union, until it has divested itself of the love of created beings." This quotation of St. John of the Cross serves as the epigraph to "Sweeney Agonistes" (1926–27) and helps to elucidate the meaning of this third passage. In addition, an earlier draft omits the adjective "blessèd" which, it seems to me, is the source of the confusion concerning the identity of the face: "And I renounce the face/renounce the voice. . . ." This draft is in the collection of King's College, Cambridge.
20. See for example, Frye, p. 74.
21. E. E. Duncan-Jones, "Ash Wednesday," *T. S. Eliot: A Study of His Writings by Several Hands,* pp. 44–5.
22. See "The Love Song of J. Alfred Prufrock," "Portrait of a Lady," "Rhapsody on a Windy Night," "The *Boston Evening Transcript,*" "Burbank with a Baedeker," and *The Waste Land,* II and III.
23. Duncan-Jones, p. 48.
24. Dante, *Purgatory,* trans. by Dorothy Sayers (Baltimore, Md.: Penguin Books, 1955), IV, 32. All quotations from Dante's *Purgatory* are from this edition.
25. See Sayers's diagram of the Mount of Purgatory, p. 62.
26. Matthiessen, p. 67.
27. Stephenson, p. 24.
28. Sayers, p. 18.
29. Eliot, "Preface," Mowrer's *This American World,* p. xiv.
30. An early draft of this passage, now belonging to King's College, Cambridge, does not contain the concrete images of the white sails and the "salt savour of the sandy earth" and seems generally vaguer and less striking.
31. This idea is stated more directly in an earlier version which reads, "Our life is in the world's decease."
32. See "The Love Song of J. Alfred Prufrock," "Rhapsody on a Windy Night," "Mr. Eliot's Sunday Morning Service," *The Waste Land,* and "The Hollow Men."
33. Drew, p. 120.
34. J. E. Cirlot, *A Dictionary of Symbols,* trans. by Jack Sage (New York: Philosophical Library, Inc., 1962), p. 145.
35. Eliot, *The Use of Poetry and the Use of Criticism,* p. 148.
36. Bradbrook, p. 24.
37. Drew, p. 127.
38. Smith, p. 134. Smith notes that Eliot mentioned this specific setting in his original draft.

NOTES TO CHAPTER IV

1. George Williamson, p. 201; Smith, pp. 251-2; Gardner, "The Landscapes of Eliot's Poetry," p. 325; Jones, pp. 269–72; and E. A. Hansen, "T. S. Eliot's 'Landscapes,' " English Studies, 50 (August, 1969), 379.
2. A similar use of these three symbols can be found in Dylan Thomas's "Fern Hill."
3. Children in leaves appear in several other poems as symbols of joyous ecstasy and innocence: "Marina," "Burnt Norton," I and V, and "Little Gidding," V.
4. Diana Steward, "A Contrast of Landscapes: 'Virginia' and 'Usk,' " T. S. Eliot: A Symposium for His Seventieth Birthday, ed. by Neville Braybrooke (New York: Farrar, Straus and Cudahy, 1958), p. 109.
5. This use of the word "still" can be found in several other poems: "Ash Wednesday," V, "Triumphal March," "Difficulties of a Statesman," "Burnt Norton," I, IV, and V, and "Little Gidding," V.
6. Steward, p. 109. Another possible interpretation of the trees is that they are the dogwood (white) and flowering judas (purple) of spring; they would function ironically as symbols of life and rebirth that are rendered sterile by the apathetic soul.
7. The ruins of the Roman walls are no longer visible, and, according to a townsperson in 1973, the site itself would soon be covered by apartment buildings. The castle ruins are now used as an enclosure for two white horses, although part of the land is worked as a garden. The owner of the property very kindly allowed me to look about at my leisure.
8. Eliot also made trips to Wales in 1937 and 1938. The report for the twenty-fifth reunion of Harvard's Class of 1910 and the original draft of "Usk" are in the collection of the Houghton Library, Harvard University.
9. Letter from Mrs. Eliot, November 22, 1977.
10. The Mabinogion, trans. by Lady Charlotte Guest (London: T. Fisher Unwin, 1902), II, 7, and I,76-7.
11. Cirlot, pp. 294, 350.
12. The Mabinogion, I, 72.
13. These lines may have been insired by Longfellow's six sonnets which preface his translation of Dante's Divine Comedy, particularly sonnets I and III:

> So, as I enter here from day to day,
>   And leave my burden at this minster gate,
>   Kneeling in prayer, and not ashamed to pray,
> The tumult of the time disconsolate
>   To inarticulate murmurs dies away,
>   While the eternal ages watch and wait.
>
> I enter, and I see thee in the gloom
>   Of the long aisles. . . .

14 "Glencoe," Encyclopaedia Britannica, 1967, X, 482.
15. Harry T. Batsford and Charles Fry, The Face of Scotland (London: B. T. Batsford, Ltd., 1933), p. 51.
16. John Buchan, The Massacre of Glencoe (London: Peter Davies, Ltd., 1933), p. 129.
17. The narrow, winding road in existence at the time of Eliot's visit has been replaced by a modern highway. However, if one turns off the highway toward the village of Glencoe, he will travel on what must be a portion of the original road. The Celtic cross is located off this road down a narrow lane leading to several small cottages.

NOTES TO CHAPTER V

1. Matthiessen, p. 99.
2. Drew, p. 147.

3. Eliot, *Selected Essays*, pp. 214, 228.
4. After completing "Burnt Norton," Eliot's intention was to write two additional poems, thus making a set of three. In a letter (XI) dated February, 1940 from John Hayward to Frank Morley, Hayward quotes Eliot as calling "East Coker" "the second of three quatuors." In a subsequent letter (XII), Hayward describes "East Coker" as "a kind of sequel [to 'Burnt Norton']." In January, 1941 (Letter XXVII) Hayward speaks of receiving "the typescript of the first draft of the third poem ['The Dry Salvages'] of Tom's trilogy." It is not until July, 1941 (Letter XXXVII) that Hayward writes of "Little Gidding" and calls the set a quadrologue: "Tom has completed the first rough draft of the final poem of the Quadrologue." (This Hayward-Morley correspondence is in the collection of King's College, Cambridge.) The first collected edition of all four poems with the title *Four Quartets* was published by Harcourt, Brace in New York on May 11, 1943. The first English edition was published on October 31, 1944 in London by Faber and Faber.
5. See "The Story of Sir William Kyte," *The Gentleman's Magazine*, 44 (1774), 171–2.
6. For a number of years, the manor was used as a school for disadvantaged boys. However, the school closed in 1973, and extensive renovations were begun. Upon their completion, Lord Sandon took up permanent residence there.
7. Frye, p. 88.
8. Gardner, p. 159.
9. All the details—the center, the order, the circle—suggest the condition of perfection.
10. Eric Thompson, *T. S. Eliot: The Metaphysical Perspective* (Carbondale, Ill.: Southern Illinois University Press, 1963), p.100.
11. Eliot, "The Significance of Charles Williams," *The Listener*, 36 (December 19, 1946), 895.
12. Eliot, *Selected Essays*, pp. 357–8.
13. Sir Kenneth Clark, *Landscape Into Art* (London: John Murray, 1949), p. 4.
14. C. A. Bodelsen, *T. S. Eliot's Four Quartets: A Commentary* (Copenhagen: Rosenkilde and Bagger, 1966), p. 40.
15. See "Ode to Memory," *Maud*, "The Hesperides," "Locksley Hall," and "The Lotos-Eaters."
16. For an interpretation of the experience as belonging to a child, see David Perkins, "Rose Garden to Midwinter Spring: Achieved Faith in the *Four Quartets*," *Modern Language Quarterly*, 23 (1962), 43–4.
17. McLuhan, "The Aesthetic Moment in Landscape Poetry," p. 175.
18. Sayers, p. 294.
19. For a diagram of the celestial rose, see Sayers and Barbara Reynolds, trans., Dante's *Paradise* (Baltimore, Md.: Penguin Books, 1962), p. 323. All quotations from Dante's *Paradise* are from this edition.
20. Hugh Kenner points out that Eliot himself once indicated that the specific station is "the Gloucester Road Station, near the poet's South Kensington headquarters, the point of intersection of the Circle Line with the Piccadilly tube to Russell Square. Whoever would leave the endless circle and entrain for the offices of Faber and Faber must 'descend lower,' and by spiral stairs if he chooses to walk." *The Invisible Poet: T. S. Eliot*, p. 300.
21. For an opposing view, see Bodelsen, p. 53. He states that the names have "no special significance" other than being "the name-boards of stations."
22. Drew, p. 158.
23. See Smith, p. 265.
24. Ibid., p. 266.
25. H. W. Hausermann, " 'East Coker' by T. S. Eliot," *English Studies*, 23 (August, 1941), 109.
26. Gardner, p. 164.
27. Smith, p. 268.

28. Sir Rupert Hart-Davis, "Address in Tribute to the late Mr. T. S. Eliot at the Memorial Service," *T. S. Eliot: Poet* (East Coker-Yeovil: Swift Printing, 1972). This pamphlet is available at St. Michael's Church and contains a foreward by the vicar, the poem "East Coker," and the memorial service for Eliot with the address by Sir Rupert. Two photographs of East Coker taken by Eliot himself are in the collection of King's College, Cambridge.

29. Raymond Preston, *Four Quartets Rehearsed* (New York: Haskell House, 1966), p. 24.

30. Bradbrook, p. 63.

31. Arthur Mizener, "To Meet Mr. Eliot," *T. S. Eliot: A Collection of Critical Essays*, ed. by Hugh Kenner (Englewood Cliffs, N. J.: Prentice-Hall, Inc., 1962), p. 25.

32. Gardner, p. 166.

33. A. Conan Doyle, *The Hound of the Baskervilles* (New York: Grosset and Dunlap, 1902), p. 107.

34. John M. Bradbury, *"Four Quartets:* The Structural Symbolism," *The Sewanee Review*, 59 (1951), 263.

35. Preston, p. 32.

36. My major source of information on the Cape Ann settings is a personal visit made in May, 1974. I saw the Eliot house, the Dry Salvages, and the town of Gloucester; quite by accident I happened upon Our Lady of Good Voyage Church and immediately recognized it as the shrine of Part IV. Other sources of information on the area include Howarth's *Notes on Some Figures Behind T. S. Eliot;* John D. Boyd's *"The Dry Salvages:* Topography as Symbol," *Renascence*, 20 (Spring, 1968), 119–33; and Samuel Eliot Morison's "The Dry Salvages and the Thacher Shipwreck," *The American Neptune*, 25 (October, 1965), 233–47.

37. Eliot, *The Use of Poetry and the Use of Criticism*, pp. 78–9.

38. Morison, pp. 234–6.

39. Melvin Copeland and Elliott Rogers, *The Saga of Cape Ann* (Freeport, Maine, 1960), pp. 132–3, as quoted by Boyd, p. 124.

40. John Hayward's letter (XXVIII) to Frank Morley, dated January, 1941. This letter is found in the collection of King's College, Cambridge.

41. Morison, pp. 233–4.

42. Copeland and Rogers, as quoted by Boyd, p. 123.

43. Morison, pp. 234–5.

44. Eliot makes this statement in a letter to Morison, quoted by Morison, p. 246.

45. Eliot, "Preface," James B. Connolly's *Fishermen of the Banks* (London: Faber and Gwyer, 1928), p. vii.

46. In an early draft of "The Dry Salvages" (received by Harcourt, Brace before the poem's publication in the *New English Weekly* on Feb. 27, 1941) Eliot had included an additional headnote which specifically mentioned Gloucester: "The Gloucester fishing fleet of schooners, manned by Yankees, Irish or Portuguese, has been superseded by the motor trawlers." This draft is in the collection of the Houghton Library, Harvard University.

47. Morison, p. 234.

48. Eliot, "Preface," Connolly's *Fishermen of the Banks*, pp. vii–viii.

49. Boyd, p. 126.

50. John Hayward's letter (XXVII) to Frank Morley, dated January, 1941. This letter is found in the collection of King's College, Cambridge.

51. This early draft of the speech is in the collection of King's College, Cambridge. The final version appears in *To Criticize the Critic*, entitled "American Literature and the American Language." See pp. 43–60.

52. M. W. Childs, "From a Distinguished Former St. Louisan," *St. Louis Post-Dispatch*, 15 October, 1930.

53. Eliot, "Preface," Mowrer's *This American World*, p. xiv.

54. Eliot, "The Influence of Landscape upon the Poet," p. 422.

55. Ibid.

56. From an early draft of the address given at Washington University in 1953 and later published as "American Literature and the American Language."

57. The flood of 1927 covered 26,000 square miles, cut off communications, and killed 214 people.

58. Staffan Bergsten, *Time and Eternity: A Study in the Structure and Symbolism of T. S. Eliot's Four Quartets* (New York: Humanities Press, 1973), p. 221.

59. Howarth, p. 121.

60. Bodelsen, p. 86.

61. Morison, p. 236.

62. A similar idea is found in John Donne's poem, "A Hymne to God the Father," in which the poet laments both the original sin of man in general, "that sinne where I begunne,/Which is my sin, though it were done before," and the daily, personal sins "through which I runne,/And do run still: though still I do deplore." See *The Complete Poetry and Selected Prose of John Donne,* ed. by Charles M. Coffin (New York: Random House, 1952), p. 270.

63. Bodelsen, p. 101.

64. J. Henry Shorthouse, *John Inglesant* (New York: The Macmillan Company, 1903), pp. 52–5.

65. Bradbrook, p. 27.

66. Preston, p. 53.

67. The date of Eliot's visit is given in Hayward's notes for the French translation of *Four Quartets.* The dates of the two restorations are given in the pamphlet, *Little Gidding: An Illustrated Guide to the Church,* which can be secured at the chapel. According to the pamphlet, the restoration of 1714 was carried out by John Ferrar, the son of Nicholas Ferrar's brother, and that of 1853 was undertaken by William Hopkinson.

68. Geoffrey Chaucer, "General Prologue to the Canterbury Tales," *The Works of Geoffrey Chaucer,* ed. by F. N. Robinson (Boston: Houghton Mifflin Co., 1957), p. 17.

69. Preston, p. 52.

70. See Hayward's notes for the French translation of *Four Quartets, Quatre Quatuors,* trans. by Pierre Leyris (Paris: Editions du Seuil, 1950).

71. "The Story of Sir William Kyte," *The Gentleman's Magazine,* p. 172.

72. Drew, p. 54.

73. See Hayward's notes for the French translation of *Four Quartets.*

74. This handwritten draft is one of numerous drafts of "Little Gidding" belonging to Magdalene College, Cambridge.

75. Eliot, *To Criticize the Critic,* p. 128.

76. Sayers's translation of the line is similar to Ciardi's:

> When he put out his hand to me, I stared
> At his scorched face, searching him through and through,
> So that the shrivelled skin and features scarred

> Might not mislead my memory. . . .

See Dante, *Hell,* trans. by Sayers (Baltimore, Md.: Penguin Books, 1949), XV, 25–28. Eliot would, of course, have read Dante in Italian rather than in an English translation.

77. Henry James, "The Jolly Corner," *The Short Stories of Henry James,* ed. by Clifton Fadiman (New York: Random House, Inc., 1945), pp. 633, 635.

78. This draft of the ghost's speech is in the collection of Magdalene College, Cambridge.

79. This draft is in the collection of Magdalene College, Cambridge.

80. Lines 236–9 have always evoked for me Dickinson's "There's a certain Slant of light" because of the similar winter late afternoon settings. In both, the setting suggests the passage of time and man's mortality. However, in Dickinson's poem

the emphasis is on the gloom and depression created in the speaker by his (her) sudden awareness of transience; in Eliot's it is on the speaker's realization that divine love overcomes the limitations of time.

81. Similar meanings are found in the "running stream" in "Journey of the Magi," the fountains and springs in "Ash Wednesday," IV, "the running streams" in "East Coker," III, and the waterfall in "The Dry Salvages," V.

82. George Williamson, p. 233.

83. Sayers, *Paradise*, p. 349.

84. John Hayward's letter (XXXVIII) to Frank Morley, dated August, 1941. This letter is found in the collection of King's College, Cambridge.

85. Eliot, *To Criticize the Critic*, p. 134.

NOTES TO CONCLUSION

1. Gardner, "The Landscapes of Eliot's Poetry," p. 320.

2. Eliot, *Selected Essays*, p. 368.

3. Ibid., p. 214.

4. Gardner, "The Landscapes of Eliot's Poetry," p.329.

Bibliography

BOOKS

Batsford, Harry, and Charles Fry. *The Face of Scotland.* London: B. T. Batsford, Ltd., 1933.

Baudelaire, Charles. *Oeuvres Complètes.* Paris: Bibliothèque de la Pléiade, 1961.

Bergsten, Staffan. *Time and Eternity: A Study in the Structure and Symbolism of T. S. Eliot's Four Quartets.* New York: Humanities Press, 1973.

Betjeman, Sir John. *The City of London Churches.* London: Pitkin Pictorials, Ltd., 1972.

Blamires, Harry. *Word Unheard: A Guide through Eliot's Four Quartets.* London: Methuen and Co., Ltd., 1969.

Bodelsen, C. A. *T. S. Eliot's Four Quartets: A Commentary.* Copenhagen: Rosenkilde and Bagger, 1966.

Buchan, John. *The Massacre of Glencoe.* London: Peter Davies, Ltd., 1933.

Buckley, Jerome Hamilton. *Tennyson: The Growth of a Poet.* Cambridge, Mass.: Harvard University Press, 1960.

Cattaui, Georges. *T. S. Eliot.* Translated by Claire Pace and Jean Stewart. New York: Funk and Wagnalls, 1966.

Chaucer, Geoffrey. *The Works of Geoffrey Chaucer.* Edited by F. N. Robinson. Boston: Houghton Mifflin Co., 1957.

Cirlot, J. E. *A Dictionary of Symbols.* Translated by Jack Sage. New York: Philosophical Library, Inc., 1962.

Clark, Sir Kenneth. *Landscape Into Art.* London: John Murray, 1949.

Conrad, Joseph. *Conrad.* Edited by Morton Dauwen Zabel. New York: The Viking Press, 1947.

Cook, E. C. *London and Its Environs.* Llangollen: Darlington and Co., n.d.

Dante. *Hell.* Translated by Dorothy Sayers. Baltimore, Md.: Penguin Books, 1949.

———. *Inferno.* Translated by John Ciardi. New York: The New American Library, 1954.

———. *Paradise.* Translated by Dorothy L. Sayers and Barbara Reynolds. Baltimore, Md.: Penguin Books, 1962.

———. *Purgatory.* Translated by Dorothy L. Sayers. Baltimore, Md.: Penguin Books, 1955.

Donne, John. *The Complete Poems and Selected Prose.* Edited by Charles M. Coffin. New York: Random House, 1952.

Donoghue, Denis. *The Ordinary Universe.* New York: The Macmillan Company, 1968.

Doyle, Sir Arthur Conan. *The Hound of the Baskervilles.* New York: Grosset and Dunlap, 1902.

Drew, Elizabeth. *T. S. Eliot: The Design of His Poetry.* New York: Charles Scribner's Sons, 1949.

227

228 · Bibliography

Eliot, T. S. *Collected Poems: 1909–1962*. New York: Harcourt, Brace and World, Inc., 1963.
———. *For Lancelot Andrewes*. Garden City, N.Y.: Doubleday, Doran, and Co., Inc., 1929.
———. *On Poetry and Poets*. New York: Farrar, Straus and Cudahy, 1957.
———. *Poèmes: 1910–1930*. Translated by Pierre Leyris. Notes by John Hayward. Paris: Editions du Seuil, 1947.
———. *Poems Written in Early Youth*. New York: Farrar, Straus and Giroux, Inc., 1967.
———. *Quatre Quatuors*. Translated by Pierre Leyris. Notes by John Hayward. Paris: Editions du Seuil, 1950.
———. *Selected Essays*. New York: Harcourt, Brace and World, Inc., 1950.
———. *To Criticize the Critic*. New York: Farrar, Straus and Giroux, Inc., 1965.
———. *The Use of Poetry and the Use of Criticism*. Cambridge, Mass.: Harvard University Press, 1933.
———. *The Waste Land: A Facsimile and Transcript of the Original Drafts*. Edited by Valerie Eliot. New York: Harcourt, Brace, Jovanovich, Inc., 1971.
French, Warren. *The Twenties: Poetry, Fiction, Drama*. Deland, Fla.: Everett-Edwards, 1976.
Frye, Northrop. *T. S. Eliot*. New York: Barnes and Noble, 1966.
Gardner, Helen. *The Art of T. S. Eliot*. New York: E. P. Dutton and Co., Inc., 1959.
Headings, Philip. *T. S. Eliot*. New York: Twayne Publishers, Inc., 1964.
Howarth, Herbert. *Notes on Some Figures Behind T. S. Eliot*. Boston: Houghton Mifflin Co., 1964.
James, Henry. *The Short Stories of Henry James*. Edited by Clifton Fadiman. New York: Random House, Inc., 1945.
Jones, Genesius. *Approach to the Purpose: A Study of the Poetry of T. S. Eliot*. New York: Barnes and Noble, 1964.
Kenner, Hugh. *The Invisible Poet: T. S. Eliot*. New York: MacDowell, Obolensky, Inc., 1959.
Kermode, Frank. *Romantic Image*. London: Routledge and Kegan Paul, 1957.
Langbaum, Robert. *The Poetry of Experience*. New York: W. W. Norton and Co., Inc., 1957.
Leavis, F. R. *New Bearings in English Poetry*. London: Chatto and Windus, Ltd., 1932.
Lewis, Wyndham. *Blasting and Bombardiering*. Berkeley: University of California Press, 1967.
———. *Men Without Art*. New York: Russell and Russell, Inc., 1964.
Mabinogion, The. Translated by Lady Charlotte Guest. London: T. Fisher Unwin, 1902.
Matthiessen, F. O. *The Achievement of T. S. Eliot*. New York: Oxford University Press, 1959.
Nicolson, Harold. *Tennyson: Aspects of His Life, Character and Poetry*. Boston: Houghton Mifflin Co., 1923.
Pitt, Valerie. *Tennyson Laureate*. Toronto: University of Toronto Press, 1963.
Preston, Raymond. *Four Quartets Rehearsed*. New York: Haskell House, 1966.
Quennell, Peter. *Baudelaire and the Symbolists*. London: Weidenfeld and Nicholson, 1929.
Raymond, Marcel. *From Baudelaire to Surrealism*. London: Peter Owen Limited, 1957.
Richardson, Joanna. *The Pre-Eminent Victorian*. London: Jonathan Cape, 1962.
Sencourt, Robert. *T. S. Eliot: A Memoir*. New York: Dodd, Mead and Company, 1971.
Shorthouse, J. Henry. *John Inglesant*. New York: The Macmillan Company, 1903.
Smidt, Kristian. *Poetry and Belief in the Work of T. S. Eliot*. Oslo: I Kommisjon Hos Jacob Dybwad, 1949.
Smith, Grover. *T. S. Eliot's Poetry and Plays: A Study in Sources and Meaning*. Chicago: The University of Chicago Press, 1956.
Stephenson, E. M. *T. S. Eliot and the Lay Reader*. London: The Fortune Press, 1944.

Tennyson, Alfred. *The Complete Poetical Works.* Edited by W. J. Rolfe. Cambridge, Mass.: The Riverside Press, 1898.

Thompson, Eric. *T. S. Eliot: The Metaphysical Perspective.* Carbondale, Ill.: Southern Illinois University Press, 1963.

Turnell, Martin. *Baudelaire: A Study of His Poetry.* Norfolk, Conn: New Directions, n.d.

Unger, Leonard. *T. S. Eliot: Moments and Patterns.* Minneapolis: University of Minnesota Press, 1956.

Wheelwright, Philip. *The Burning Fountain.* Bloomington, Ind.: Indiana University Press, 1954.

Willey, Basil. *More Nineteenth Century Studies.* New York: Harper and Row, 1956.

Williamson, George. *A Reader's Guide to T. S. Eliot.* New York: The Noonday Press, 1953.

Williamson, Hugh Ross. *The Poetry of T. S. Eliot.* London: Hodder and Stoughton, 1932.

Wilson, Edmund. *Axel's Castle.* New York: Charles Scribner's Sons, 1931.

ARTICLES

Aiken, Conrad. "King Bolo and Others." *T. S. Eliot.* Edited by Tambimuttu and Richard March. London: Frank and Cass Co., Ltd., 1965.

Beringause, A. F. "Journey through *The Waste Land.*" *South Atlantic Quarterly,* 56 (1957), 79-88.

Boyd, John. "*The Dry Salvages:* Topography as Symbol." *Renascence,* 20 (Spring, 1968), 119-33.

Bradbrook, M. C. "T. S. Eliot." *British Writers and Their Work.* Edited by Bonamy Dobree. Lincoln, Neb.: University of Nebraska Press, 1965.

Bradbury, John M. "*Four Quartets:* The Structural Symbolism." *The Sewanee Review,* 59 (1951), 254-70.

Brooks, Cleanth. "T. S. Eliot: Thinker and Artist." *T. S. Eliot: The Man and His Work.* Edited by Allen Tate. New York: Delacorte Press, 1966.

———. "*The Waste Land:* An Analysis." *T. S. Eliot: A Study of His Writings by Several Hands.* Edited by B. Rajan. New York: Haskell House, 1964.

Carey, Sister M. Cecilia. "Baudelaire's Influence in *The Waste Land.*" *Renascence,* 14 (Summer, 1962), 185-92.

Childs, M. W. "From a Distinguished Former St. Louisan." *St. Louis Post-Dispatch,* 15 October, 1930.

Coghill, Nevill. "Sweeney Agonistes." *T. S. Eliot.* Edited by Tambimuttu and Richard March. London: Frank and Cass Co., Ltd., 1965.

Day, Robert A. "The 'City Man' in *The Waste Land:* The Geography of Reminiscence." *PMLA,* 80 (1965), 285-90.

Duncan-Jones, E. E. "*Ash Wednesday.*" *T. S. Eliot: A Study of His Writings by Several Hands.* Edited by B. Rajan. New York: Haskell House, 1964.

Eliot, T. S. "A Brief Introduction to the Method of Paul Valéry." *Paul Valéry's Le Serpent.* London: The Criterion, 1924, pp. 7-15.

———. "The Influence of Landscape upon the Poet." *Daedalus,* 89 (Spring, 1960), 420–22.

———. "London Letter." *The Dial,* 70 (June, 1921), 686–91.

———. "London Letter." *The Dial,* 71 (October, 1921), 452–5.

———. "A Prediction in Regard to Three English Authors." *Vanity Fair,* 21 (February, 1924), 29, 98.

———. "Preface." Edgar A. Mowrer's *This American World.* London: Faber and Gwyer, 1928, pp. ix–xv.

———. "Preface." James B. Connolly's *Fishermen of the Banks.* London: Faber and Gwyer, 1928, pp. vii–viii.

———. "The Significance of Charles Williams." *The Listener*, 36 (December 19, 1946), 894–5.

———. "The Three Provincialities." *The Tyro*, No. 2 (Spring, 1922), 11–13.

Gardner, Helen. "The Landscapes of Eliot's Poetry." *Critical Quarterly*, 10 (Winter, 1968), 313-30.

Hansen, E. A. "T. S. Eliot's 'Landscapes.' " *English Studies*, 50 (August, 1969), 363-79.

Hart-Davis, Sir Rupert. "Address in Tribute to the late Mr. T. S. Eliot at the Memorial Service." *T. S. Eliot: Poet*. East Coker-Yeovil: Swift Printing, 1972.

Hausermann, H. W. " 'East Coker' by T. S. Eliot." *English Studies*, 23 (August, 1941), 108-10.

Kenner, Hugh. "The Urban Apocalypse." *Eliot in His Time*. Edited by Walton Litz. Princeton: Princeton University Press, 1973.

Langbaum, Robert. "New Modes of Characterization in *The Waste Land*." *Eliot in His Time*. Edited by Walton Litz. Princeton: Princeton University Press, 1973.

Martin, Jay. "T. S. Eliot's *The Waste Land*." *A Collection of Critical Essays on The Waste Land*. Edited by Jay Martin. Englewood Cliffs, N. J.: Prentice-Hall, Inc., 1967.

McLuhan, Herbert Marshall. "Introduction." *Tennyson: Selected Poetry*. New York: Holt, Rinehart, and Winston, 1956.

———. "Tennyson and Picturesque Poetry." *Essays in Criticism*, 1 (July, 1951), 262-82.

———. "The Aesthetic Moment in Landscape Poetry." *English Institute Essays*. Edited by Alan Downer. New York: Columbia University Press, 1952.

Mizener, Arthur. "To Meet Mr. Eliot." *T. S. Eliot: A Collection of Critical Essays*. Edited by Hugh Kenner. Englewood Cliffs, N. J.: Prentice-Hall, Inc., 1962.

Morison, Samuel Eliot. "The Dry Salvages and the Thacher Shipwreck." *The American Neptune*, 25 (October, 1965), 233-47.

Perkins, David. "Rose Garden to Midwinter Spring: Achieved Faith in the *Four Quartets*." *Modern Language Quarterly*, 23 (1962), 41-45.

Rajan, B. "The Overwhelming Question." *T. S. Eliot: The Man and His Work*. Edited by Allen Tate. New York: Delacorte Press, 1966.

———. "The Unity of the Quartets." *T. S. Eliot: A Study of His Writings by Several Hands*. Edited by B. Rajan. New York: Haskell House, 1964.

Ransom, John Crowe. "Gerontion." *T. S. Eliot: The Man and His Work*. Edited by Allen Tate. New York: Delacorte Press, 1966.

Sickels, Eleanor M. "Eliot's *The Waste Land*, I, 24-30, and *Ash Wednesday*, IV-VI." *The Explicator*, 9 (October, 1950), Item 4.

Spender, Stephen. "Remembering Eliot." *T. S. Eliot: The Man and His Work*. Edited by Allen Tate. New York: Delacorte Press, 1966.

Stange, Robert G. "Tennyson's Garden of Art: A Study of 'The Hesperides.' " *Critical Essays on the Poetry of Tennyson*. Edited by John Killham. London: Routledge and Kegan Paul, 1960.

———. "Tennyson's Mythology: A Study of 'Demeter and Persephone.' " *Critical Essays on the Poetry of Tennyson*. Edited by John Killham. London: Routledge and Kegan Paul, 1960.

Steward, Diana. "A Contrast of 'Landscapes': 'Virginia' and 'Usk.' " *T. S. Eliot: A Symposium for His Seventieth Birthday*. Edited by Neville Braybrooke. New York: Farrar, Straus and Cudahy, 1958.

"The Story of Sir William Kyte." *The Gentleman's Magazine*, 44 (1774), 171-2.

Tate, Allen. "On *Ash Wednesday*." *T. S. Eliot: A Collection of Critical Essays*. Edited by Hugh Kenner. Englewood Cliffs, N. J.: Prentice-Hall, 1962.

Waterston, Elizabeth. "Symbolism in Tennyson's Minor Poems." *Critical Essays on the Poetry of Tennyson*. Edited by John Killham. London: Routledge and Kegan Paul, 1960.

Index